The Urbanization of European Society in the Nineteenth Century

Edited and with an introduction by

Andrew Lees
Rutgers University—Camden

and

Lynn Lees
University of Pennsylvania

D. C. HEATH AND COMPANY
Lexington, Massachusetts Toronto London

Published simultaneously in Canada.

Printed in the United States of America.

International Standard Book Number: 0-669-95992-8

Library of Congress Catalog Card Number: 75-36347

The Urbanization of European Society in the Nineteenth Century

PROBLEMS IN
EUROPEAN CIVILIZATION

Under the editorial direction of
John Ratté
Amherst College

CONTENTS

I THE GROWTH OF CITIES

II NINETEENTH- AND TWENTIETH-CENTURY VIEWS OF THE BIG CITY: POSITIVE AND NEGATIVE

III THE URBAN MIDDLE CLASSES

IV THE URBAN LOWER CLASSES

INTRODUCTION

The Growth of Cities and the Conflicting Perceptions of Urban Life

Cities arose in the civilizations of the ancient Near East long before the start of what is commonly regarded as European civilization. Indeed, the Latin origins of the very word "civilization" imply the presence of cities. Except for the early Middle Ages, urban history has continued to be of central importance for European history as a whole. Cities have been sources of ideas and centers of power, theaters of innovation and instruments of control, and much else besides.

Their central position in civilized societies made them objects of concern and controversy from early times. In classical antiquity, Latin writers such as Cicero, Sallust, and Tacitus and the poets Horace and Juvenal all expressed their disgust with Rome as a source of moral corruption and cultural decline. Two millennia later, in eighteenth-century Europe, while French Physiocrats such as Quesnay voiced the fear that the growth of Paris would impoverish the rest of the country, Voltaire and Adam Smith argued that cities were indispensable for cultural, social, and economic progress.[1]

During the nineteenth century, there was a pronounced change in the nature of European cities, their place in European society as a whole, and the intensity of the controversies they generated— controversies that have given rise to some of the most interesting

---

[1] Hans Oswald, *Die überschätzte Stadt: Ein Beitrag der Gemeindesoziologie zum Städtebau* (Olten and Freiburg im Breisgau, 1966), p. 69; Raymond Williams, *The City and the Country* (New York, 1973), pp. 46–48; Edith Pfeil, *Grossstadtforschung* (Bremen-Horn, 1950), pp. 20–21; Carl Schorske, "The Idea of the City in European Thought: Voltaire to Spengler," in Oscar Handlin and John Burchard, eds., *The Historian and the City* (Cambridge, Mass., 1963), pp. 96–98.

scholarship to be produced recently in the area of European social history. Let us consider each of these themes in turn.

The most obvious new element in European urban history during the nineteenth century was rapid urban growth. Although cities had existed for thousands of years, the sizes of their populations had been fairly stable. To be sure, the port city of Liverpool had tripled between 1730 and 1773, and there were other cases of comparable growth, but such expansion was the exception rather than the rule. In contrast, when we examine the period of a hundred years or so after 1800, we find that increases in the size of individual cities amounting to 400 or 500 percent or even more were not at all uncommon. Consider some of the cities in the three European countries which had the largest urban populations by the end of the century, the countries on which the readings in this book concentrate. In Great Britain between 1801 and 1901 London grew from about 900,000 (the exact figure depends on which of several definitions of the city is employed) to over 4.5 million, and Manchester expanded from 75,000 to over half a million. In Germany, Berlin's population rose from 197,000 in 1816 to a little over 2 million in 1905, while Essen's went from under 4,000 to almost 230,000 between 1810 and 1905. In France, Paris grew roughly fivefold between 1801 and 1901, from half a million to over 2.5 million, and Lille went from 55,000 to almost 200,000.

As a result of such population growth, there was a dramatic increase in the number of big cities. Whereas at the start of the century only London had close to a million inhabitants, by 1900 not only Paris and Berlin but also Barcelona, Vienna, Moscow, and St. Petersburg had passed the million mark. The increase in the number of cities with populations of 100,000 or more was equally striking: from 23 to 143.

The growth in the size of cities was dramatic not only in absolute numbers and in percentages but also in relation to the growth of the total European population. There were about twice as many Europeans in 1900 as there had been a hundred years earlier, but the increases between these two dates in the numbers of people living in cities of any given size were considerably greater. Consequently, the urban population suddenly began to account for a larger and larger portion of society as a whole. For instance, the proportion of Europeans living in cities numbering 100,000 or more, after having fluctuated between approximately 2 and 3 percent between 1600 and

1800, jumped to 4.8 percent by 1850 and to 12.3 percent by 1900. If, as was frequently done in the nineteenth century, we regard the total urban population as consisting of everyone living in settlements of 2,000 or more inhabitants, we find that during the second half of the century several European countries reached the point where more of their citizens lived in cities than in the countryside and that most of those which had not yet crossed the dividing line were approaching it quickly. It was not just that cities grew. Society itself was becoming urbanized.[2]

What caused this massive redistribution of the European population? Differences between urban and rural birth and death rates do not help us answer that question. In most places throughout most of the century, natality was lower and mortality higher among city-dwellers than among residents of the countryside. In fact, most cities, especially on the Continent, not only would have failed to keep up in percentage terms with the total population but also would have failed to grow very much even in absolute terms if they had had to depend upon natural increase alone.

The key to urban growth was migration, the result of the city's ability to attract the surplus rural population. London, Paris, and Berlin each received thousands—and sometimes tens of thousands—of migrants every year from smaller cities and towns, for which they or their parents had earlier abandoned their homes in villages or on the land.

Men and women migrated to cities largely because it was there that they could find the best-paid employment. The major stimulus to urban migration was the prospect of personal economic advancement. The fact that cities were able to hold out this promise was intimately linked to the progress of industrialization. Industry gravitated increasingly toward the cities, in turn attracting migrants in search of work. To be sure, many cities grew because they were commercial centers, and others owed much of their expansion to their position as national capitals, but it is inconceivable that Europe would have urbanized to anything like the extent that it did without

---

[2] Most of the statistics in this and the preceding paragraph have been accumulated from the following sources: Brian Mitchell and Phyllis Deane, *Abstract of British Historical Statistics* (Cambridge, Eng., 1962), pp. 24–27; entries on individual cities in Erich Keyser, *Bibliographie zur Städtegeschichte Deutschlands* (Cologne and Vienna, 1969), Philippe Dollinger, *Bibliographie d'Histoire des villes de France* (Paris, 1967), and the eleventh edition of the *Encyclopaedia Britannica* (London, 1911); and Charles Tilly, *An Urban World* (Boston, 1974), p. 39.

the Industrial Revolution. It is particularly noteworthy that some of the fastest-growing cities were manufacturing centers: between 1801 and 1901, Manchester, the center of the English cotton industry, grew by 673 percent, while Essen, the home of the Krupp iron and steel dynasty, from 1810 to 1905 grew by 5,874 percent!

Industrialization meant that the urban scene was not only quantitatively but also qualitatively different from what it had been in earlier centuries. The subtle and not so subtle social implications and some of the physically visible consequences of industrialization will concern us at greater length later. It suffices at this point to emphasize that the industrial city—"Coketown," to use the term invented by Charles Dickens and employed by Lewis Mumford in one of the selections reprinted below—was something radically new. While nineteenth-century London and Paris, despite their rapid growth, might plausibly be regarded as expanded versions of something still recognizable from earlier times, Manchester and Essen, with their somber factories and their endless blocks of workers' housing, were quite different from any city that had previously existed.

So far we have emphasized the common elements in European urban development, but national differences are equally important to bear in mind. There was considerable national variety with respect to the pace and extent of urbanization. Whereas Great Britain's thirty big cities (i.e., cities numbering 100,000 or more) accounted for 28.4 percent of her population in 1891, Germany's twenty-eight accounted for 14 percent, and France's twelve were the home of 11.9 percent.[3] The readings in the first part of this book illuminate what was peculiar about the urbanization of each of these countries. England is the subject of a chapter on the period 1801–1891 from a classic work by Adna Weber. Weber links England's urban primacy—indicated by the fact that as of 1851 it was the only country in which more than 50 percent of the population lived in cities—quite clearly to the processes of economic transformation, in which England also took the lead. Pierre Sorlin treats the growth of French cities between 1840 and 1914, emphasizing the gap between France on the one hand and Great Britain and Germany on the other, which was traceable to its

[3] Paul Meuriot, *Des agglomérations urbaines dans l'Europe contemporaine: Essai sur les causes, les conditions, les conséquences de leur développement* (Paris, 1897), p. 32. After Great Britain, the countries with the greatest proportions of their populations living in cities of 100,000 or more were The Netherlands (17.5 percent), Denmark (17.4 percent), and Belgium (15.6 percent). All other European countries ranked below France, the last in line being Russia, with 3.5 percent.

relative economic backwardness. Urbanization in France was much slower and less far-reaching. Finally, Wolfgang Köllmann's essay on "The Process of Urbanization in Germany at the Height of the Industrialization Period" takes up German developments in 1871. Köllmann shows how Germany's accelerated industrial advance during the years between that date and 1910—which enabled it to challenge and overtake Britain in many areas of production—led to an extremely rapid expansion of cities during these years. Urbanization in Germany was both late and intensive.

By the middle of the nineteenth century, the growth of cities had proceeded far enough so that an urban Europe was clearly foreseeable as the likely long-range outcome of current trends. The English example provided a model that other countries appeared likely to follow, more or less quickly, depending upon their particular economic and social circumstances. One result was a growing concern among intellectuals with the consequences of Europe's ongoing demographic transformation. More and more thinkers began to ponder both the opportunities and the problems inherent in city life, expressing sharply divergent views of the burgeoning big city.

Two of the earliest writers to evaluate big cities within a context of general attitudes toward modern society were an English historian and clergyman, Robert Vaughan, and a German journalist and sociologist, Wilhelm Heinrich Riehl, both of whose works are excerpted below. Writing in the early 1840s, Vaughan proudly hailed the nineteenth century as the Age of Great Cities. Vaughan fell heir to the view of cities voiced earlier by Voltaire and Adam Smith. A good liberal in matters of politics, economics, and religion, he believed that cities nurtured political responsibility and private associations, that they stimulated learning and the arts, and that on balance they improved the moral fiber of their inhabitants. A decade later, the politically and socially conservative Riehl took a position that was the extreme opposite of Vaughan's. For Riehl, the city was a source of corruption—a monstrosity, which lured young men and women away from small villages and farms only to destroy them spiritually and in some cases economically as well. Although there had been a healthy sense of community in the smaller cities of yesteryear, Riehl felt, the big city of the nineteenth century spelled doom for European civilization.

The opinions voiced by Vaughan and Riehl—both of whom were widely read—recur again and again in later writing on cities, but not all writing about urban life was as highly opinionated as theirs. Concomitant with the rise of the social sciences, there was an increasing flood during the late nineteenth century of highly empirical studies of the city. The works of Charles Booth and Seebohm Rowntree in England and a large number of new German periodicals specializing in urban affairs are only some of the examples that come to mind.[4] As a result of the spate of empirical investigations, some of the persisting general commentary on cities reflected a more balanced outlook than was possible for either Vaughan or Riehl. Adolf Weber, a young German economist writing at the very end of the period with which we are concerned, took such a middle position. The lecture of his from the early twentieth century included herein affords an interesting comparison with the writings of those earlier authors, addressing itself to the issues they had raised but arriving at a final position that incorporated a variety of elements from both sides of the argument. For Weber, the big city had much to recommend it, especially as an instrument of economic growth and a disseminator of high culture. But much of the urban population lived under ghastly conditions, and crime and other forms of social pathology seemed to increase in urban settings. What was to be done? Weber answered that question by enjoining his listeners ''to retain what is good in the big city and to combat what is evil'' through a program of urban reform. There was no way of returning to a rural paradise. One had to make the best of the world as it was and as it was destined to become.

More than half a century later, American as well as European historians can look back with the benefit of hindsight at the developments which Vaughan, Riehl, Weber, and others discussed. But the concerns that informed the perceptions of contemporaries are still very much alive in the historical literature, and the debate about the quality of urban life in nineteenth-century Europe continues. Lewis Mumford, one of the most distinguished analysts of cities in America today, harks back to some of the same ideas articulated by Riehl in his assessment of ''Coketown.'' Mumford paints a grim picture of the physiognomy of the nineteenth-century industrial city, which he ironically calls a ''paleotechnic paradise.'' The product

---

[4] Charles Booth, *Life and Labour of the People in London* (17 vols.; 3rd ed.; London, 1902–1903); Benjamin Seebohm Rowntree, *Poverty: A Study of Town Life* (London and New York, 1901). On the German side, see the *Statistisches Jahrbuch deutscher Städte*, ed. M. Neefe (Breslau, 1890–), and *Kommunale Praxis: Zeitschrift für Kommunalpolitik und Gemeindesozialismus* (1901–22), along with numerous other periodicals.

of aimless and uncontrolled expansion, the industrial city was characterized by the factory, the railroad, and the slum, and it was "a no-man's-land of social life." In contrast, H. J. Dyos and Michael Wolff—one an Englishman, the other an American, and both editors of a magisterial recent work on Victorian cities—contend that on balance the nineteenth-century city was a force for good. In an excerpt from an essay of theirs with which we conclude our sampling of general attitudes toward cities, they argue that "in the modern world . . . the path of progress has been an urban one. The very existence of the city has been a demonstration of the capacity, however uneven, to lift human effort beyond subsistence and a preoccupation with the brute facts of mere existence; and the urbanization of the whole population is an index, however crude, of rising standards of material welfare. Here is a measure of our civilization." Robert Vaughan would have agreed heartily.

Many of the disagreements over the nature of urban life in the past have arisen not only from conflicting values but also because different commentators have chosen to look at quite different parts of the total picture. One's judgments about the quality of urban experience vary dramatically depending on whether one is focusing on a Parisian slum-dweller in the 1830s, a Sheffield steelworker in the 1880s, or an entrepreneur in Barmen around 1900. Not only did European cities change strikingly between the early and the late nineteenth century, but each city functioned differently throughout the period for upper- and lower-class residents. Death and disease rates were decidedly higher among workers; dissimilar types of education, housing, and urban services were provided for rich and poor; and each social and ethnic group had its own networks and territory. By concentrating upon specific times, places, and sections of the urban population, historians enable us to understand the highly variegated nature of the urban scene. Parts III and IV of this book represent an effort to enable the reader to test various general opinions about cities against some of the best recent scholarship produced by such historians.

Urban history is not a unified genre, either in subject matter or in method. Just as sociologists, economists, and geographers study cities in different ways, and see different things in cities, so do historians. What unity there is in this field emerges from certain common themes and interests, which can be seen most clearly in the work of urban social historians. Those who concentrate upon the

European middle classes, for example, deal with many of the same topics, and the images they present of urban elites have many similarities. In the selections we have included from the works of Wolfgang Köllmann on Barmen, Adeline Daumard on Paris, and Francis Sheppard on London, we encounter representatives of the urban middle classes in their roles as businessmen, property-owners, and consumers of culture. Despite differences in structure and cultural heritage, the Barmen, Parisian, and London middle classes emerge as self-confident, relatively cohesive elites who kept their hands on the levers of local power. United by sets of social norms, they lived vastly different lives from their social inferiors, intermarrying with their own kind and frequenting separate sets of institutions. Their culture dominated the urban milieu in the past, and European cities today bear their stamp. A walk through Paris, Manchester, or Vienna leads one to the nineteenth-century creations of the middle-class residents, who planned and generally paid not only for their own residences but also for new town halls, railroad stations, libraries, department stores, and other public or quasipublic buildings.

Most historians of urban society—like social historians generally—have a decided preference for studying workers. With or without the impetus of Marxian ideology, the new social historians concentrate on the masses rather than the elites. Their predisposition to do urban history "from the bottom up" adds a valuable corrective to existing literature, most of which examines cities "from the top down." Historians of the urban lower classes focus on a number of common topics: physical conditions in the city, work and wages, the structure of workers' family and social life, and their psychological responses to the city. These are the themes they commonly treat.

What they have to say on these and related subjects points in a number of different directions. One major debate concerns migration. Since nineteenth-century cities grew primarily because of immigration rather than natural increase, one's view of new arrivals and their ability to adapt to urban life becomes a central part of any interpretation of cities. Many historians have borrowed heavily from the sociologists Robert Park and Louis Wirth and have expressed decidedly negative views of the consequences both of migration and of urbanization.[5] Park's image of migrants as marginal men who were

[5] Robert E. Park and Ernest Burgess, *The City* (Chicago, 1925); Robert E. Park, "Human Migration and the Marginal Man," *American Journal of Sociology* 33 (1928): 881–893; Louis Wirth, "Urbanism as a Way of Life," *American Journal of Sociology* 44 (1938): 1–24.

limited to superficial social relationships and isolated from other citizens has been widely influential. In the works of Oscar Handlin, migration emerges as a profoundly unsettling and uprooting experience, destructive of the migrant's cultural and familial life.[6] Louis Chevalier, in *Laboring Classes and Dangerous Classes,* amplifies this theme by arguing that the process of urbanization, the consequent crowding, and high mortality forced workers into pathological forms of behavior. The demographic pressures of urban life had adverse psychological consequences and recruited men into the dangerous classes.

More recent treatments of urban workers in the nineteenth century, such as Michael Anderson's study of Preston in 1851, deny these connections between migration, isolation, and pathological behavior. Pointing out that most migrants had moved only a short distance, Anderson shows how the chain migration of relatives and friends provided newcomers with ready-made structures to ease their adaptation to urban life and to provide services in time of need. Other works, such as Sidney Pollard's study of Sheffield, show how the presence in cities of workers' organizations, schools, and churches helped to integrate workers into an urban environment. Although Pollard admits the physical problems of city life, he shows how these conditions improved during the later nineteenth century. For lower-class Berliners, as Hsi-Huey Liang demonstrates, migration to the city brought economic, social, and cultural opportunities that outweighed the disadvantages of living in a huge tenement.

This concentration upon the positive attractions of the city and upon migrants' means of adaptation parallels the concerns of urban sociologists seeking to extricate themselves from the shadows of Park and Wirth by formulating alternative views of migration and urban life.[7] Much urban history, in terms of the questions asked and the interpretations advanced, lies very close to urban sociology or urban anthropology. Models and terminology are borrowed, as are methods. Demographic techniques are particularly useful to the urban historian who wishes to ground his study of a particular city in

[6] Oscar Handlin, *The Uprooted* (Boston, 1951), and *Boston's Immigrants, 1790–1880* (rev. ed.; Cambridge, Mass., 1959).
[7] Charles Tilly and C. Harold Brown, "On Uprooting, Kinship, and the Auspices of Migration," *International Journal of Comparative Sociology* 7 (1967): 139–164; Peter C. W. Gutkind, "African Urbanism, Mobility, and the Social Network," *International Journal of Comparative Sociology* 6 (1965): 48–60; Herbert Gans, *The Urban Villagers* (New York, 1963); Michael Young and Peter Willmott, *Family and Kinship in East London* (London, 1957).

an analysis of its population. Some recent urban history is in fact a kind of social science history, linked by methods and hypotheses to other disciplines. Anderson's work on Preston draws explicitly upon sociological theory and uses historical data to investigate a standard sociological topic, urban kinship relations. His book is a prime example of urban histories that investigate social processes that take place in cities, rather than attempting to describe the functioning of the city as a whole. Other urban histories make social structure the focus of their work. Daumard's study of the Parisian bourgeoisie and Chevalier's discussion of Parisian workers are books that deal with urban life indirectly through the analysis of one social group. Although virtually all urban histories of this sort focus upon one city, the authors are usually interested in comparing their results with those of other historians in order to make general statements about social structure or social processes.

Urban social history usually relies heavily on statistical analyses of the urban population. Since the great bulk of the population left no memoirs, diaries, letters, or autobiographies, the historian cannot depend solely upon such sources in reconstructing their life experiences. Instead, he must piece together the history of a social group from the individual entries in censuses, wills, deeds, and tax and institutional records. By moving away from the particular case and by counting, the historian acquires the ability to generalize with precision about the structures and patterns of urban social life. Such work has been widely touted as the New Urban History, largely because of its use of quantitative methods or social science theory.[8]

These urban social histories contrast both in terms of methods and subject matter with more general urban histories, which form the bulk of the work in the field. Books such as Sheppard's history of London spring from the still vital tradition of European local history, in which civic pride and breadth of outlook combine to produce studies surveying urban institutions, culture, and political and economic life. The methods and sources employed are traditional: the historian searches local archives for material on a town and its citizens, weaving it together to tell the story of the city's development. Since the emphasis falls upon specific details, generalizations about urbanization or social processes are usually absent. At best

[8] Stephan Thernstrom and Richard Sennett, eds., *Nineteenth-Century Cities* (New Haven, 1969); Leo F. Schnore, ed., *The New Urban History* (Princeton, 1975); Stephan Thernstrom, "Reflections on the New Urban History," *Daedalus*, no. 100 (1971): 359–375.

this type of urban history introduces the reader to a wide variety of urban themes and captures the unique flavor of a particular city; at worst it degenerates into an antiquarianism in which description triumphs over analysis.

Historians themselves reflect the highly variegated nature of cities in their diverse methods and subjects. There is no commonly accepted model of what an urban history should be. This severely hampers one's ability to compare one city with another, and as long as urban historians produce local histories almost exclusively, the task of comparison will not be done by those writing specialized work in the field. This puts an extra burden upon the student of cities, who must find his own way of moving from London to Paris to Berlin and from the city of the workers to that of the bourgeoisie. Every reader must be his or her own urban historian.

We have omitted almost all of the original footnotes from the selections reprinted below. Most of the footnotes in the volume are our own, as is all of the material in English within brackets in the texts themselves. We have renumbered tables and charts where necessary so that within each selection the series starts with the number one. British spellings have been Americanized.

We thank the following colleagues and friends who have helped us in preparing this volume: Keith Davies, Evan Davis, H. J. Dyos, William H. Hubbard, John Ratté, and Peter N. Stearns.

Conflict of Opinion

Europe is becoming sick as a result of the monstrosity of its big cities.
WILHELM HEINRICH RIEHL

It is not only true that from cities good laws, liberal arts, and letters, have, in the main, their origin, but no less true that spontaneous efforts in the cause of public morals, and in the aid of the necessitous . . . are found almost exclusively among citizens.
ROBERT VAUGHAN

The big city poses extraordinarily important and difficult challenges for us, challenges which we must meet unless we are willing to see the culture which we cherish give way gradually to a new kind of barbarism.
ADOLF WEBER

Between 1820 and 1900 the destruction and disorder within great cities is like that of a battlefield. . . . Industrialism, the main creative force of the nineteenth century, produced the most degraded urban environment the world had yet seen; for even the quarters of the ruling classes were befouled and overcrowded.
LEWIS MUMFORD

The promise of modernity, however distant, is abundance and equality, the material and ideological products of the dual revolution in England and France in the late eighteenth century, and the city is its exponent, if not its redeemer.
H. J. DYOS AND MICHAEL WOLFF

I THE GROWTH OF CITIES

Adna Ferrin Weber

URBAN GROWTH IN ENGLAND AND WALES IN THE NINETEENTH CENTURY

One of the first major comparative works in the field of urban studies was published by an American, Adna Ferrin Weber, in 1899. Weber, who spent his life as a government statistician, began his career with this study. The book, a revised version of his Columbia Ph.D. thesis, is an impressive synthesis of the available statistics on urban growth and urban populations, which has yet to be superseded. In this selection he explores the close relationship between industrialization and urbanization in England and Wales.

From many points of view, England offers superior advantages for the study of the distribution of population and the causes affecting the same. England was the pioneer in the modern industrial movement and is even now the typical industrial country. For while the aggregate output of machine- or factory-made products in the United States exceeds that of England, it does not constitute so large a proportion of the entire national product. A smaller percentage of Englishmen and Scotchmen are devoted to agricultural pursuits than of any other nation of the world. The latter being the only workers who are of necessity resident in scattered habitations, it will be worth while to ascertain under what conditions the remainder of the population has dwelt.

Unfortunately, the English statistics present serious difficulties to the classification of dwelling-centers. This is chiefly the fault of the historical English method of local government, distributing the various functions to a variety of independent authorities over different areas and thus producing a chaos of boundaries and officials. In 1871, the 938 dwelling-centers which were taken to represent the urban population of England and Wales were thus classified: municipal boroughs, comprising cities and towns to which charters of incorporation had been granted and were later governed by the Municipal Corporations Reform Act, 224; local board districts established either under the Public Health Act of 1848 or under the Local Government Act of 1858, 721 (including 146 municipal boroughs); places

From Adna Ferrin Weber, *The Growth of Cities in the Nineteenth Century* (Ithaca: Cornell University Press, 1899), pp. 40–57.

which had improvement, paving, lighting or other commissions under (special) local Acts, 88 (including 37 municipal boroughs); other "towns" of some 21,000 population, 96. But these "towns" not under a regular municipal authority had no recognized boundaries, and "the Superintendent Registrar of the District in each case distinguished the houses which in his opinion might properly be considered within the limits of the town."

Such was the condition of affairs in 1871. In the earlier censuses there were still fewer places which had definite and recognized boundaries; such being the boroughs alone. But a borough might be either municipal or parliamentary. And sometimes there was a vast difference between the limits of the two; for example, Wolverhampton, the municipal borough, had a population of 49,985 in 1851, but a population of 119,748 dwelt within its parliamentary boundaries. All of which tended to confuse the statistician.

In 1872, however, legislation simplified matters considerably. By the Public Health Act of 1872, it was enacted that all municipal boroughs, local board districts and towns with improvement commissions, should henceforth be termed "urban sanitary districts," and to these authorities were transferred all the powers and duties previously exercised by any other authority in the districts under the provisions of acts relating to local government, the utilization of sewage, the removal of nuisances, the regulation of common lodging houses, baths and wash houses and the prevention of disease. These powers connected with sanitation, which have since been augmented, are so important and, in fact, so essential a part of city government, that the English urban sanitary district may well be considered the typical urban community. To the original urban sanitary districts of 1872, others have been added from year to year, being carved out of the great area comprised in the rural sanitary districts as rapidly as an agglomeration of peoples becomes of sufficient magnitude to require urban sanitary regulations. The number of urban sanitary districts in the Census of 1891 was 1,011, of which only 194 had less than 3,000 inhabitants. Their aggregate population constituted 71.7 percent of the entire population of England and Wales; only 1.3 percent of the population dwelt in urban districts smaller than 3,000.

With these explanations, . . . Table 1 is put forward to show the degree in which the population was concentrated at the different periods in the present century.

Table 1

Classes of cities	1801		1851		1891	
	No.	Population	No.	Population	No.	Population
Over 20,000	15	1,506,176	63	6,265,011	185	15,563,834
10,000–20,000	31	389,624	60	800,000	175	2,362,376
5,000–10,000	60	418,715	140	963,000	262	1,837,054
Total 5,000+	106	2,314,515	263	8,028,011	622	19,763,264
Total under 5,000	—	6,578,021	—	9,899,598	—	9,239,261
Grand total	—	8,892,536	—	17,927,609	—	29,002,525

In the ninety years covered by the table, over 20 millions of people were added to the population of England and Wales; but while the rural inhabitants (those dwelling in places of less than 5,000) increased from 6.6 million to 9.2 million, the town-dwellers increased from 2.3 million to 19.8 million. That is, of the total increase of 20 million, about 17.4 million, or 80 percent, fell to the towns and cities. It is, moreover, noticeable that the increase of the rural population took place entirely in the first half of the century, and later turned into an actual decrease. Some 800,000 more people are classed as belonging to the rural population in 1851 than in 1891; so that while in some countries much is said of a rapid growth of cities, causing the rural population to suffer a *relative* decline, in England there is a decrease in the absolute numbers of the rural inhabitants. The decline began in 1861, as may be seen in the following percentages of decennial increase or decrease calculated from the figures of Table 2 [p. 8]:

	Urban	Rural
1851–61	21.9%	+1.88%
1861–71	28.1	−5.86
1871–81	25.6	−3.84
1881–91	18.5	−2.76

It does not follow from this that there has been a rural depopulation in England in the strict sense of the term; for the aggregate rural population of a country may diminish either as a result of emigration or as the result of the growth of hamlets and villages into towns and cities. The increase in the mere number of cities is remarkable. In 1891 England and Wales contained 360 urban sanitary districts, or towns, of 10,000 and more inhabitants; in 1881 there were 123; in 1801, 45; and in 1377, with a population nearly one-fourth as great as that of 1801, only two cities, London with almost 35,000 inhabitants and York with about 11,000. Nine towns are believed to have had a population of 5,000 or more, and 18 a population of not less than 3,000 in lieu of the present number of 817 in a population about fourteen times as large. In 1377 the population of these 18 towns formed 8 percent of the entire population. In 1688 the towns, according to Gregory King, contained one-fourth of the population. But such estimates are extremely crude, as appears from Arthur Young's observation in 1770 that half the population was urban; whereas Table 1 shows that not more than one-third of the population could properly be called urban even in 1801.

The question of rural depopulation in England has been frequently discussed by the English statisticians and will not be entered into here, at any length, since this paper is concerned with the relative increase or decrease of the country as compared with the city. Dr. Ogle's investigation covered the seventeen registration counties in which more than 10 percent of the population were devoted to agricultural pursuits, with the exception of the two mining counties of Cornwall and Shropshire. Defining as the rural population the inhabitants of all districts in these counties except urban sanitary districts of 10,000 and upwards, he found that it aggregated 2,381,104 in 1851 and 2,358,303 in 1881. The loss is scarcely perceptible. And even if the rural population be restricted to sanitary districts of less than 5,000, it shows a decrease of only 2.1 percent in the entire period.

There are fifteen English counties which reached their maximum population in 1841 or at some other census prior to 1891. Their aggregate loss from the year of maximum to 1891 is 133,600, and of this loss 46,570 or over one-third is found in Cornwall, where the cause is not agricultural depression, but failure of the tin mines. All this does not imply a rural depopulation, which connotes a great scarcity of farm labor. Nevertheless, it is somewhat startling to read in the preliminary census report of 1891 (p. vi) that in the preceding decade there was a decline of population in 271 out of the 632 registration districts in England and Wales; and that in 202 of the 271 there had also been a decline in the decade 1871–81. And even Dr. Ogle admits that hard times, the use of labor-saving machinery and the conversion of arable into pasture land have caused the farmers to reduce their labor force.

But the decrease of the rural population in England is less significant than the great urban increase already indicated in Table 1 and set forth in greater detail in Table 2. Looking at the movement of population as a whole it is seen what a considerable change in the conditions of life has taken place during the century. The population of cities of 20,000 or more inhabitants has multiplied tenfold, while the remainder of the population has not quite doubled. A table of percentages will present the facts embodied in Table 2 more graphically [see Table 3].

In 1851 the urban population constituted 50 percent of the whole; in 1891, 72 percent. This increase, moreover, was not in the smaller cities, since the cities of 20,000 and over account for 18.5 of the 22 percent increase. The increase has not been divided equally among the three classes of cities over 20,000 shown in the table, for London has gained only 2.34 percent, while the other "great cities" have gained 7.9 percent and the middle-sized cities 9.34 percent. London, in fact, grew no more rapidly than the small cities, i.e., those having between 2,000 and 20,000 inhabitants. While, then, there has been a concentration of population in cities of at least 20,000 population, it is not a form of concentration carried to the extreme; for London's population is barely holding its own in the general growth of population, and is dropping behind the population of provincial and middle-sized cities. These latter cities are indeed constantly recruited from the next lower order of cities, but even when such manner of growth is excluded and the comparison confined to a fixed number of towns, it will not be found that population is concentrating in one great metropolis very rapidly. An English statistician, Mr. R. Price Williams, has, happily, summarized the population in a certain number of towns at each census from 1801 to 1871, using, in nearly all cases, the same territorial limits. While many considerable cities of 1871 were mere villages in 1801, and therefore a part of the rural population, for present purposes this fact may be neglected. Taking the rate of increase as given in Mr. Williams's brilliant paper in the *Journal of the Royal Statistical Society,* and comparing them with the rate of increase for the entire country as the average or standard (100), interesting results are obtained [see Table 4].

It will be noticed that the urban population of Mr. Williams's calculations has uniformly exceeded in its rate of increase the average of the entire country; while the rural population, being the complement of the urban population in the general total, has of course fallen below the average. The smaller towns, it is worth noting, have

TABLE 2
Distribution of Population in England and Wales

	London	Other cities of 100,000+		Cities of from 20,000 to 100,000		All cities 20,000+		Aggregate urban Population[a]		Aggregate rural population	Total population
								Towns	Population		
1801	864,845	—	—	14	641,331	15	1,506,176	—	—	—	8,892,536
1811	1,009,546	2	210,484	15	619,370	18	1,839,400	—	—	—	10,164,256
1821	1,225,694	3	393,330	24	870,242	28	2,489,266	—	—	—	12,000,236
1831	1,471,941	5	791,315	37	1,203,624	43	3,466,880	—	—	—	13,896,797
1841	1,873,676	5	1,039,942	48	1,695,045	54	4,608,663	—	—	—	15,914,148
1851	2,362,236	8	1,678,551	54	2,224,224	63	6,265,011	580	8,900,809	8,936,800	17,927,609
1861	2,803,989	11	2,211,075	60	2,652,558	72	7,667,622	781	10,960,998	9,105,226	20,066,224
1871	3,254,260	12	2,617,726	90	3,671,982	103	9,543,968	938	14,041,404	8,670,862	22,712,266
1881	3,834,354	19	3,864,821	125	4,754,326	145	12,453,501	967	17,636,646	8,337,793	25,974,439
1891	4,232,118	23	5,021,856	161	6,309,860	185	15,563,834	1,011	20,895,504	8,107,021	29,002,525

[a] The urban population from 1851 to 1871 consists of "municipal boroughs, towns of improvement acts, and towns of some 2,000 or more inhabitants, without any organization other than the parish vestry" (*Census of 1871*, Introd., p. xxxi). In 1881 and 1891 it consisted of the urban sanitary districts.

TABLE 3
Percentage of Population of England and Wales

	London	Other great cities	Cities 20,000– 100,000	All cities 20,000+	Urban districts	Rural districts
1801	9.73	0.	7.21	16.94	—	—
1811	9.93	2.08	6.10	18.11	—	—
1821	10.20	3.27	7.35	20.82	—	—
1831	10.64	5.71	8.70	25.05	—	—
1841	11.75	6.52	10.63	28.90	—	—
1851	13.18	9.40	12.42	35.00	50.08	49.92
1861	13.97	11.02	13.22	38.21	54.60	44.40
1871	14.33	11.50	16.20	42.00	61.80	38.20
1881	14.69	14.91	18.40	48.00	67.90	32.10
1891	14.52	17.30	21.76	53.58	72.05	27.95

also grown less rapidly than the population of England and Wales in its entirety, except in the single decade 1811–21. The 98 cities other than London which had a population in excess of 20,000 in 1871, have far outstripped the small towns and rural districts; but even their rapid growth is inferior to the expansion of the sixteen "great cities," in every decade except the last. There is therefore a regular progression in the rate of growth, beginning with the villages and scattered population in the country districts and proceeding through the several classes of towns to the largest cities.

Levasseur, observing a similar phenomenon in France, formulated the law that "the force of attraction in human groups, like that of matter, is in general proportionate to the mass." If London be classed with the other English cities of 100,000, Levasseur's rule will hold good for England. But London's population is properly a class by itself and is so treated in the tables. London might be expected to grow more rapidly than the provincial cities, just as Paris does. But such is not the case in a single decade of the century. Moreover, in the last decade represented by Mr. Williams's figures, the great cities were outstripped by the middle-sized cities. This tendency has become even more manifest in the subsequent periods, as appears in the table for 1881–91 [see Table 5].

It thus appears that the largest growth is in the cities of from 20,000 to 100,000 inhabitants, with the classes 100,000 to 250,000 and

TABLE 4
Proportionate Decennial Increase

	London[a]	Other great cities[b]	All cities of 20,000+ exc. London	Small towns[c]	Total urban population[d]	Total rural population[e]	Pop. of England and Wales
1801–11	131	150	140	91	122	84	100
1811–21	117	163	147	105	126	81	100
1821–31	126	239	190	95	143	66	100
1831–41	122	202	182	86	138	67	100
1841–51	167	209	195	82	158	46	100
1851–61	157	172	165	61	137	61	100
1861–71	121	131	152	83	132	64	100

[a] London—the registration district.
[b] Other great cities—the 16 cities which, in addition to London, had over 100,000 inhabitants in 1871.
[c] Small towns—places which contained, in 1871, a population of 2,000–20,000.
[d] Urban population—the population at the various censuses of all towns with 2,000 or more inhabitants in 1871.
[e] Rural population—the remainder.
Some of these figures agree with the calculations of Sir Rawson W. Rawson, in the *J. of Stat. Soc.*, 43: 500.

TABLE 5
Urban Sanitary Districts

Population	No.	Mean percentage of increase of population
London	1	10.4%
250,000–600,000	5	7.2
100,000–250,000	18	19.9
50,000–100,000	38	22.8
20,000–50,000	123	22.1
10,000–20,000	175	18.9
5,000–10,000	262	11.5
3,000–5,000	195	6.6
Under 3,000	194	3.6
Total urban	1,011	15.4
Total rural	—	3.0

10,000–20,000 in close company. The urban districts under 3,000 have gained little more than the rural districts and the small towns (3,000–10,000) and the six great cities have increased less than the general population. That the villages should be falling behind is not surprising, but it at first seems strange that the very largest cities should manifest so slow a growth. The six cities are:

	Increase or decrease of population
London	10.4%
Liverpool	−6.2
Manchester	9.3
Birmingham	9.4
Leeds	18.9
Sheffield	14.0

Leeds and Sheffield alone rise above the general rate (11.65) for England, while Liverpool has actually lost! Yet nobody believes that Liverpool is decaying; the explanation of the matter is simple enough: the growing business of the city requires the transformation of dwellings into stores and the dispossessed persons move away from the center of business. As there is little more room within the municipal limits most of these people live in the environs, but are no longer counted in Liverpool. This process is going on in nearly all the great cities, as will appear later. But as it is comparatively recent that such cities as London have reached "the point of saturation," it does not affect the conclusion that in England the largest urban aggregation has exerted a weaker power of attraction than the class of "great cities." The concentration of population has not been carried to its utmost point in the England of the nineteenth century.

There now arises the question of the causes that influenced the distribution of population in England and Wales in the direction shown by the preceding analysis. The tables of Mr. Price Williams show that the maximum urban increase was in 1811–21; but this was balanced by a similarly large increase in the rural districts, so that the concentration was not so great then as later. Table 3 shows that the entire period of 1821 to 1851 was a period of concentration in cities, and in this period the two decades 1821–31 and 1841–51 are especially marked. The earlier decade saw the rise of the sixteen "great cities"; the second decade, the expansion of London.

The charts accompanying the article of Price Williams already referred to clearly show that most of the great English cities attained their maximum rate of growth in 1821–31, which was in some cases phenomenal. Brighton's[1] increase, for example, was 69.7 percent, Bradford's 65.5, Salford's 55.9, Leeds's 47.3, Liverpool's 45.8, Manchester's 44.9, Birmingham's 41.5, Sheffield's 40.5. Thus eight of the twelve "great cities" of 1871 owe their largest decennial increase to the causes at work in 1821–31. With the exception of Bristol, all the eight cities are in the manufacturing district in the North; and Bristol is a port in an adjacent county. It may therefore be conjectured that the period was marked by a great expansion of the manufacturing industries; and it was indeed at this time that the cotton trade began to assume large dimensions. The number of pounds of cotton imported was in—

1781	5,198,775
1785	18,400,384
1792	34,907,497
1813	51,000,000
1832	287,800,000
1841	489,900,000

"Though 1800 marks the beginning of a continuous expansion in both cotton and woolen manufactures, it was not until about 1817, when the new motor had established itself generally in the large

---

[1] Weber means to refer here to Bristol rather than to Brighton.—Eds.

centers of industry and the energy of the nation was called back to the arts of peace that the new forces began fully to manifest their power." It must therefore be clear to every mind that the decade under discussion (1821–31) presents in England a typical instance of the effect which the growth of manufactures and the development of the factory system, or system of centralized industry, has upon the distribution of population [see Table 6].

TABLE 6
Decennial Increase of Population

	Lancashire	Rural districts	Urban districts	Small towns (2,000–20,000)	Large towns (20,000+)
1801–11	23.02%	20.44%	25.07%	19.40%	26.37%
1811–21	27.09	20.20	32.37	25.44	33.08
1821–31	26.97	13.29	36.46	19.44	39.95
1831–41	24.70	12.51	31.73	19.07	33.94
1841–51	21.84	12.67	26.37	14.35	28.23
1851–61	19.61	20.46	19.23	20.77	19.01
1861–71	16.06	14.86	16.58	19.91	16.12

The noteworthy feature of Lancashire's growth is the concentration of population in the large cities which was going on throughout the period 1801–51, and especially in the decade 1821–31, when the great expansion of the textile industry took place.

The marked concentration of population in 1821–31 was, then, produced by the industrial changes affecting the cities of northern England. In the succeeding decade the concentration continued, at a somewhat diminished rate, under the same influences. But in 1841–51 was reached the most notable period of concentration in the century. Table 4 shows that London's rate of increase reached its maximum at this time, but that alone does not fully account for the effect. A more detailed analysis, as follows, shows that the middle-sized cities were even more influential in their action on the general result:

	Average Eng. and Wales	London	Other great cities (100,000+)	82 cities, 20,000–100,000	Towns, 2,000–20,000	Total urban
1821–31	100	126	239	150	95	143
1841–51	100	167	209	182	82	158

The counties in which the urban population (i.e., cities of 20,000 and upwards) increased most in 1841–51 are as follows:

	Percent
Monmouth	78.7%
Bedford	65.0
Chester	48.8
Glamorgan	45.3
Lincoln	44.7
Average of the 82 cities	23.2%

As to the influences on the growth of the city population of Monmouth and Glamorgan counties there can be no doubt. Glamorganshire contains the great coal-fields and iron mines of South Wales, and it was the iron industry that built up its three largest cities, Merthyr Tydvil, Cardiff, Swansea, and the iron-smelting seat, Newport in Monmouth. It is to be regretted that the development of the iron industry in the North cannot also be traced; but the iron deposits and the smelting-centers there are mainly in Yorkshire and Lancashire, where the other factors of previously established manufactures complicate the study.

Outside the iron districts the cities that showed the highest rates of increase in this period were ports. Thus in Lincolnshire, the growth was mainly in Grimsby, a rival of Hull; Cheshire's high rate is due almost wholly to Birkenhead, a port on the Mersey opposite Liverpool. Of the ten cities that grew most rapidly in 1841–51, seven were seaports.[2]

Now commercial statistics show that English trade experienced a very considerable impetus about this time,[3] and the stimulus came

---

[2] Birkenhead (port), Hanley in Staffordshire, Torquay (p), Grimsby (p), Cardiff (p), Newport (p), Southport (p), Luton in Bedfordshire, Hythe (p), Merthyr Tydvil. Bradford is excluded as being one of the sixteen "great cities."

[3] The following are the statistics of imports and exports in million pounds sterling:

	Imports	Exports
1785	14.27	13.66
1795	20.10	22.23
1810	39.30	43.57
1825	44.21	56.32
1830	46.30	69.70
1835	49.03	91.16
1840	67.49	116.48
1845	85.30	150.88
1850	100.47	197.31
1855	123.60	116.70
1860	210.53	164.52

These figures are not to be depended on absolutely; and in 1854 the method of from the opening of railways, which was of course accompanied by a great expansion of the iron industry. The first railroad, the Liverpool and Manchester line built by George Stephenson, was opened in September 1830. Its effect on the distribution of population was not immediate, owing to the slowness with which the system developed. But by 1840 the United Kingdom possessed 800 miles of railways, and construction was then going on so rapidly that by 1850 the number of miles had risen to 6,600. The census of 1851 is therefore the first one to show the effects of the new transportation methods on the distribution of population. Contemporaneously with the beginnings of railway enterprise occurred the establishment of the iron industry, the leading events of which were the substitution of hot for cold blast in 1829 and the adoption of raw coal in place of coke in 1833, so that it was not much before 1840 that the production of iron assumed large dimensions.[4]

The conclusion is therefore unavoidable that it was the opening of railways, with the concomitant development of the iron industry, and expansion of domestic and foreign commerce under free trade, which occasioned the great concentration of population in the decade 1841–51, in the seaports and iron-producing districts. This explains why London, Wolverhampton and Portsmouth, alone of the seventeen great cities attained a higher rate of growth in 1841–51 than in 1821–31. Wolverhampton was a center of the Staffordshire iron-manufacturing district, and the three other cities were great seaports. It has already been shown that the middle-sized cities whose growth contributed so much to the high degree of concentration in 1841–51 were either seaports or iron-centers.[5]

valuation was changed, which probably had some effect. Up to 1800 the data refer to Great Britain; thereafter to the United Kingdom. But making allowance for all uncertainties, it would still appear that a great expansion of trade began about 1835–40. Between 1835 and 1850 the imports doubled in value, and the exports more than doubled; and this was in a period of falling prices. The repeal of the Corn Laws and adoption of a free-trade policy in 1846, favored a larger foreign trade.

[4] The following are the statistics of the pig iron production in Great Britain and Ireland:

1790	68,000 Tons.
1800	158,000 Tons.
1810	305,000 Tons.
1820	400,000 Tons.
1830	700,000 Tons.
1840	1,396,000 Tons.
1850	2,250,000 Tons.
1860	3,827,000 Tons.

[5] The *Census of 1851* classified 212 cities, and computed their rate of growth during the

Since 1851 the process of concentration has sensibly diminished. As already indicated, this is due in part to the overflow of municipal boundaries in the greater cities where a small area was already filled. This movement and the growth of small suburban towns account for the recent tendency of city growth to center in the smaller cities. Cf. Table 5.

half century 1801–51. It is interesting to note that the highest rate was that of the watering places, as appears below:

No.	Class.	Increase percent, 1801–51
15	Watering places	254.1%
51	Manufacturing places	224.2
28	Mining and hardware places	217.3
26	Seaports (exc. London)	195.6
1	London	146.4
99	County towns (exc. London)	122.1
212	Cities	176.1%

Pierre Sorlin

FRENCH SOCIETY, 1840–1914: THE BIG CITIES

Pierre Sorlin, a French academic, has written extensively on French political and social history and on the social history of Soviet Russia. In this selection from his survey of French society between 1840 and 1914, he describes the complex but regular, staged migration along well-defined paths that led to the transformation of the largest French cities. Each city had its own sphere of influence, which was based upon transportation routes and earlier migration as well as economic ties.

The contrast between traditional society, still close to the old regime, and modern society, leading to the industrial era, was especially evident in urban development. Under the July Monarchy, one Frenchman out of four lived in a city; on the eve of the war [World War I], the cities contained almost half of the population (Figure 1).

From Pierre Sorlin, *La société française*, Vol. 1: *1840–1914* (Paris: B. Arthaud, 1969), pp. 12, 101–109. Reprinted by permission of the publisher. Translated by the editors.

FIGURE 1. The Population of France, 1841-1911.[a]

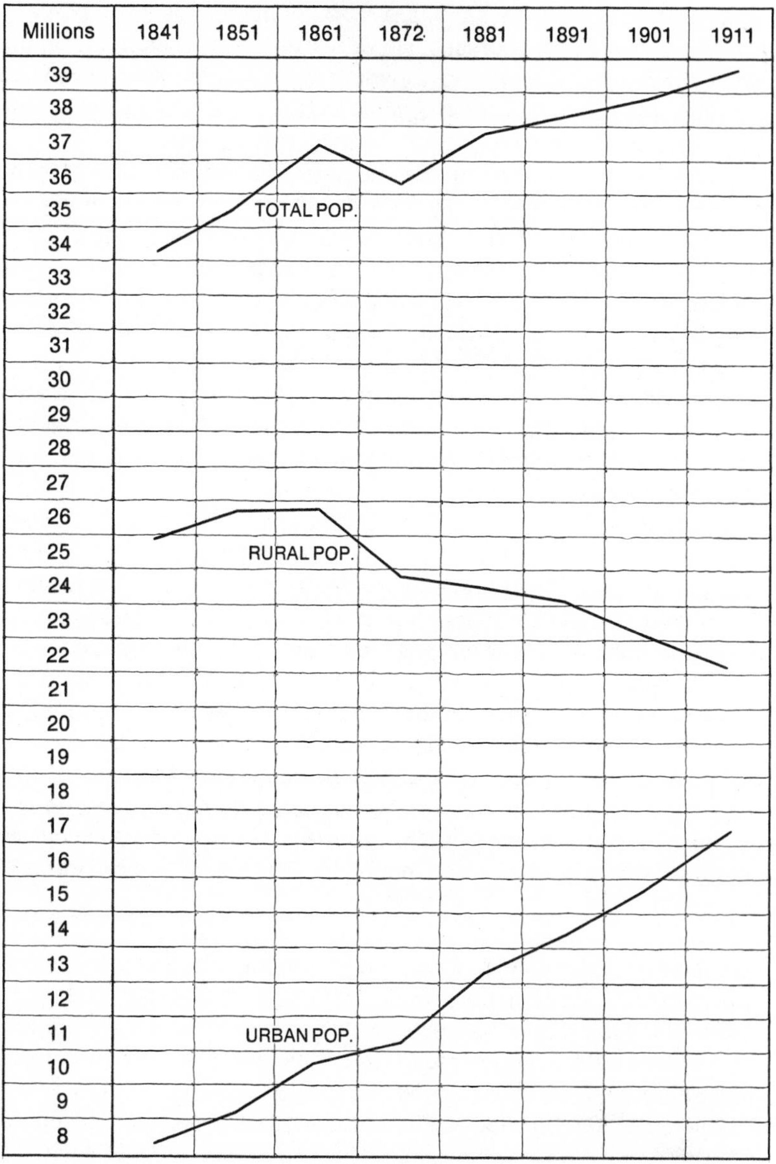

Millions	1841	1851	1861	1872	1881	1891	1901	1911

TOTAL POP.

RURAL POP.

URBAN POP.

[a]The urban population is defined as everyone living in towns numbering 2,000 inhabitants or more. — Eds.

Moreover, this proportion was not extraordinary: in comparison with Great Britain or Germany, an increase of 80 percent seems moderate. But . . . our country possesses two rather different types of cities; the small towns, close to the rural world, were transformed slowly; in contrast, the extremely rapid transformation of the big cities bears comparison with the English or German metropolises.

Statistics do not suffice for defining the big city; there is no dividing line, although a city of 100,000 persons can scarcely be considered "small." Rather than numbers, it is appropriate to consider the speed of growth: the big city expands rapidly, sometimes discontinuously, but with very great thrusts, which mark the sudden progression of some activities. Spatial growth is another criterion. Before 1840, most French cities seemed to be enclosed in a corset beyond which they dared not expand. At best they had some suburbs, appendages that were poorly linked to the main area of settlement. Often they retained a wall that marked their limits and prevented all growth.

Under the July Monarchy[1] these traditional frontiers were crossed. The territorial conquest must not be confused with the demographic change. In reality these were two different phenomena. The distinction is easy to maintain in the case of Lille or Lyon. The population of these two cities began to grow at the start of the century. Under the July Monarchy, Lille's growth exceeded 30 percent. This rapid development had no impact on the geography of the city: the two cities remained crowded, one inside its ramparts, the other between its rivers. After 1850, geography changed along with population: both the population and the area of Lyon doubled during the second half of the nineteenth century; Lille, breaking through its fortifications, acquired space to the south equal to that which it had formerly occupied.

The cities annexed the neighboring communes.[2] Henceforth they consisted of extremely diverse neighborhoods. The suburbs, a typically modern phenomenon, took the place of the old residential areas. The suburb is not an exterior appendage: it is a fragment of a city, welded into a large mass, having its own life, but continually interacting with the main center.

The cities encroached on the countryside. This fact, taken for

---

[1] The reign of Louis Philippe, 1830–1848.—Eds.
[2] Communes are the French equivalents of townships.—Eds.

granted today, shocked contemporaries. It explains Verhaeren's horror at "the tentacular city, a greedy octopus and a tomb," as well as the view of life as indefinitely reverberating and prolonged, which Jules Romains attempted to express: now the city was in motion.

In the middle of the nineteenth century the small cities predominated heavily. They comprised the greater part of the urban population, while the centers with populations of 50,000 or more included only one Frenchman out of twenty. Then the big cities began to swell: under the Empire[3] they gained 1.8 million inhabitants, and the Third Republic brought them 3.4 million more;[4] between 1841 and 1911 they quadrupled. If there was an upsurge of cities in France it was at this level, and not in the provincial centers. Henceforth the fifteen cities with populations of 100,000 or more stood clearly apart. They had a distinctive appearance and their own problems, and they assumed a special place in the life of French society.

The growth of the urban population resulted in part from natural increase. Working-class families continued to have large numbers of children up until the end of the Empire: at Rouen around 1880 the only really big families, numbering at least seven persons, were those of the cotton workers. Everywhere there was an especially large gap between rich and poor areas: the birth rate was twice as high in Buttes-Chaumont as in the area around the Opera.[5]

But these birth rates were counterbalanced by high mortality rates, which often reached the level of 30 per thousand. On the other hand, starting in 1890 the poorer classes started to follow the example of the bourgeoisie: by 1911 the birth rate had fallen below 25 per thousand in Lille, Roubaix, and Rheims. For now, we need not dwell on this problem, but it is important to emphasize the decline of fertility in the cities. In the final analysis the natural increase was not very important. In Marseilles it came to only 10,000 persons for the entire nineteenth century. In 1911, 60 percent of the inhabitants of Rouen and 65 percent of the inhabitants of Marseilles and Paris had been born outside the city where they lived. Accordingly it is immigration that explains the growth of the big cities, and the process by which urban populations were formed is the first problem to study.

The geographic origins of the city-dwellers are not without interest.

[3] 1851–1870.—Eds.
[4] The Third Republic lasted from 1871 to 1940, but Sorlin here means the period 1871–1914.—Eds.
[5] Buttes-Chaumont was working-class, and the area around the Opera was well-to-do. Both districts are in Paris.—Eds.

Setting the capital to one side, it is clear that most immigrants had not left their native department:[6] they had merely slipped from the periphery toward the chief town of the area. In Marseilles, 35 percent of the inhabitants had been born in the lower Rhône Valley, while only 30 percent came from other districts. Moreover, these proportions are distorted by the fact that the port attracted foreigners. If one counts only Frenchmen, barely a tenth of the inhabitants of Lille, an eighth of the inhabitants of Lyon and of Toulouse, and a seventh of the inhabitants of Marseilles had spent their childhood in another department.

This simple observation permits us to understand more fully who the city-dwellers were. Only rarely had they come directly from the countryside. Certainly there were some peasants who had abandoned their villages in order to take a job in an urban business: one encountered them in Paris, in Havre, and in Roubaix. But they were exceptions. Generally the process had two or three stages, almost always with an intermediary passage through a secondary town. Contrary to an often-repeated legend, it is not true that the city attracted rustics at the end of the nineteenth century; instead, it scared them, and they risked it only after a certain amount of preparation.

Each center had its sphere of attraction, which was not the same as its zone of economic influence. The inhabitants of Marseilles were recruited in Corsica, in lower Languedoc, in the Cevennes Mountains, and in the departments of Pyrénées-Orientales and Basses-Alpes. In the last two cases one cannot invoke commercial or financial ties by way of explanation. In reality it is especially necessary to take account of the state of communications and of the existence of regional groups that had already settled in the midst of the big cities: the immigrants went where they hoped to meet compatriots. Paris was no exception: its radius of attraction simply extended farther. Vast areas—Poitou, Aquitaine, the lower Rhône Valley, and the Mediterranean Midi—resisted the charms of the capital. Aside from some poor departments in the Massif Central, it was the East and the Parisian basin that supplied Paris. The progress of migration toward the capital was complex, but it obeyed the same rules as the other movements of population.

At the end of the ninteenth century and at the start of the twen-

[6] The departments are administrative subdivisions of France.—Eds.

tieth, a current of continuous emigration developed in Languedoc. It was directed essentially toward the area around Marseilles, but it paused in the countryside or in the secondary towns of Arles, Salon, and Aix-en-Provence. The next generation ventured toward Marseilles itself, and then from there moved toward Paris. A sort of relay was necessary before the banks of the Seine were reached.

Only foreigners chose the major centers at the outset. In 1911, 40 percent of them were to be found in four cities: Paris, Lille, Marseilles, and Nice. The 200,000 foreigners in the department of the Seine vanished in a population of which they constituted less than one-thirtieth. Their presence occasionally elicited reactions from unemployed workers, but it was not really perceptible. In contrast one cannot ignore the 100,000 Italians in Marseilles or the 50,000 Belgians in Lille, since in both cases it was a matter of a fifth of the inhabitants. These cities, like Nice, already had their foreign districts.

Migration toward the big cities was not a continuous movement. Instead it is possible to distinguish between periods of more and less rapid migration. Starting in the first half of the nineteenth century, especially between 1830 and 1840, one notices a period of rapid growth. The tendency varied considerably from region to region. Such ports as Rouen, Le Havre, and Marseilles grew only a little, and Nantes even experienced a slight decline. Lyon and Nancy gained less than 15 percent. On the other hand, the population of Bordeaux grew by a half, and that of Toulouse by two-thirds, while that of Saint-Etienne doubled. There is nothing surprising about the growth of the capital of the department of the Loire [Saint-Etienne]: around 1830 it was a small city with fewer than 30,000 inhabitants; the establishment of textile and metallurgical factories and the growth of the ribbon trade attracted hundreds of rural artisans who settled in the city. The situation of the two metropolises of the Southwest was not so simple. Industry was almost nonexistent there: owing to its port, Bordeaux had several shipyards, but in Toulouse there were only some artisans producing clothing and daily necessities. In fact, commercial activities were the only ones that expanded continuously. Aquitaine and the valley of the Garonne were rich agricultural areas at the time. The farmers tended naturally toward the regional centers where they went to make their purchases. Stores selling textiles and novelties, foodstuffs, and luxuries began to be established. Some of the big land-owners began to find it agreeable to live in town during the winter. Worldly life was active, both cities had theaters and paint-ing exhibitions, and the university of Bordeaux had an influence throughout all of western France.

. . . During the July Monarchy, Paris already exercised considera-ble powers of attraction. In fifteen years, from 1831 to 1846, its population went from 780,000 to 1.05 million inhabitants, growing by more than a third. France had never experienced such a rate of growth, and the phenomenon was abnormal. Neither the political role nor the industrial and commercial functions of the capital justified this development. Masses of the unemployed, of artisans without work, went to Paris hoping to find jobs. At mid-century the police counted 50,000 nomads who had nothing to do and nowhere to live and just managed to get by. In addition, large numbers barely pro-cured the necessities and lived on the edge of misery. Epidemics, such as the cholera of 1832, ravaged the capital, where the disinher-ited were legion. Terrible insurrections took place in 1832 and 1848 because Paris had too many poor people, threatened by famine and sickness.

Under the Second Empire the capital no longer led the way. For two decades, the [other] big cities grew at the expense of the middle-sized centers. It is pointless here to give statistics and to try to make distinctions, since everything points in the same direction. Toulouse and Bordeaux, which continued to surge forward, were imitated by Marseilles, Lyon, Lille, and Nantes. The only notable exception was Rouen, which was hit hard by a crisis in the cotton trade and gained scarcely 1,500 inhabitants in twenty years.

The statistics of this period are distorted by the annexations of suburban communes, which greatly augmented the numbers of in-habitants. This tendency to enlarge the limits of the commune de-serves emphasis. It shows clearly that by 1855 the older cities had reached the saturation point; henceforth they had to expand. Lyon set the example in 1851 by including Guillotière, Croix-Rousse, and Vaise; Lille followed suit in 1858, Paris in 1859.

The heyday of the big cities was between 1852 and 1865 (see Figure 2). This was the period when construction projects were un-dertaken everywhere. The railroads reached the principal centers and created jobs; for a decade Bordeaux was occupied with the con-struction of lines linking the city with Paris and Cette; Lyon had to redevelop Perrache and build a tunnel in order to establish a rail

FIGURE 2. Three Types of Urban Population Growth.[a]

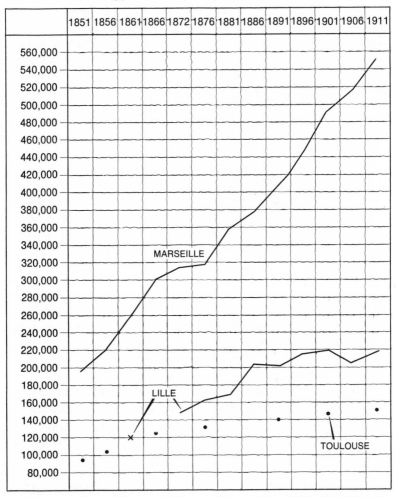

[a]Owing to geographical additions in 1858, figures for the population of Lille begin in 1861.— **Eds.**

connection with Paris; Marseilles transformed Joliette; Lille constructed new walls; and everywhere there were new streets and avenues.

During this period a clear hierarchy of the important centers
began to emerge. Around 1850, ten cities had between 100,000 and
200,000 inhabitants. Starting in the 1850s Lyon and Marseilles started
to outstrip the others. When Napoleon III fell, each of them had more
than 300,000 inhabitants. No other city reached this size before the
middle of the twentieth century. While the other centers specialized
in industry, like Lille or Rouen, or in commerce, like Bordeaux and
Toulouse, the two principal metropolises multiplied their activities.
They went through, somewhat later, the difficulties which the capital
had experienced under Louis Philippe. In Lyon, Guillotière, a vast
area almost totally alien from the center of the city and separated
from it by the Rhône River, and in Marseilles the areas of Saint-
Lazare and Longchamp were inundated by the new arrivals, unfortunate artisans, unemployed workers, and tradesmen attracted by the
hope of bigger profits.

Growth began to slow around 1865. The slowdown affected every
city, and this exact coincidence is important. It proves that with the
modern means of communication the big cities evolve in identical
ways. When the principal construction projects were completed, the
feverish growth of the middle of the century subsided; soon war
threatened, and the fear of hostilities led to a slowdown of activity
everywhere.

Only the capital (Figure 3) started once again to grow rapidly at
the start of the Third Republic. It gained another 850,000 inhabitants
during the last thirty years of the century, and its suburbs, unimpor-
tant up to that time, numbered a million by the start of the twentieth
century. One can discern phases of relatively slow growth, especially
during the depressed period after 1882, but there was no reversal of
the trend. Each year, between 15,000 and 20,000 persons settled in
the capital. Sometimes the approach of an exceptional event, such as
the exposition of 1900, or exceptional prosperity, such as was evident
between 1910 and the war, precipitated the migration, and at these
times there were as many as 40,000 new arrivals [per year].

The rest of the country reacted less quickly (Figure 2). Some cities
experienced only slow growth up to the war: Toulouse gained fewer
than 1,000 persons each year, and during the Third Republic it grew
by only 12 percent. The growth of Rouen and of Saint-Etienne was

FIGURE 3. The Growth of the Population of Paris and Its Suburbs.[a]

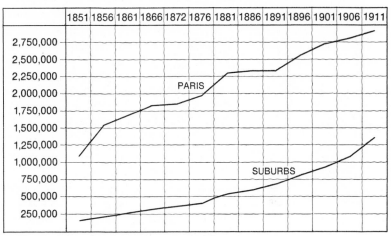

| | 1851 | 1856 | 1861 | 1866 | 1872 | 1876 | 1881 | 1886 | 1891 | 1896 | 1901 | 1906 | 1911 |

PARIS

SUBURBS

[a]The population of Paris is for the area within the boundaries of 1859.

scarcely greater. Migration toward the cities did not slow down, but it was counterbalanced by departures. Cities numbering between 100,000 and 150,000 inhabitants were way-stations: the inhabitants of Rouen went to Havre or to Paris, the inhabitants of Saint-Etienne to Lyon. Eventually they also went to the major industrial centers. Between 1872 and 1901 Lille registered a gain of 40 percent; starting from a level close to that of Toulouse, it moved well ahead, thanks to its factories. Then the decline began: 15,000 persons left between 1901 and 1906. Lille had been a halting-place, which people abandoned in favor of neighboring cities or the capital. Ultimately only Lyon and Marseilles retained their vitality. The Mediterranean port even out-stripped its rival. Each year 6,000 to 8,000 people entered the city, and, as in the capital, the start of the twentieth century was marked by an acceleration of population growth.

Urban development in nineteenth-century France was not a simple phenomenon. Country-dwellers did not move constantly to the cities: they experienced periods of doubt and hesitation. The movement was dominated by the growth of the capital. Whereas in sixty years Paris only doubled, the department of the Seine, that is, the whole metropolitan area of which Paris was the center, tripled. Aside from

Marseilles, no other center experienced comparable expansion. Only beyond a distance of 800 kilometers did the attraction of the capital diminish. The growth of Paris preceded that of the other cities. It certainly was not uniform, but it was continuous, without phases of interruption, which was rarely the case elsewhere.

Frenchmen migrated unceasingly to Paris, and the periods of crisis did not discourage them. They were more suspicious of the other cities, from which they turned away during the difficult years. Each of the regional metropolises enjoyed its period of success, more or less prolonged but never permanent.

The city was attractive because it offered jobs. Immigration reached its height for all of the urban centers during the epoch of large construction projects, at the start of the Empire. Between 1866 and 1876 Marseilles seemed immobile. This was the time when the textile and food industries were threatened by competition, when the traffic in the port declined, when manual laborers and dockers were laid off. But the upsurge of Mediterranean commerce with the opening of the Suez Canal, and the multiplication of shipments toward the colonies, brought about an economic revival, and immigration resumed immediately.

The correlation between the availability of work and the level of migration is not perfect. We have already indicated that the peasants had few illusions concerning the fate that awaited them in the city. On the other hand, we shall see that at the lowest echelons wages in the capital did not differ significantly from those in the rest of the country. Economic considerations were not the only ones.

In addition, there was the matter of transportation. People went to the cities because they could get there. The railroads regulated migration. Before 1840 it was primarily single people who left for the city. Thereafter, entire families moved together. Sometimes the influence of the railroad was very clear: Bordeaux experienced its most rapid development after 1853, that is, after the arrival of the train; the situation was similar in Nantes, where 20,000 people arrived during the decade after the opening of the train station.

The existence of a group originating from the same region was a powerful attraction. The role in Paris of the migrants from Auvergne and Brittany is too well known for us to dwell upon. To a lesser extent the same thing happened in Marseilles: immigrants from the Alps were assured of finding work in the urban transportation industry or with the PLM.[7] Those from the Vaucluse became tradesmen. Corsica provided civil servants, and Drôme and Ardèche furnished domestic servants.

Here we take up again the matter of employment, but from another perspective. The new arrivals had a greater chance of being hired wherever some compatriot could show them the ropes and shorten the preliminary proceedings. The departments of Corrèze, Aveyron, and Lozère poured out their excess population on the capital. Logically, Lyon and Marseilles would have received a portion of this flow, but the layout of the French railway network, combined with the presence of colonies that had sprung from these three departments, meant that Paris had priority.

French workers in the nineteenth century were haunted by unemployment. In the urban centers, industries took turns, and the rise of one compensated for the decline of another. Construction was undertaken as the growth of population generated services and trade. At equal wages the chances for work were greater in a large city than in a provincial city or in the countryside, and this is the primary explanation for the magnitude of the migrations toward the great centers.

[7] The Paris-Lyon-Marseilles Railroad.—Eds.

Wolfgang Köllmann

THE PROCESS OF URBANIZATION IN GERMANY AT THE HEIGHT OF THE INDUSTRIALIZATION PERIOD

Wolfgang Köllmann, Professor of History at the Ruhr University of Bochum in the Federal Republic of Germany, is a leading historian of modern German social and economic development. The article reprinted below is one of several studies of demographic changes in the nineteenth and twentieth centuries written by Köllmann. This article, which focuses on the late nineteenth and early twentieth centuries, emphasizes both the extremely rapid pace of urbanization in Germany—determined in large part by the extreme rapidity of industrialization—and the complexity of the changes in social structure that accompanied urban growth.

The process of accelerated urbanization apparent in Germany from the mid-nineteenth century was a phenomenon which accompanied and had its origin in industrialization. Admittedly, in the eighteenth century certain areas had shown a quite considerable growth in urban population due almost entirely in particular cases to the growth of industry in the age of mercantilism. But this earlier increase in urban population remained under the jurisdiction of the "town" government, still largely medieval in character, which underpinned the social position of the burghers in the narrower sense and that of privileged citizens and protected aliens, and which, thanks to the relatively high financial and social status needed to acquire "citizenship" and to the rigidity of the guild constitution, to which only those granted special exemption were not subject, impeded progress rather than furthered it; so that the more significant phenomenon of this period was the emergence of industry in rural areas (e.g. Silesia, Saxony, Berg and Mark) which reached the first stages of development into urban-artisan structures. In any case this growth created both conditions of residence and the impulse for "new" urban development. It was with the developments set in motion by the abolition of the older municipal constitutions—beginning with the reforms of the early nineteenth century under the direct or indirect influence

From *The Journal of Contemporary History*, Vol. 4, No. 3 (1969), pp. 59–76. Reprinted by permission of Sage Publishers Ltd.

of the French Revolution and the economic doctrines of classical liberalism which informed the municipal administrations of the middle of the century, culminating in the removal of the old privileges and the establishment of the legal equality of all subjects and the gradual elimination of guild and trade restrictions designed to discourage migration—only with these steps was it possible to remove the obstacles to urban development by the time the 1871 imperial constitution was promulgated, while at the same time the older forms of industrial activity gave way to new ones as a result of the transformation of production introduced by the technical revolution.

Gunther Ipsen, developing the ideas of Werner Sombart and Gottlieb Gassert, regarded industry as the true builder of cities of the modern age. Since the town as the industrial center of primary producers presupposed or necessitated the existence of secondary producers such as artisans, builders, retail and wholesale traders, and services providing banking and transport, cultural activities, catering, etc., as well as the presence of the free professions and administrators, all of them activities which from one center serve a fairly broad hinterland, this meant a balancing out of industrial and nonindustrial employment whereby, according to the "double job law" valid at least for the period of industrial expansion, every 100 new jobs in the "primary" sector necessitated another 100 in the "secondary" sector. If urban growth in Germany in the period of industrialization was governed by this "law," industry became the chief agent changing the role and function of the city. Although the towns, and especially the large towns, with the exception of a few new and exclusively industrial settlements, continued to excercise their functions as administrative and commercial centers, these became secondary to their function as centers of production. Industry took over the town and reshaped it.

The demographic conditions for the process of urbanization can be traced to the initial period of industrialization before the middle of the century, which was marked by a growing discrepancy between labor potential and the availability of work. Despite considerable regional differences, it can be said for Germany as a whole that the increase in population could not be absorbed by the existing agrarian and industrial economy. Even emigration brought no significant relief. The resultant phenomenon of severe overpopulation and its social consequence of mass poverty (pauperism) were only slowly

TABLE 1
Urbanization in Germany, 1871–1910.

	Urban dwellers as percentage of total Reich population	
	1871	1910
Towns with more than 100,000 inhabitants	4.8	21.3
Towns with 10,000 to 100,000 inhabitants	7.7	13.4
Towns with 5,000 to 10,000 inhabitants	11.2	14.1
Parishes with 2,000 to 5,000 inhabitants	12.4	11.3
Parishes with fewer than 2,000 inhabitants	63.9	39.9

overcome in the wake of industrialization which began to gather momentum after 1850 and brought relief from the pauper existence of the early industrial worker. However, the existence of an uprooted and propertyless surplus population increased the willingness to move in search of work. Mass emigration was only one symptom of this new mobility, which also encouraged a far greater measure of internal migration into the industrial centers with their new and constantly increasing opportunities for employment.

Although the process of urbanization began around the middle of the century it reached completion essentially between 1871 and 1910. It brought about a shift in the population which doubled the proportion of city dwellers. In 1871, 23.7 percent of the population lived in communities of over 5,000 inhabitants; by 1910 this figure had risen to 48.8, while the share of the rural population, including those living in country market towns, fell from 75 to 50 percent of the population. By far the sharpest was the rise in the population of large cities (+ 443 percent), but here it must be remembered that in most cases the town boundaries, once they took in neighboring parishes, were revised accordingly. These mergers were an attempt to contain the city area within the new boundaries, provided the expanded cities did not themselves become parts of a larger conurbation, as was the case in the Ruhrgebiet. This conurbation, marked off by a provincial boundary, never became one administrative entity, whereas in 1920 the Berlin conurbation became a single municipality by the incorpo-

ration of Charlottenburg, Neukölln, Schöneberg, Wilmersdorf—
these four were statistically already large towns in 1910—Köpenik,
Lichtenberg, and Spandau, and 56 villages and 29 communities
under manorial domain.

Considerable differences appeared in the various regions depending
on the existing economic structure. Whereas in 1871 the agrarian
east, but also the southwest and Westphalia, showed approximately
the same degree of urbanization, but was far below that of the Rhine
Province and Saxony, which had progressed farthest during the early
period of industrialization, variations were more marked by 1910:
urbanization remained highest in the Rhine Province, where almost
three-quarters of the population lived in urban centers, and of these
over half in large cities. Next came Westphalia, although in this area
the tendency was still towards towns of small and medium size. It
must be remembered that the process of urbanization here was concentrated chiefly in the west (i.e. the eastern part of the Ruhrgebiet
and the ore-bearing and cutlery manufacturing districts of the Sauer-
land), while the equivalent density in the Rhine Province was reached
in the western part of the Ruhrgebiet, the Bergisches Land, along the
banks of the Rhine and in the industrial area of the lower Rhine as
far west as Aachen. But it is significant that the proportion of town
dwellers in Westphalia already exceeded that in Saxony, although in
the latter the number of big-city inhabitants was almost three times
as high. In contrast to these three highly industrialized areas the
agrarian east, and more especially East Prussia, lagged farther behind. But even in the commercially and industrially advanced southwest urbanization was only half that of the Rhine Province. It is true
that the difference between these areas and East and West Prussia
had widened, particularly in regard to large and medium-sized
towns, but the economic structure of Baden and Württemberg, based
principally on small-scale and light industry, caused the proportion of
urban population to lag behind.

The growth of urban population in the phase 1871–1910 shows
that one part of the southwest region was advancing towards the
level of the industrially most developed regions, and although it did
not reach that level, the urban population in Baden at least had
increased in the same proportion as in the areas of older industrial
concentration, that is in Saxony and the Rhine, whereas in the east it
was considerably lower and Württemberg also lagged behind. The

TABLE 2

	Total population (000's)			Urban population (000's)			As % of total population increase
	1871	1910	Percent increase	1871	1910	Percent increase	
East Prussia	1,822.9	2,064.2	13.2%	217.2	554.2	155.2%	139.7%
West Prussia	1,314.6	1,703.5	29.5	208.8	533.7	155.6	83.5
Saxony	2,556.2	4,806.7	88.2	832.2	2,902.6	236.8	92.0
Westphalia	1,775.2	4,125.1	131.9	373.2	2,617.1	601.2	95.5
Rhine Province	3,579.3	7,121.1	99.2	1,387.4	4,806.7	246.5	96.5
Baden	1,461.6	2,142.8	46.6	224.8	811.3	260.9	86.1
Württemberg	1,818.5	2,437.6	34.6	300.9	872.2	189.9	92.3

highest figures were reached in Westphalia, where mining and heavy industry accelerated the process of urbanization. This bears out Ipsen's view that the decisive factor for the course of urbanization and the growth of large cities was large-scale industry. But in all areas the town absorbed almost the entire population surplus of the region. In Saxony, the Rhine Province, and Westphalia the urban population of 1910 was even greater than the total population of the Reich in 1871. At the same time this meant stagnation among the rural population. In the countryside, including rural market towns with fewer than 5,000 inhabitants, the population had already declined by 1871; jobs in the country, including those in local government and public utility undertakings, were already filled, so that the natural population increase necessarily made their way to the towns.

If the growth rate of the population for the period 1871–1910 for the Reich as a whole is compared with the population of the individual regions in 1871, we should get a rough idea of the growth rate of their population. In the case of Westphalia, to quote just one example, the increase between 1871 and 1910 was approximately 2.8 million, which means that not even half the increase in urban population could have come from the area itself. The corresponding calculation for East Prussia would show that the loss through migration from the agrarian northeast after 1871 was greater than its natural increase, although a small part of this increase did serve to develop its own urban areas.

To what extent and with what speed the development of an industrial complex was possible can be seen in the (extreme) example of Gelsenkirchen in Westphalia. As a town it did not exist before 1903, when it was formed by the amalgamation of seven parishes which around the middle of the eighteenth century had been farming villages centering on a country market town (Alt-Gelsenkirchen). In 1856 the Hibernia and Shamrock mining company sank its first shaft. The result was a sudden and striking increase in population, by 400 percent in the 13 years 1858–71, and by 300 percent in the following 14 years. Then the rate slowed down: it took 25 years to treble again, when the increase at least after 1895 was basically due to the expansion of the local light and service industries. These were confined to Gelsenkirchen itself. Services for the surrounding area were supplied by the older centers of urban life in the Ruhrgebiet.

The population of Gelsenkirchen grew tenfold between 1871 and 1910. No other town in this period recorded such an increase in size, except the suburbs of Berlin which expanded to city proportions. Of the 37 cities examined by Schott it was Kiel, developed from 1871 onwards as the German empire's naval base, which showed the highest growth rate with a ratio of 1:5.5. Then, with a ratio of between 1:5.0 and 1:4.0, came the Saxon textile town of Plauen im Vogtland; the Rhineland metropolis of Düsseldorf, an offshoot of the Ruhrgebiet with its emphasis on steel smelting and heavy industry (at the same time it housed the headquarters of many large industrial concerns), and the two Rhineland coal and steel centers of the Ruhrgebiet, Essen and Duisburg. Then, with a ratio of between 1:4 and 1:3.5 came the inland port of Mannheim, also the center for the southwest German engineering industries; the Westphalian coal and steel town of Dortmund; Saarbrücken, center of the Saarland mining industry; and Nuremberg with a variety of medium-scale industries. Among these nine fastest-growing towns there were then four centers of mining and heavy industry, four more dependent on iron and engineering, and only one textile town. This indicates the relative importance of the various industries for urbanization during the height of industrialization. Mining, heavy industry, and engineering predominated over the other branches of industry as factors promoting the growth of urban population. Of the textile towns only Plauen, and Chemnitz especially, received new and decisive impulses from the expansion of the engineering industry, while the other west German textile towns of Elberfeld (1:2.3), Barmen (1:2.25), Krefeld (1:2.1) and Aachen (1:1.8), where industry continued largely as medium- and small-scale enterprises, were incapable of further growth on such a scale.

Urbanization results from internal migration; it became possible only through the high proportion of population released from the agrarian surplus before the middle of the century. The total movement between town and country can be measured only in a few censuses. Particularly revealing is the 1907 census, which also covers the professional and industrial distribution of the population.

It gives us a picture of the state of urbanization towards the end of our period. Even though, in accordance with the census definition of "town," the inhabitants of market towns with 2,000 to 5,000 people are included in the urban population and cannot be assessed separately, the exodus from country to town is clearly perceptible. The data showing the movement into the country of those born in the towns and vice-versa give a balance in favor of country-to-town migration of around 8.3 million people. The ratio varies in the different regions. Rhineland-Westphalia, the area of most intensive urbanization, shows the smallest degree of town-to-country migration but the highest degree of country-to-town migration, while east Germany shows the highest degree of migration to the country together with the lowest degree of migration to the towns. Pomerania, Mecklenburg, and East Prussia, the areas with the smallest urban population of all, show that the ratios in east Germany were determined above all by movement between rural market town and village. Here no medium- or large-scale enterprises were developing to attract the people of the surrounding area, while in the Rhine Province and Westphalia urban expansion dictated the degree of migration by the rural population. Just so the growth of Greater Berlin spread far beyond the boundaries of the city of Berlin (defined only in 1920) to include the large number of migrants from the rural areas of Brandenburg, while Saxony emerged in second place in respect of intensive urbanization.

In this way the town drained people not only from its immediate hinterland (insofar as the agglomeration did not overspill into this), but also from a wider area, stretching at times roughly to the boundaries of the province or state; it also attracted migrants from further afield, and even from foreign countries. For the large towns in 1907—statistics are available only for these—the ratios between natives, those born in neighboring parishes and adjacent regions, and those born further afield or abroad, vary between 6.5:2.5:1.0 for Aachen and 3.7:4.0:2.4 for Bochum. In general it can be seen that where the industrial city is less able during its expansion to draw upon a surrounding area of a similar commercial or industrial pattern, its proportion of long-distance migrants and immigrants will be correspondingly higher. This was the case in the northwestern ports of Kiel, Altona, Hamburg, and Bremen, and in the cities of the Rhine-Main area, Wiesbaden, Frankfurt, and Mannheim, and a number of industrial centers in agrarian areas such as Kassel, whereas the central German towns of Dresden, Leipzig, Chemnitz, Plauen, and Halle, as centers of a sprawling industrial belt, had the smallest proportion of long-distance migrants, and the towns of the Ruhrgebiet, despite the extreme case of Gelsenkirchen, had only an average intake of long-distance migrants.

Not only did the town absorb the population surplus of the country, but the birth-rate of migrants from the country helped further to accelerate the growth of the urban population. A fall in the birth rate, characteristic of the new industrial population, did begin in the industrial centers, but the mortality rate also fell due to the relative predominance of the younger age-groups and perhaps also to better conditions of hygiene and supply services available earlier and more extensively, so that in general the surplus of live births was probably above the average for the total population. These facts put the proportion of natives to migrants within the urban population in a somewhat different light. The only insight into this is given by the national census of 1900 which reveals the approximate age composition for the native and nonnative born. In the towns selected the migrant population exceeded the native born by proportions varying from 12.5 to 17.6 percent, and of these Krefeld, where the migration period had virtually ended fairly early, showed the lowest proportion, while Dortmund at a period of most active migration showed the highest. Even clearer criteria for measuring the impact of migration can be found by projecting the growth of a given population and then comparing it with the population count of a later census. To cite here two examples: the population of Barmen, excluding migrants and applying the rate of population growth for the Reich between 1871 and 1910, would have risen from 75,074 to 115,924, while in reality it rose to 169,214. The population of Gelsenkirchen would have risen from 16,023 to 24,742, whereas in reality it grew to 169,513. In the case then of Barmen and Gelsenkirchen an estimated increase of 53,290 and 144,771 respectively can be traced to migration. In Barmen (the increase through migration for Gelsenkirchen cannot be measured) this is more than three times the increase of 16,555 which came from migration alone. Only in comparisons of this kind does the high mobility of the German population fully reveal its importance for urbanization.

In interpreting the urbanization process as a whole as a shift of population from country to town, it should be remembered that internal migration was not confined to country-to-town migration, but that this movement continued in migration from one town to another. The investigations of Heberle and Meyer emphasize the importance of these migratory processes "in particular for the chief towns in densely populated areas." The readiness for mobility was further increased by the unsatisfactory nature of the circumstances in which the newcomers frequently found themselves at first, for the only jobs immediately open to them were those rejected by the native inhabitants, and also by the competition in production which led to the ruthless ousting of those less suitable or less willing. From this it is clear that the population turnover of the towns was considerably higher than their gains through migration, so that the degree of mobility and that of gain through migration were independent of each other. Thus, of the towns of the Rhineland and Westphalia, the cities in the Ruhrgebiet showed a far higher mobility than those of the Rhine, while the gains through migration in the Westphalian towns of this zone—Dortmund and Bochum—were up to three times greater than those of the Rhineland towns of Essen and Duisburg. A similar difference is seen between the Rhine towns of Düsseldorf and Cologne, while Krefeld and Aachen at the end of their industrialization period—Aachen having registered only minimal gains through migration and Krefeld actual losses—showed a far smaller turnover of migration. The special position of Gelsenkirchen in the Ruhrgebiet might be explained not least by its mono-industrial structure, while it is important to note that the migrants from northeastern Germany, recruited for the mining industry and provided with living accommodation in the town of their destination, were presumably more inclined to settle down in the first town they moved to than those who had come without such advance guarantees.

The peak period of industrialization meant a shifting of the population of Germany in favor of the town and above all the large town, by migration and the regrouping of communities whose status was changed because of their population growth. Thus between 1882 and 1907 the large towns increased by 8.5 million inhabitants, and the rural, small, and medium-sized towns increased by 8.4 million, whereas the rural population in 1907 had decreased by 0.4 million. These changes were accompanied by social changes—greater horizontal mobility (internal migration) and greater vertical mobility (social rise and fall). It was in the town, above all in the large town, that this new social order took shape, so that consideration of the process of urban growth must include an understanding of the changes in social as well as economic structure. In this sense industrial urbanization is to be understood as "a cumulative process with rising incidence and more differentiated structures." Here too it resulted from the instability of rural conditions after the reforms of the early nineteenth century and was a consequence of rural overpopulation. This rural population surplus, poverty-stricken and propertyless, threatened the stability of the agrarian social structure at its foundations, a process of disintegration in agrarian society which the new capacity of industrial society for integration was able to check. The basic conditions of "isolation and solidarity" which gave rise to "essentially functional structures of a new kind" were responsible for the reshaping of a society whose structure was determined by performance and availability.

Here the lines of horizontal and vertical mobility converge. Socially, migration from country to town almost always meant divorce from the agrarian structure and integration into an artisan-industrial order. Social rise or fall within this order frequently entailed a change of town; and intertown migration too has to be seen as a result of this kind of social mobility. The exodus from the country served still further to restore the stability of the agrarian structure. The village, relieved of its population surplus, recovered the self-sufficiency it had had under the older order whose survival and security continued to be guaranteed by the continuing capacity for absorption of the constantly expanding industrial sector.

The social composition of the German nation as it developed in the peak industrialization period revealed three occupational hierarchies: the agrarian order of the countryside and the industrial order of the town, both held together by the third, the public sector, which covered national and local administration and the churches. The distinctive feature of this social structure, in addition to the multiplicity of its groups, was the freedom of movement between them, for rigid barriers existed only between the agrarian upper and middle classes, and between the different ranks of the bureaucracy, demarcated by education and official position. The structure of the village remained relatively inflexible, while the industrial structure may be seen to reflect that of the mobility of society. At least the chances of social betterment, despite the equal danger of a fall in social position, were in each individual case a reality, from the possibility of promotion within the company to the chance of independence or an expanding sphere of authority right to the most senior posts. Not infrequently a rise of this sort coincided with the emergence of the new generation who were able to take advantage of the many kinds of educational opportunity offered by the town.

The ranks of the industrial lower classes were expanded chiefly from the agrarian lower classes, the industrial middle classes from the industrial lower classes, and the industrial upper classes from the

FIGURE 1. Diagram of Social Structure and Mobility at the Height of Industrialization.

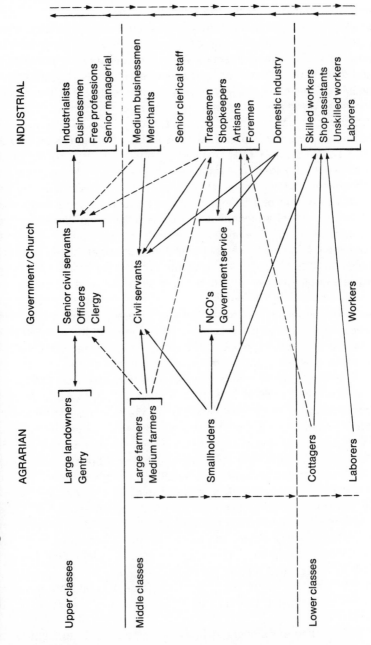

industrial middle classes. The latter, however, also came into close contact with the administrative and agrarian upper classes, and a change of employment in the civil service afforded at every level the possibility of a change in social status. But despite such possibilities, and despite continuing family ties between the rural migrant and his people at home, the majority necessarily had to find their place in the industrial world and accommodate themselves to it. This was how the decisive changes in social structure brought on by urban growth occurred, while it was precisely the isolation of the individual and the depersonalization of relationships, so often lamented by social critics, which provided the impulse for the new independence and self-assertion which made change of social position possible and helped to further it. This again applied principally to the large town, while in small- and medium-sized towns older social patterns based on rank and privilege and on closer personal contact frequently continued to prevail over more material considerations. This kept social conflict at a low level, whereas in the large towns it found full expression in industrial and political disputes, and in social and political agitation. The growing dualism between social mobility and social antagonism was from the first inherent in the urbanization process seen as the process of social change and the emergence of new social structures, while at the same time it marked the instability of these new structures and the will to change them.

Only crude categories can be deduced from statistics. Even so, in the rather short span of 1895–1907, a relatively late phase of the peak industrialization period, they trace for us the essential changes in the main groups: the decline in numbers of those employed in the country in agriculture and forestry and the increase in industrial occupations even in small- and medium-sized towns. Here the vacuum left by the loss of rural laborers was filled by the increased help given by members of the family. The number of relatives who did help, shown by statistics as increasing from 1.7 to 3.4 million—in other words doubling—was attributable not only to better statistical records and improved census methods but to the fact that "more work must have been done by relatives." This makes it clear that migration from the country had passed beyond the point of relieving the rural population by releasing its surplus; the growing shortage of rural labor necessarily meant increased pressure at the other end of the scale on the family.

The decline in numbers of those self-employed in agriculture and forestry can be explained partly by the change in status of many communities as a result of population growth, and by fundamental structural changes in the economy and society, for in the two urban spheres the number of self-employed rose by 33,000, partly because small-scale economy passed from being a primary to a secondary occupation, just as in general such marginal forms of activity can bring changes without radically altering the social position. In contrast the decline of those self-employed in industry and handicrafts points to processes of industrial concentration, and the change in the ratio of self-employed to dependent workers points the same way: in the countryside it widened between 1895 and 1907 from 1:2.5 to 1:3.8, and in the towns from 1:4.1 to 1:6.0. Trade and transport show the same change to a lesser extent, from 1:1.2 to 1:1.15 in the country and from 1:1.8 to 1:2.4 in the towns. A particularly large part was played in this development by the above-average increase in the number of white-collar workers as a new but not independent group within the middle classes; the differences in their rate of growth as between the smaller and the larger towns were greater than the corresponding differences for the industrial workers. The same was true of the growth in the public services and free professions.

Migration and regrouping also caused a decline in the numbers of those engaged in agriculture and forestry among the wage-earning rural population as a whole. This decline corresponded to the expansion of industry and handicrafts. It was chiefly the rural crafts which suffered most from that expansion; in the country trade and transport also gained ground, while their proportion in the urban population remained almost unchanged. In the small and medium-sized towns the declining proportion of workers in agriculture and forestry was fully balanced by an increase of those employed in industry and handicrafts, which in these towns accounted for the large majority of the wage-earning population. This may be due to the fact that many of the medium-sized towns owed their expansion to the development of a few large-scale concerns in one industry but lacked the capacity to provide more than local services for the hinterland. This was the case of the Ruhr towns of Herne, Wanne-Eickel, Oberhausen, Hamborn, or the textile towns of Saxony. These services were responsible for the higher proportion of those in the cities employed in trade and transport, but also in the public services and professions.

If these occupational ratios are interpreted in their social aspect, the importance gained by the industrial sector through the decline of

TABLE 3
Social-Occupational Distribution: 1895, 1907 (selected groups)

		1895		1907		Percent increase (+) or decrease (−)
		000's	%	000's	%	
In the countryside						
Agriculture	Independent	2,232	25.7%	2,131	24.6%	−4.5%
& forestry	Laborers	3,342	37.4	2,930	33.8	−9.6
Industry	Independent	692	8.0	579	6.7	−16.3
& crafts	Clerical	45	0.5	85	1.0	+88.9
	Workers	1,707	19.7	2,100	24.2	+23.0
Trade and	Independent	215	2.5	216	2.5	+0.5
transport	Clerical	20	0.2	34	0.4	+70.0
	Workers	230	2.7	290	3.3	+26.1
Casual						
labor		65	0.7	64	0.7	−1.5
Public ser-	Independent	143	1.6	147	1.7	+2.8
vice and	Clerical	32	0.4	43	0.5	+34.4
professions	Workers	45	0.5	47	0.5	+4.4
Total		8,668	100.0	8,666	100.0	—
In small and medium towns (from 2,000 to 100,000 inhabitants)						
Agriculture	Independent	326	5.1%	354	4.3%	+8.6%
& forestry	Laborers	460	7.2	434	5.2	−5.7
Industry	Independent	788	12.4	762	9.2	−3.3
& crafts	Clerical	143	2.2	345	4.2	+141.3
	Workers	3,013	47.4	4,287	51.7	+42.3
Trade and	Independent	391	6.2	456	5.5	+16.6
transport	Clerical	114	1.8	188	2.3	+64.9
	Workers	519	8.2	748	9.0	+44.1
Casual						
labor		226	3.6	203	2.4	−10.2
Public ser-	Independent	193	3.0	246	3.0	+27.5
vice and	Clerical	104	1.6	149	1.8	+43.8
professions	Workers	81	1.3	118	1.4	+45.7
Total		6,358	100.0	8,290	100.0	+30.4
In large towns						
Agriculture	Independent	11	0.4%	16	0.3%	+45.5%
& forestry	Laborers	22	0.8	25	0.5	+13.6
Industry	Independent	293	11.0	389	8.5	+32.8
& crafts	Clerical	76	2.9	256	5.6	+236.8
	Workers	1,180	44.4	2,073	45.1	+75.7

TABLE 3 (continued)

		1895		1907		Percent increase (+) or de- crease (−)
		000's	%	000's	%	
		In large towns				
Trade and	Independent	238	9.0%	340	7.4%	+42.9%
transport	Clerical	128	4.8	283	6.2	+121.1
	Workers	373	14.0	660	14.4	+76.9
Casual labor		141	5.3	204	4.4	+44.7
Public ser-	Independent	96	3.6	166	3.6	+72.9
vice and	Clerical	59	2.2	105	2.3	+78.0
professions	Workers	41	1.5	72	1.6	+75.6
Total		2,658	100.0	4,589	100.0	+72.6

the agrarian sector becomes clear, although there is little differentiation within the upper and middle classes. As early as 1895 the agrarian sector employed altogether less manpower than the industrial sector, but 12 years later it accounted for a full third less than the industrial lower classes alone. The ratio of the upper and middle to the lower agrarian classes shifted slightly in favor of the upper and middle classes (1895 1:1.45 and 1907 1:1.35), an indication of the newly achieved relative stability, whereas in industry we can distinguish somewhat greater shifts in favor of the lower classes (1895 1:2.51 and 1907 1:2.71). These however were not large enough to be seen as a fundamental change. The social structure of the German nation in this phase of the industrial age was fully formed by the first decade of the twentieth century.

The process of urbanization, inseparable from the development of industrial society, provided the framework for a decisive change in the life of the individual and of social groups. Stage by stage, as industrialization encroached on the agrarian sector, the entire population was engulfed by urban ways of life and more especially the life of the big city. The romantics who criticized the city for its apparent anonymity, its equally apparent coincidence of isolation and human concentration, and the allegedly dwindling vigor of the urban population, obscured understanding of the significance of this transformation. These critics saw agrarian ways of life in the initial period of industrialization as unchanged and stable, since they judged from the new and relative stability which followed from the migration of the population surplus into the town. This view misinterprets the importance of the urbanization process in contemporary development. It not only led to even greater centers of human concentration, but also provided the frame for the new social structures of the industrial age; their structures never became too rigid to prohibit change, but by their very flexibility and adaptability offered the individual greater opportunities for development and advancement, and for making his own way in society—perhaps for the first time in history.

II NINETEENTH- AND TWENTIETH-CENTURY VIEWS OF THE BIG CITY: POSITIVE AND NEGATIVE

Robert Vaughan

THE AGE OF GREAT CITIES

Robert Vaughan was a Congregationalist clergyman who held the chair of history at University College of London University from 1834 to 1843. He wrote extensively on the history of theology, on English political history, and on contemporary affairs. In The Age of Great Cities, *he employed his historical learning to formulate the classic nineteenth-century defense of the urban phenomenon. In Vaughan's eyes, big cities were great not only by virtue of their size, but also by virtue of the qualities they embodied and the progressive developments they stimulated.*

Our age is preeminently the age of great cities. Babylon and Thebes, Carthage and Rome, were great cities, but the world has never been so covered with cities as at the present time, and society generally has never been so leavened with the spirit natural to cities. . . .

Yes—cities, and their resources, must soon become, in a greater degree than ever, the acknowledged wealth and power of nations. Philosophers are beginning to see this; cabinets are obliged to act upon it; and monarchs cannot conceal from themselves that it will be to their interest to conform to this new current in human affairs. Thus the feudal temper, which rested its dominion upon the sword, is giving place to the spirit of a civilization which aims at dominion by means of intelligence, industry, order, law, and liberty. It will not be upon the sovereign and his nobles, or upon the chief and his vassals, that the states of Europe in the future will depend for the means of safety. As nations come to abound in great cities, they learn to become their own defenders, and their own rulers.

In forwarding these great moral results, science is lending her influence in many powerful forms. The new and speedy communication which will soon be completed between all great cities in every nation of Europe, will necessarily tend to swell the larger towns into still greater magnitude, and to diminish the weight of many smaller places, as well as of the rural population generally in social affairs. Everywhere we trace this disposition to converge upon great points.

From Robert Vaughan, *The Age of Great Cities: Modern Society Viewed in its Relation to Intelligence, Morals and Religion* (London: Jackson and Walford, 1843), pp. 1, 90–91, 101–103, 105–106, 108–109, 116–117, 130–131, 136, 141–142, 145, 146–147, 152–153, 254–255.

It avails nothing to complain of this tendency as novel, inconsiderate, hazardous. The pressure toward such an issue is irresistible, nor do we see the slightest prospect of its ceasing to be so. . . .

On Great Cities in their Connection with the Designs of Providence

It is a poet of our own who has said—"God made the country; man made the town." In this saying there is a portion of truth, but it does not contain the whole truth. As commonly understood, its effect is to substitute error in the place of truth.

Even the country, in the greater part, is no longer seen as it would appear if wholly devoid of the agency of man. In the absence of what man has done upon it, the surface of the earth must have remained barren, or have degenerated into a monstrous wilderness. No visible hand beside could have prevented it from becoming the home of every rank production, and of every unclean thing.

Nor should it be forgotten, that it was as much a part of the purpose of the Creator with regard to man, that he should build towns, as that he should till the land. If the history of cities, and of their influence on their respective territories, be deducted from the history of humanity, the narrative remaining would be, as we suspect, of no very attractive description. In such case, the kind of picture which human society must everywhere have presented, would be such as we see in the condition, from the earliest time, of the wandering hordes of Mongolians and Tartars, spread over the vast flats of central Asia. In those regions, scarcely anything has been "made" by man. But this most happy circumstance, as it seems to be accounted—this total absence of anything reminding you of human skill and industry, has never been found to realize our poetic ideas of pastoral beauty and innocence. It has called forth enough of the squalid and of the ferocious, but little of the refined, the powerful, or the generous.

Thus the manifest tendency of the half-truth contained in the saying adverted to, is not to convey a true impression so much as a false one—and how large a portion of the error in the world may be traced, in this manner, to partial announcements of truth! If this saying has any meaning, it must mean, that man in the city, is in a less favorable condition for the development of his nature, than man in the field; that in prosecuting the higher arts which flourish in cities, he is not so much in his place as in attending to the more limited arts which relate to pasturage and cattle. But where is the man of sense that would not as soon think of reasoning to the first quadruped he should meet upon the village road, as to the head that could really mean to insinuate such a notion?

If anything be certain, it would seem to be certain, that man is constituted to realize his destiny from his association with man, more than from any contact with places. The great agency in calling forth his capabilities, whether for good or for evil, is that of his fellows. The picturesque, accordingly, may be with the country, but the intellectual, speaking generally, must be with the town. Agriculture may possess its science, and the farmer, as well as the landowner, may not be devoid of intelligence; but in such connections, the science and intelligence, in common with the nourishment of the soil, must be derived, in the main, from the studies prosecuted in cities, and from the wealth realized in the traffic of cities. If pasturage is followed by tillage, and if tillage is made to partake of the nature of a study and a science, these signs of improvement are peculiar to lands in which cities make their appearance, and they become progressive only as cities become opulent and powerful. In this sense we might venture to change the language of our poet a little, and say, "Man makes the country, where art makes the town";—and in so saying we should make a much nearer approach toward the truth. . . .

Every living thing, from the hyssop that springeth out of the wall to the noblest of the animal creation, has its appointed development; and in the discipline, expansion, and force of the human faculties, as realized in the civic associations of mankind, we see the development which has been manifestly assigned to human nature. In such relations the aptitudes of the human mind are placed under due culture, and man is assisted in making his nearest approach toward the fullest use of his capabilities.

It is felt, accordingly, to be against nature, that any community of minds, or that any solitary mind, should be disposed to retrace the steps which have once led from barbarism to refinement. Nor do men always sufficiently remember how much of the habit of mind which qualifies them to enjoy their seasons of seclusion and repose, has been derived from those more busy scenes of life, which give a new keenness and compass to the power of observation, and open a new world of susceptibilities in the heart.

Great cities may possibly become too large, as great capitalists may become too rich, and as great landholders may become too powerful; but who can be competent to lay down any general rule in such matters? Will not the ever-changing pressure of circumstances always determine for itself between the expedient and inexpedient in such cases? Can it be wise, can it be just, to seem to repudiate a system, because it is not necessarily exempt from the evils of fluctuation, or from occasional excess? Is the good influence to be accounted as nothing, even while immeasurably outweighing the evil, simply because the good is not wholly secure against an admixture of evil? . . .

On Great Cities in their Connection with Physical Science

Looking to great cities in their relation to physical science, we may safely speak of this branch of intelligence as deriving all its higher culture, if not its existence, from the ingenuities which are natural to men in such associations. Cities are at once the great effect, and the great cause, of progress in this department of knowledge. The monuments of Thebes and Persepolis, of Athens and Rome, are as so many mutilated treatises on the science of the ancients. Next to the memorials of mind transmitted to us in the literature of an ancient city, are those presented in its monuments. In the latter we trace the developments of thought, reasoning, imagination, and taste, no less certainly than in the former; and in consequence of the peculiar visibility which attaches to them, they bring a susceptible spirit into the nearest possible fellowship with the spirits of remote times. Cities which can hardly be said to have had a literature at all, have risen to extraordinary magnificence purely as the effect of science; and in our time, the moldering fragments which bespeak their scientific skill furnish almost the only direct testimony to their power and character, and in some cases to their existence.

Every region that has become the home of such cities has become the home of an improved agriculture. This has resulted in part from the wealth of cities; but still more from their mechanical and scientific skill. In this manner it has often been reserved to cities to convert the desert into a garden, and to give to the richer soils of the earth the aspect of a paradise. . . .

On Great Cities in their Connection with the History of Political Science

If the influence of great cities on the progress of natural science is thus manifest, their tendency to foster just and enlightened views in relation to political science is no less obvious. Every municipal body must have its local regulations, and its local functionaries to carry them into effect. As those regulations have respect to the common interest, it is natural that they should be the result of something like common deliberation, and common consent. If it be reasonable that laws relating to the common interest should seem to emanate from the common will, it is further reasonable that the common will should reserve to itself the power of choosing its own executive.

In this manner a popular character naturally attaches to municipal law and municipal authority. Every such community is constantly under the influences which dispose it to imbibe the spirit, and to take up the forms of a commonwealth. In proportion as a nation becomes a nation of towns and cities, this spirit, and these forms, are likely to become more prevalent and more fixed. Cities are states upon a small scale, and are of necessity schools in relation to the policy most in harmony with the genius of a people. Political knowledge never diffuses itself more wholesomely among a people, than when it results, in this manner, slowly and steadily, from circumstances and experience; and when its principles are to be brought out upon a large scale, by men who have worked them successfully on a smaller scale. . . .

On Great Cities in their Connection with Art

. . . It is not disputed, that in any land where there are flourishing cities, the territorial aristocracy will be distinguished as patrons of the beautiful in art. But whence has this aristocracy derived the wealth by means of which it indulges so largely in the gratification of those tastes? Whence has it derived these tastes themselves? And whence came the men of genius possessing the power to minister to those tastes? On these questions, it is not too much to say, that as the town has made the country, giving to its lands a beauty and value they would not otherwise have possessed; so the citizen has made the noble, by cultivating in him a taste for art, which would not otherwise have formed a part of his character. For it must be obvious that the country which should be purely agricultural, producing no more than may be consumed by its own agricultural population, must unavoidably be the home of a scattered, a rude, and a necessitous people, and its chiefs be little elevated above the coarse untaught mass of their dependants. Burgesses produce both the useful and the ornamental, and minister in this manner both to the need and the pleasure of nobles and kings. What they sell not at home they send abroad. In either case, wealth is realized; lands become more valuable; public burdens can be borne; and along with the skill which produces embellishment, come the means by which it may be purchased.

In this manner, the baron has been elevated by the burgess, and courts have been refined by cities. During no small interval in the history of modern Europe, the social position of citizens in these respects was in advance of the social position of courtiers. We see little in the picturesque beauty and brilliancy of the feudal mansions and royal palaces of the sixteenth century, which had not existence, in the public edifices, if not in the private dwellings, of the great commercial cities on the Continent some centuries earlier. . . .

It appears, then, that the ornamental arts owe their existence to the same causes which give existence to cities; and that society becomes possessed of the beautiful in art, only as cities become prosperous and great. It has appeared, moreover, that while there are advantages and disadvantages pertaining to the different forms of civil society, as regards their influence on art, it is a fact, that the popular states of antiquity have supplied the models in relation to this high department of civilization, which the more aristocratic, and the monarchical states of later times, have been content to imitate or mutilate, but which they have never been known to improve.

On Great Cities in their Connection with Literature

. . . Great cities also, which have raised our nobles from the condition of men almost wholly occupied in conducting petty and barbarous wars, to become the patrons of art and literature, have now raised a large portion of our people from their former state of ignorance and sensuality, to their present measure of acquaintance with letters, and with the means of mental improvement. From cities both classes have derived their intelligence, and all the pleasures connected with it; and upon cities both classes depend for the continuance of the state of things thus produced. Even now, the multitude who are employed in making contributions to our popular literature, look to find their readers much more among traders and artisans than among farmers and peasants. In all calculations on this very material point, the experience of such men prompts them to look with special interest to the population of our great cities. . . .

In conclusion, then, it is manifest, that men possess nothing deserving the name of literature until they begin to build cities; that literature, the offspring of society as it obtains in cities, derives its character from the state of that society, varying with it in all the stages of social progress; and that the effect of commerce in augmenting small towns into great cities has been, to give to literature in our own age, a much more popular character than has attached to it in any preceding time. Let the influence of a commercial spirit on modern nations cease, and popular literature will cease. Let the great cities of Europe be accounted an evil, and let the course of legislation be to depress and subdue them, reducing them to the state of so many passive victims in the hands of the masters of the soil, and the consequence of such an ingrate policy must be, the destruction of literature in every form, and the return—the retributive return of an unlettered barbarism.

On the Effect of Association in Great Cities with Regard to Popular Intelligence

Every intelligent person must have observed, that apart from any technical or direct means of instruction, there is much in the nearer, the more constant, and the more varied association, into which men are brought by means of great cities, which tends necessarily to impart greater knowledge, acuteness, and power to the mind, than would have been realized by the same persons if placed in the comparative isolation of a rural parish. As we pass from the town to the country, from the crowd to the comparative solitude, we soon become sensible to another kind of diminution than that which meets the eye. It is soon perceptible that men are losers in intelligence, in proportion as they are losers in the habit of association. In the population of a village, we see a small circle of persons, and little variety of occupation. With this monotony of pursuit, we find a similar monotony of character. The dull have little chance of being roused to shrewdness; and those who are not dull, possess little inducement to bestow their attention on anything deserving the name of mental cultivation.

In the processes of agriculture, there is much which, to an observant mind, should be highly suggestive and interesting. But it is painful to mark how completely devoid of any susceptibility of this nature are the minds usually engaged in such avocations. This observation applies much too generally even to the farmer himself. But with regard to the whole class below him, it is always a matter of agreeable surprise if we find in them any degree of capacity above the low average required in order that they may go through the round of sheer manual labor assigned to them. In the history of these men and women, the animal toil of today is followed by that of tomorrow, and amidst scenes clothed in beauty, rich in the most wonderful changes, and teeming with abundance, it is reserved to the human spirit to appear as the unnatural, the unproductive, the unlovely—as the exception, where it should be as the glory. There was a time when English prejudice—that very old and deeply besetting infirmity of our nation—could make its boast of this people as—"the finest peasantry in the world"! But the ignorance, or the dishonesty, betrayed in such boasting, has at length become too palpable to be endured even by the prejudice of Englishmen. . . .

Cities, then, are the natural centers of association. Of course the advantages derived from association are there realized in an eminent degree. Men live there in the nearest neighborhood. Their faculties, in place of becoming dull from inaction, are constantly sharpened by collision. They have their prejudices, but all are liable to be assailed. Manufactures, commerce, politics, religion, all become subjects of discussion. All these are looked upon from more points, talked about more variously, and judged of more correctly, as being matters in which many minds are interested, and on which many minds are not only accustomed to form conclusions, but to form them with a view to utterance and action. It may be the lot of very few to possess much vigor of thought, but each man stimulates his fellow, and the result is a greater general intelligence. The shop, the factory, or the marketplace; the local association, the newsroom, or the religious meeting, all facilitate this invigorating contact of mind with mind. The more ignorant come into constant intercourse with the more knowing. Stationariness of thought is hardly possible, and if its movements are not always wise, the errors of today are as lessons of experience for tomorrow. Such, indeed, is often the astuteness ac-

quired in the exercise of this greatest of free schools
of Sheffield, or the weaver of Manchester, would frequen...
any common ground, more than a match for many a u...
graduate. But does your man of technical education ever apprehend
any such rencontre with the village plowman? Or has it ever occurred
to him to reckon the plowman's assistant as superior in shrewdness to
the city apprentice? In short, nothing can be more plain, than that
the unavoidable intercourse of townsmen must always involve a system of education; and that while instruction reaches, in such connections, to a much lower level than elsewhere, minds of better capacity
naturally make the common intelligence about them the starting-
point in their own race of superiority.

It has been intimated that in towns there are greater facilities than
in the country for conducting education in its more direct and technical form. These facilities are greater in towns, partly on account of
their greater wealth, and their greater freedom from prejudice; and
partly in consequence of their more general sympathy with popular
improvement, and their comparative freedom from the discountenance or control of powerful individuals or classes. Towns are not
like villages, subject, it may be, to the oversight and guidance of a
single family, or of a single clergyman. They possess greater means
and greater liberty, and, in general, a stronger disposition to use both
in favor of education, even in behalf of the children of the
poorest. . . .

On the Presumption that the State of Society in Great Cities Must Be Favorable to Morality, from its Relation to Intelligence

If it be true that it is in the tendency of great cities to raise intelligence to its maximum, it would not be to do much honor to morality
to allege, that we must expect to see it flourish the least, where
intelligence is known to flourish the most. This would not be to say
much in favor of the connection which is thought to subsist between
morality and utility, or between the just and the reasonable. Such a
doctrine might be natural to the enemies of morality, but is hardly to
be expected from its friends. We can readily perceive how it might
happen, that the instances should be numerous, in which men seem
to become more intelligent, only that they might become more adept
in the indulgence of their vices. But that this abuse of intelligence

ould be regarded, the subject being looked upon broadly, as more natural and more probable than the use of it, is a form of delusion scarcely possible to any mind accustomed to reflection.

It is ascertained as the effect, even of the most elementary instruction, that in proportion as it reaches the people at large, it diminishes crime, creates a power of self-government, and demonstrates to the great majority brought under its influence, that the rogue's arithmetic is based on false principle, that as such it must always lead to false results, and that the most expedient course of action, even in the case of the selfish, is that, which, by conducing to character, conduces to power. Thus the man who is placed in possession of a new power to do wrong, is placed under the influence of new motives to do right. In the moral world, as in the physical, the true equilibrium of things is realized by the action of opposite forces. The sphere of our responsibility widens with every increase of intelligence, wealth, and association; but it does not widen as opening new sources of temptation, more than as presenting new considerations on the side of resisting temptation. In this manner, it is provided that the bestowments of heaven should take their own safeguards along with them, at least in such degree as is necessary to the great purposes of moral government. The greater power to do evil, is meant as a greater power to do good; and every just view of the Infinitely Good would lead us to conclude, that where he has sown the most, so as to render the abounding of good in the greatest degree practicable, there he expects to reap the most in the form of good. If it be reasonable to suppose that his designs point toward such a result, it is then no less reasonable to conclude, that the web of his moral government has been wrought so as to subserve that end, and that city life, as meant to be that of eminent intelligence, was meant to be that of eminent morality.

On the Moral Influence Peculiar to Great Cities as Opposed to the Vices Peculiar to Them

. . . If large towns may be regarded as giving shelter and maturity to some of the worst forms of depravity, it must not be forgotten that to such towns, almost entirely, society is indebted for that higher tone of moral feeling by which vice is in so great a measure discountenanced, and for those voluntary combinations of the virtuous in the cause of purity, humanity, and general improvement, which hold so conspicuous a place in our social history. It is not only true that from cities good laws, liberal arts, and letters, have in the main, their origin, but no less true that spontaneous efforts in the cause of public morals, and in aid of the necessitous, made in such manner as to embrace voluntary association, and large sacrifice of time, thought, and property, are found almost exclusively among citizens.

The feudal noble, the village esquire, and the rural incumbent, may be moral and humane persons, and their influence may be highly favorable to the morality and comfort of the circle about them. But the permanent and costly institutions designed to act as a means of abating the physical and moral evils of great cities, owe their origin, and nearly the whole of their support, to the people of the cities in which they make their appearance.

Our conclusions on this subject, therefore, will not be just, except as we place in one view with the evils which are generated by the state of society in large towns, the good also which only that condition of society is found competent to call into existence. The immorality of large towns, even when thus viewed, may be very lamentable, but the influence opposed to it will be seen to be of vast amount. The provisions which are thus made against the ignorance, the vice, and the miseries of society are so manifold, that it would require large space to explain their nature, and be tedious even to enumerate them. The oversight of this spontaneous benevolence extends to the suppression or discountenance of vice in almost every form, to the restoration of multitudes who have become its victims, to the need of the sick, the sorrows of the bereft, the condition of the homeless and the perishing, and even to the protection of the animal creation against the cruelties often inflicted upon them by the hand of man. These are among the good fruits of great cities, and they are fruits found nowhere else in such abundance, or in such maturity.

Wilhelm Heinrich Riehl

THE CITY AS A SOURCE OF CORRUPTION

Wilhelm Heinrich Riehl was a highly influential Bavarian journalist and social theorist, whose conservative opinions during and after the revolutions of 1848 earned him the favor of the Bavarian king. Consequently, in 1854 he was given a position on the official government newspaper in Munich and an honorary professorship in the university's faculty of political economy. In the same year he published the study of regional social differences in Germany from which the passages reprinted below are taken. Riehl, an heir to the nostalgic longings of the romantics, was a trenchant critic of big cities, whose opinions contrasted sharply with the pro-urban attitudes expressed by liberals such as Robert Vaughan. His views enjoyed wide currency during the later nineteenth and early twentieth centuries, after the process of urbanization he both anticipated and feared had transformed the German landscape.

Disturbing symptoms of artificiality are evident nowadays not just in recently established cities but also in many old ones that have grown enormously. Europe is becoming sick as a result of the monstrosity of its big cities. The healthy peculiar character of old England is being buried in London; Paris is the eternally festering abscess of France. . . . In the eighteenth century, every German residential city was expected to be a Versailles; now each one is supposed to become like Paris and London. Even the smallest city now desires at the very least to *impersonate* a big city, just as every citizen wants to play the part of an aristocratic gentleman. These large and small "big cities," in which all the originality of German urban life is dying out, are the swollen heads of modern civilization. As is well known, swollen heads frequently indicate a precocious and highly stimulated psyche. But one ought not to conclude from this fact that the biggest heads are always the cleverest and the most capable of living.

The fabulously rapid growth of our big cities is occurring not as a result of a surplus of births but rather through a migratory surplus. The people of the countryside and the small city migrate toward the big city. The overwhelming mass of these immigrants consists of individuals who still do not have a definite occupation or their own household but wish to make their fortune for the first time in the big

From Wilhelm Heinrich Riehl, *Die Naturgeschichte des Volkes als Grundlage einer deutschen Social-Politik*, Vol. I: *Land und Leute* (Stuttgart and Tübingen, 1854), pp. 75–82. Translated by the editors.

city. As far as they are concerned, they have gotten ahead too slowly at home, but they hope that in the big city they can reap without having sown. Certainly only a few of them discover this dreamed-of happiness, whereas the majority returns home after awhile. But in their stead even more migrants stream in, only to disappear again just as quickly. Our big cities are becoming monstrous through an increase not of the stationary but rather of the *fluctuating* population. This fact by itself should already be disconcerting to the socially-oriented statesman. Workers in luxury trades, speculators, apprentices, assistants, servants, day-laborers, and so on, are the ones who add so greatly to the numbers of such cities. It is the proletariat that flows from small cities into the big ones, in order from this vantage point to dominate both the city and the countryside. It is not the really necessary trades, the ones that serve the inescapable requirements of life, that multiply with striking rapidity in the big cities, but rather the short-lived luxury trades, on which so much of the proletariat depends. In Berlin, for example, the carpenters, masons, tanners, etc., have not increased at all since 1784, but instead have decreased; in contrast, the bookbinders, lacquerers, makers of musical instruments, etc., have become extraordinarily numerous. But the day-laborers and household servants are increasing the most rapidly of all.

For the most part, inhabitants of the countryside live together, *in families,* whereas their urban counterparts live to a great degree in solitude. This fragmentation increases all the more as the big cities increase in size. Thus, an extremely significant gap already opens up between the city and the countryside, a gap which unfortunately does not diminish at all, but rather grows continually. Owing to this circumstance the social importance of the urban population relative to that of the rural population is considerably diminished. But if statesmen neglect to consider the social factor, then the increase of the masses in the big cities will utterly destroy our entire civilization. Universal suffrage would bring about complete supremacy of the big cities over the countryside, whereas an electoral law based on residency, on a household of one's own, and on property would to a certain extent compensate for the recent preponderance of the city vis-à-vis the countryside. The dominance of the big cities will ultimately become synonymous with the dominance of the proletariat. Already in 1840 one Prussian out of forty-five was a Berliner, one Frenchman out of thirty-five was a Parisian, and one out of fifteen

Englishmen lived in London. These statistics pertaining to rural-urban migration suggest a far greater array of threats to the individual development of our entire national life than do the statistics pertaining to emigration toward distant parts of the earth, even though the latter may strike the economist as being more ominous.

The relationship between city and countryside is developing quite spectacularly in Belgium. This small kingdom is becoming increasingly a purely urban country. According to the census taken at the end of 1850, approximately every *third* Belgian was a city-dweller! Here the cities dominate the countryside, and urban industry outweighs agricultural occupations to an extent unparalleled in any other country of similar size on the European continent. The growth of cities proceeds here at a stormy pace. The population of Brussels has almost doubled within forty-five years, that of Ghent has more than doubled, and that of Antwerp has grown by at least a third. This preponderance of urban life in Belgium is by no means arbitrary or accidental; rather, it is deeply rooted in the history, in the basic nature, and in the location of the country. The constitutional system of the modern kingdom, which presupposes an identity between the concepts of "middle class" and "society," corresponds to the largely urban and industrial condition of the country and is rightly regarded as an excellent one—for Belgium. But it by no means follows from this situation that a constitution that is the best one for Belgium is necessarily the best one for Germany. In Germany, the relationships between city and countryside are quite different. Of course the abstract policies of men who are guided by general doctrines are formulated without regard for such differences between countries and their inhabitants. But it is the essential advantage of a socially-oriented policy that it gives the highest priority to such considerations.

In the big cities, which have stretched out to such a gigantic size that they lack any shape or form, the peculiar character of the city as a creative collective personality disappears. Every big city strives to become a world city, like all other big cities, shedding every distinguishing feature of nationality. Big cities are the abode of a leveling cosmopolitanism. In them, the natural differences among social groups disappear, and the modern outlook on the world, according to which there are no other "estates" besides the rich and the poor, the educated and the uneducated, is no longer a fiction; instead it is the naked truth, which has been gleaned from the pavements of the big city. The world cities are gigantic encyclopedias of the customs, the art, and the industry of all of civilized Europe. I appreciate the grounds for pride, and I recognize that the productive and inventive talents of industry, commerce, and material activity in general will reap a bountiful harvest from these encyclopedias. Wherever huge masses of men gather together, industrialism thrives, and the economist rejoices over this fact. But social health and well-being are not always to be found where the largest masses of people are; just as, on the other hand, they are not to be sought in the isolated dwellings of farmers who live in the mountains. The need is for harmonious human settlements of medium size. As is well known, the encyclopedic mentality made its appearance along with the great literary encyclopedias. This spirit has been harmful, as will be the enormous urban encyclopedias of the future. Young people are sent into the big cities in order to gain familiarity with the world. But most of them do not become more mature; instead, they become intoxicated, confused, and discontented. Whoever sees everything at once sees nothing. The denizen of the big city feels no need to wander, since he can view the world comfortably from within the city walls; he lets the world come to him instead of going to the world. And yet, travel and a *step-by-step development* of one's views concerning nature, society, and human activity are prerequisites for spiritual maturity. Whoever rummages about in the world as he would in an encyclopedia gains what he has not truly won for himself, and therefore he retains little of what he has gained.

The overwhelming majority of Germany's great men, especially in the fields of art and learning, have come from the smaller cities and the countryside. Spiritual concentration makes the great man, and this is extremely difficult to attain in the encyclopedic big city. After outstanding talents have grown to maturity in the countryside they are attracted to the big city; and yet, how frequently it is the case that such talents seem to be placed immediately in a kind of spiritual retirement, living on their laurels.

Medieval artistic activity developed in a far more original fashion than the artistic activity in our middle-sized cities. Earlier artists did not see, hear, or read too much, and therefore they could create directly from the depths of their souls. In contrast, the blight of big-cityness afflicts all our modern art. Theater in Europe has been ruined for generations by the insatiable demands of the highly urbanized Parisian public for display and spectacle. Already in Germany no really good small theater is any longer possible, inasmuch as the German philistine has been to Paris, Vienna, and Berlin and consequently evaluates the small theater in his home town from a big-city viewpoint. And yet such small theaters were once places of refuge for far purer and more national dramatic art.

Architecturally, the barracks system of modern housing construction in the big cities has done terrible damage. And yet it becomes all the more difficult to give it up as more and more "solitary people" stream daily into the big cities, while families in the countryside live almost exclusively in houses. Space can no longer be created for the majority of single workers and day-laborers in the big cities, because they do not provide sufficient profit as tenants for housing speculators. In Berlin this problem of rents is already threatening to become a "social question," and soon the authorities in such cities are going to have to build proletarian barracks whether they wish to or not. The "journeymen's hostels" in England are already barracks of this type, and people are thinking of transplanting them to Germany. They will be admirably furnished, and everything will be done to compensate the journeymen in these dwellings for the lack of family life, but they remain barracks nonetheless.

We could proceed with this exposition, in which case we would observe that the big cities exert the same disintegrating influence in the areas of music and painting. Art exhibitions, with their show-pieces, provide evidence enough of the blasé and frivolous taste of the big-city public, which demands ostentatious art above all else. Domestic and chamber music, which has real social significance, has been almost entirely suppressed by the pressure of showy big-city musical productions and by the superficial finesse which has found its shelter in these cities.

We must also, however, emphasize the other side of the coin. In the big cities, which are the ancestral seats of the luxury trades, artisanal production is beginning once again to display artistic elements that have been missing for centuries. This is a bright side of big-city life, which generally appears in a favorable light from an economic standpoint. In ages that were primarily artistic and only secondarily industrial, this merging of art and artisanal production did not pose any threat to the higher, ideal interests of artistic greatness. But in the present the situation is reversed: we are primarily industrial and only secondarily artistic. Consequently the crowd succumbs to the illusion that brilliant artisanal technique is the same thing as true artistry. This illusion, which degrades the intrinsic value of artistic genius and reduces it to being the servant of technology, is nourished to an unbelievable extent by the artistic activity of the big cities.

The ultimate conquest of technology in the field of art and the reduction of art to subservience to the luxury trades was made manifest at the Crystal Palace Exhibit in London.[1] This was the day of triumph for the ethos of the big city, celebrated in Europe's foremost metropolis. The after-effects of the exhibition are incalculable, because it is going to stimulate the confident spirit of big-city industrialism for a long time to come. In the exhibition rooms of the Crystal Palace, images of Greek gods were mounted as decoration for modern factory goods. . . . Let us beware that the ecstasy of material labor does not make us forget the higher values of spiritual creativity. . . .

It was at the time of the exhibit that people sarcastically and frivolously dismissed the "heavy and dungeon-like" Cologne Cathedral, which had still not been completed after six centuries, in favor of the showy glass building on the Thames, the "open and breezy building," which had been conjured up in only one winter. Here we could observe quite clearly the arrogance—born in the big cities—of purely technical mastery toward the creations of complete artistic genius, with its roots in the depths of spiritual life. It is not within our power to affect the widespread fame of an extraordinary engineer such as Paxton[2] one way or the other. But we must protest when people measure a first-rate work of art, which is the product of centuries of ideas and religious and artistic enthusiasm, with the industrial yardstick of London; we also protest when people judge not only a purely technological structure such as the Crystal Palace but also a work of architectural art according to the speed with which it was constructed. From this standpoint, Luca da Presto[3] would have been the greatest painter, simply because he painted more quickly than anybody else. Artistic genius has bestowed great benefits upon artisanal production, and artisans show an unseemly lack of gratitude when they seek to subordinate art to mere technology.

The simple artistic sense of beauty characterized Greek antiquity.

---

[1] An international industrial exposition, held in 1851.—Eds.
[2] Sir Joseph Paxton, the architect who designed the Crystal Palace.—Eds.
[3] An imaginary artist.—Eds.

But just at the time when this aesthetic sensibility was at its height, Hellas collapsed morally, politically, and socially. In the Middle Ages the mysticism of religious life, in conjunction with a splendid social structure, produced that spiritual impulse toward creativity which built our cathedrals. But once again, when the construction of these gigantic temples was at its height, medieval civilization collapsed. The predominantly industrial spirit of the nineteenth century has produced the marvelous colossi of the modern big cities and erected that proud industrial hall of fame in the greatest of them. Those cities and that great hall correspond to one another, both of them being "open and breezy dwelling-places." But a more highly developed flowering of industrialism will take place in the future, and this will lead to the collapse of the modern world of the big cities. These cities, together with even more fabulous halls of industry than the one which we have seen, will remain only as torsos, "with scaffolding on the top," like the Cologne Cathedral. Inasmuch as world history has tragically judged bygone times, we have no right to pat ourselves on the back, frivolously using the narrow standards of our own times, and cry out, "Look and see how great we are."

Adolf Weber

THE CULTURAL AND SOCIAL SIGNIFICANCE OF THE BIG CITY

Adolf Weber, who retired from the University of Munich in 1947, was one of twentieth-century Germany's outstanding economists. His publications, amounting to over fifty books and more than a hundred articles, treated a wide range of economic problems. One of his earliest books was a nontechnical discussion of urban social problems. Published in 1908, it was based on a series of lectures Weber delivered at an adult education center while he was on the faculty of the University of Bonn. The introductory chapter, reprinted below, not only summarizes recurrent attitudes toward cities in nineteenth-century literature, but also presents Weber's own balanced views concerning the benefits as well as the costs of urbanization.

. . . What is meant by the term "big city"? All cities with a population of more than 100,000 inhabitants deserve this title.

Half a century ago there were still only six cities in Germany with 100,000 inhabitants: Berlin, Hamburg, Munich, Breslau, Dresden, and Cologne. Of these, only Berlin (450,000) numbered more than 200,000 souls. Today in Germany we have forty big cities, of which seventeen have populations of 200,000 or more. In 1900 Germany had more big cities than there were in all of Europe a hundred years earlier. In 1800 there were twenty-two cities numbering 100,000 or more, and their total population amounted to 4 million inhabitants, whereas Germany alone in 1900 possessed thirty-three such cities, with a total population of more than 9 million. The big cities have increased immensely during the last generation. In 1871, about 5 percent of the inhabitants of the German Empire lived in big cities; in 1880, 7 percent; in 1890, 12 percent; in 1900, more than 16 percent. Today it may be assumed that if one includes those suburbs which are directly influenced by a big city, more than a quarter of the German population lives in big cities.

Even more striking than the statistical growth of the urban population is the increased influence the big city exerts on our intellectual and economic life in general. It would be silly if we failed to acknow-

From Adolf Weber, *Die Grossstadt und ihre soziale Probleme* (Leipzig: Quelle und Meyer, 1908), pp. 1–20, 133–134. Reprinted by permission of the publisher. Translated by the editors.

ledge that the influences emanating from the big city are by no means uniformly favorable, but it would be just as silly to preach a crusade against the big city in general.

The big cities are the consequence of our economic development, which is intimately bound up with the immense quantitative and qualitative augmentation of material forces—on the one hand, with a population increase unknown to earlier centuries, and on the other, with the marvelous skill these newly gathered masses of men have shown during the last century in subordinating nature to their own purposes. Accordingly, the essence of the problem of the big city must be stated as follows: *to retain what is good in the big city and to combat what is evil.*

If we wish to study modern big-city life, perhaps we shall do well to begin by considering the views of those whose vocation it is "to sympathize with the sorrows and the joys of human life": our imaginative writers. Perhaps the reader is familiar with Peter Rosegger's social novel, *Blessings of the Earth: Private Sunday Letters of a Farmhand.*

Hans Trautendorffer, the economics editor of a newspaper named *The Continental Post,* a city-dweller and a fully cultivated man, bids farewell to the city as a result of a foolish bet and moves in midwinter to the countryside, to work as a farm laborer. In a mountain pasture, in the house of a man named Adam, he finds a job. Having been spoiled by urban life, he must now perform hard work, in return for which he receives scanty room and board, but he grits his teeth and sticks it out in order to win the bet. Sundays he sits in his room, which gets its only heat from an adjoining stall for oxen, and writes letters on a small bench to a friend in the big city, letters in which he describes his experiences during the preceding week. One blow after another strikes the family which has taken him in. Soon the farmhand becomes the trusted friend of the family. He comes to recognize the dark sides of rural life and he yearns increasingly for the city, feeling "homesickness for intellectual life." And yet none of this overwhelms him; on the contrary, he comes to feel that "cultural humanity" is not diminished but rather enhanced in the countryside, and he subsequently forgets that only a wager brought him there. He begins to love the land and agricultural work for their own sake. He contemplates jubilantly the growth and the decline of the marvelous magic that nature produces in the woods and the fields. "The farmer knows that it is spring when the grass begins to grow again," he writes to his friend, "whereas in the city the concerts gradually resume, the gardeners clean up the lawns in the parks, the winds stir up the dust in the streets, and the tailors introduce the spring season with some sort of foolish new fashion." The young urbanite turned farmhand feels growing love in his heart, not only for the natural open spaces but also for the people who live there. One senses clearly that he is speaking from the heart when he praises the peasantry's readiness to make sacrifices and its quietly patient love, which borders on the heroic. "The peasantry displays energy and spiritual activity of which the arrogant simpleton in a dress coat is totally ignorant." It is no surprise that Trautendorffer permanently gives up his city jacket and dons the smock of a peasant instead.

Maxim Gorki's novel, *Three Men,* provides an excellent counterpart to this novel. Ilya, the hero of the novel, moves from the countryside to the city at the age of ten. He sees the city from a distance, its houses densely crowded together. The sun has just risen, and in its rays the windows of the houses mirror one another, giving a special splendor to the whole scene. "O, how pretty that is," says the boy softly to himself. Then we see how the boy's life unfolds in the big city. Soon the child perceives that life is far more pleasant in a village than it is in the city. In the village, one could go where one pleased, wandering around in the fields and pilfering food from trees and bushes. But in the city one has to stay cooped up in narrow dusty courtyards or in ugly row-houses. And how quiet and peaceful it is in a rural homeland! Everyone has the same occupation and everyone knows one another, whereas in the city everyone is pushy and quarrelsome and nobody pays any heed to other people.

Gorki then shows how the boy's life deteriorates, how he is seduced and corrupted by the influences of the big city, until finally he even commits murder. When the police come to arrest him, they offer not to place him in chains, if he swears "by God" that he will not flee. He answers somberly, "I do not believe in God," and then he breaks loose. He is found again at the foot of a cliff with a fractured skull, having put an end to his own life.

Gorki and Rosegger, two quite different authors, depict two quite different human lives, but the basic point of both novels is the same: to indict the social life of the modern big city. But these two are not the only ones who make such complaints. If we take any writer of the most recent period who has looked at modern life with his eyes open, we will continually encounter a similar pessimism when it comes to a discussion of life in the big city.

Here, where I am speaking of the views of writers concerning urban life, we think perhaps of another writer, who rendered judgment on the city several generations ago. In his poem "A Stroll," Schiller says with regard to the city:

> Look, the competing forces struggle there passionately.
> Their conflicts produce much, but by working together
>   their achievement is still greater.
> A thousand hands are animated by a single spirit,
>   and only one heart, glowing with one sentiment,
>   beats in a thousand breasts,
> Beats for the fatherland and glows with affection
>   for the ancestral laws.

No *modern* big city will dare to assert that these verses of Schiller's are a motto it has faithfully observed. Concord and harmony have not reigned in big-city life for a long time; all too often, discord and strife make themselves felt, with fateful consequences. In so many faces we meet today in the big city, we seem to be able to discern thoughts similar to those which Gerhard Hauptmann, in his poem "On the Night Train," put into the mouths of modern proletarians:

> For you we have built houses of gold,
> While we ourselves live out in the cold.
> We make your clothes, we bake your bread,
> But all too soon we shall be dead.
> We wish to smash our chains,
> We wish revenge, revenge. . . .

I have heard many people complain, "Yes, it is a pity that the good old days are gone." But these "good old days" had their dark sides nonetheless. In particular, the city-dweller in those days by no means enjoyed an exclusively bright and blissful existence. How did the old cities look at that time, and how did people live in them?

Let us begin with externals. The streets were generally quite filthy. According to a traveler, even in Berlin in 1800—a time when our capital numbered 200,000 inhabitants—people always had to cover their noses with a handkerchief when they walked in the streets.

People were in the habit of throwing everything into the streets; especially in the morning, someone who was walking around outside inevitably breathed in foul odors. Dead cats, dogs, and even horses were permitted to lie for half a day on the streets. Whereas today the big city is bathed in extremely bright electric light during the nighttime, people in the cities used to have to make do with small street-lanterns, which were mounted at the side of the street on wooden posts in order to provide just a bit of illumination. The cautious city government took care that the street-lamps did not burn too long, fearing that otherwise they would use up too much of their scanty oil supply. When people went out, they therefore attached small lanterns to themselves, so that the way home would be lit up. The illumination within buildings was just as primitive. Here, people used tallow candles, which became dirty in a quarter of an hour and continually had to be cleaned. Naturally there were still no electric trolley cars, which seem to be indispensable in modern cities and, with their rattling noises, have become characteristic of our urban street life. Instead, people in the good old days could still enjoy the cheerful sound of the posthorn and also perhaps the reassuring sing-song of the good old night watchman, who traipsed in the evening through the streets, and every hundred paces blew into his horn and cried out:

> Now listen all you gentlemen,
> The clock has struck the hour of ten.
> Extinguish every fire and light,
> Then our city will be all right,
> And praise God the father.

Perhaps the old night watchman, as the artist Skarbina depicted him in his lithograph "Now listen all you gentlemen . . ." is the best landmark of the old-fashioned city.

But however cheerfully the urban life of yesteryear may be portrayed, modern men would hardly feel satisfied if a magician took away from them the conveniences of the modern big city and in return gave them the "charms" of the city as it existed over a hundred years ago.

Even internal conflicts were not at all rare in the old days. Then, as well as now, there were social questions in the cities: the troubles of servants, conflict between employers and employees, and the need for housing. As for happy and joyful public spirit in the city, listen to Dr. Arnold Mallinckrodt, who at the end of the eighteenth century asked why the German free cities were not as happy as would have been expected of independent republics. His answer was as follows:

> *Lack of public spirit and patriotism, love of routine and idleness, mistrust by the citizens toward the city councils, despotism by one man or by a few individuals, ineffective judicial procedures, sloppy accounting systems, negligent police, bad methods of caring for the poor, envy, ill-will, and luxury are all at fault.*

One cannot really object to this. Men have always believed in the reality of the good old days. They see the past through rose-colored glasses, whereas the present appears to be more dismal than it really is. Of course we must not go to the other extreme and depict the past in overly somber hues in order to make the present appear to radiate all the more brightly. Perhaps we can strike the proper balance by saying that the modern city is in far better shape than the old cities in terms of its *external* milieu and its *external* life. But profound *inner* conflicts were exceptions in earlier times, whereas today they have become the rule.

In general one has to be extremely cautious in comparing German cities of the period before the nineteenth century with modern big cities. It is a matter of comparing two entirely different social phenomena. If one is looking for a counterpart to our modern big cities, ancient Rome during the last years of the republic provides the best example. An Italian historian, G. Ferrero, said quite rightly a short while ago, "Similar phenomena produced the same moral and political consequences as are evident today: intellectual unrest, a weakening of traditional values, a general relaxation of discipline, the enervation of authority, moral disorder and confusion." At that time, as is the case today in the big cities, certain moral feelings—an energetic feeling of independence for example—became more refined, whereas other moral characteristics—such as pity and sympathy, love for the place of one's birth, and trust in God—faded and disappeared.

But let us return to the present. Let us seek as men of the present to take stock of what the modern big city means for our cultural life.

I have already indicated that the modern big city arose inexorably as a response to the economic needs of the present, and that its most noteworthy benefits are therefore economic in nature. The big city is a creation of our modern economic culture; in turn, it helps mightily to sustain economic life through the part it plays in the magnificent increase of wealth which is taking place nowadays. People crowd together in the big city so that they may share tasks more effectively. We have in contemporary economic life a marvelously extensive division of labor, and this division of labor functions much better where men are crowded together than it does where they live isolated from one another. Consequently the production of goods is cheaper in a big city, and the productivity of labor is greater. Consumption in the big city is mass consumption, and for this reason urban demands can be satisfied less expensively than can the demands of individuals in the countryside and the smaller cities. Related to this is the fact that an ever-increasing share of the national wealth gravitates toward the big city and that increasingly the directors of our productive forces move there as well. The corporations, the banks, and the stock exchanges are centered in the big city, and more of them are moving in all the time. They are followed by numerous newly rich provincials, who come partly in order to enjoy the pleasures of the big city and partly in order to increase their wealth through "speculation." In 1851 the most highly taxed individual in Berlin had an income of 64,000 Talers, whereas in 1905 there were already two hundred and fifty Berliners whose income exceeded that figure. In 1851 in Berlin there were only six millionaires, whereas in 1900 there were six hundred and thirty-eight. This concentration of wealth in the big city certainly has its social drawbacks, but from a purely economic viewpoint it also has advantages. Being so highly concentrated, capital can be better controlled, and above all it can be better channeled into the most profitable areas for investment and utilized most effectively from an economic viewpoint.

But it is not only *capital* that derives great benefits from the big city. The economic *intelligence* of the individual frequently develops to a greater extent here than it does in the small provincial city or on the land. Artisans cannot specialize and develop their techniques to the same extent in the provinces as they can in the big city. Moreover, in the big city the tradeschools of the big artisans' associations frequently have at their disposal especially capable technical teachers and outstanding instructional materials. The sharp competition on the one hand, and on the other hand the manifest success of those who are the most proficient, provide invigorating incentives to those who have spent their lives in the provinces in a state of lethargy. An outstanding industrialist, Oechelhäuser, once said with some justification, "The tempo of thought and action rises in proportion to the size of the population."

There is no question that *economically* the big city signifies progress, and for this reason it seems to me that its right to exist is already established, despite its obvious drawbacks in other respects.

Every man strives toward both material and ideal goals, toward an increase of his external goods and toward an improvement of his innermost being as a man. Now certainly it is easier to make material progress than to advance ideally and spiritually. But when there is disharmony, one should not try to eliminate it by giving up material progress; instead, one should make every effort to utilize mankind's material accomplishments in order to rise still higher spiritually and morally. Until the big city makes progress in this direction, it will not yet deserve the honorific title that some have already bestowed upon it: "the center of the most advanced culture."

How do matters stand with regard to the spiritual and moral progress of humanity in the big cities? I accept the answer of the geographer Ratzel: "As long as there have been big cities, they have taken the lead in their countries with respect both to what is good and to what is bad." But, I hasten to add, the modern big city of the present hinders the spiritual and moral progress of our nation to a far greater degree than it facilitates such progress. I do not wish to deny that there is more *restless energy* in the big city than elsewhere, or that broad segments of the urban population seem to be infused with an intense *craving for education*. The fact that we have made such great strides in the *struggle for political freedom and equal rights* is in no small measure the result of agitation in the big city. Nor can it be denied that the *"social conscience"* in the big city, though not entirely spontaneous, is especially sensitive.

But all of this cannot make up for the *deeply-rooted social discontent,* the *moral sickness,* and the regrettably *low spiritual level* of a large part of the big-city population.

Nowhere is the difference between rich and poor more deeply felt, and nowhere does the perception of this difference inflict more painful wounds than in the big city. People observe how quickly wealth is sometimes accumulated, but they overlook the fact that almost as often it is lost just as quickly. He who is fortunate joyously flaunts his good luck in public, while he who is unfortunate sneaks out of the city in which he can no longer be happy and becomes a part of the proletariat elsewhere. And who feels the great contrasts in the world of business most deeply? The *children,* from whom these contrasts are supposed to be hidden as long as possible. The children see with amazement that the rich live in luxury without working, while their father puts in a hard day at work and still remains poor. This may be one of the reasons for the absence of sensitive feelings in the big city. Pleasure and profit are the concepts that shape the life of a big-city family. And what is a family anyway in the big city? The man and the woman are in the factory, and the children are left on their own to roam the streets—"blinded today and blind tomorrow," already sacrificed to the big city.

Nevertheless the urban smoke and fumes continue to tempt new hordes away from the green land. They are attracted by the tenements, the department stores, and the factories, blinded by the deceptive glitter, behind which bitter misery awaits so many hopeful migrants. Even if they manage to support themselves, many remain strangers to the big city, although they may lack the courage to admit this. As strangers, they slave away among strangers, far from their homeland, devoid of the most beautiful thing in the world next to parental love, *devoid of feeling for the homeland.*

The new migrants to the city do not provide the advance notice of their arrival which would be required if the necessary dwellings were to be provided for them in time. They come in varying numbers, and as a result there is insufficient space to accommodate both the old and the new urbanites in housing that satisfies their needs. From time to time the *housing question* becomes especially acute, and people realize how much misery is encompassed by this social question.

Because the patterns of migration and economic development vary so much in the different big cities, each of which has its peculiar commercial characteristic, economic life in general is much less stable in the big city than it is in a really large community, such as the whole state. One is far more likely, therefore, to hear valid complaints in the big city about *unemployment* and hard times.

The extent to which *social discontent* is increasing in the big city is indicated by the numbers of votes cast for the Social Democratic Party. In the twenty-six big cities of the German Empire which already numbered more than 100,000 inhabitants at the time of the occupational census of May 14, 1893, the Social Democrats received 861,000 votes in the Reichstag elections of July 1903. On the other hand, the number of big-city workers who voted for the Social Democrats has been reckoned at 582,000, so that 300,000 of the 861,000 votes came from the so-called middle-class elements. Nevertheless, this social discontent has its advantages, since there is ultimately no progress without discontent.

Much more regrettable is the *moral filth* in big-city streets and bars. With the best will in the world, one still cannot find anything good to say about this phenomenon. A number of years ago the well-known Social Democratic leader, Kautsky, voiced the opinion that "whoever has the opportunity of getting to know young people in the big city must, unless he is already contaminated by their attitudes, be revolted by the brutality and the vulgarity of their manner of thinking and talking. Our youth do not talk about anything except smutty jokes and other obscenities; they boast of doing things of which decent people would be deeply ashamed."

Crime statistics reveal the consequences of these attitudes. According to the reports in the *Statistical Yearbook of German Cities,* the ratio of persons convicted of crimes or misdemeanors to the total population in cities with at least 50,000 inhabitants during the years 1898–1902 was 38 percent greater than the ratio in the rest of the Empire. For adult males, the ratio was 36 percent above the national average in these cities; for adult females, 68 percent greater; and for youths, 67 percent greater.

For every 10,000 persons in the civilian population who were old enough to be held responsible for their actions, the following numbers were convicted in the courts:

Period	Large Cities	Germany as a Whole
1898–1902	152.4	120.9
1883–1887	129.0	101.1

The yearly averages for the numbers of persons convicted of particular crimes per 10,000 responsible inhabitants during the period 1898–1902 are as follows:

Nature of Crime	Large Cities	Germany as a Whole
Assault and threats against officials	7.8	3.3
Dangerous bodily injury	19.2	25.2
Theft	34.8	22.1
Fraud	9.5	5.4
Other crimes and misdemeanors	81.2	54.5
Total	152.4	110.5

In Berlin, according to an official survey taken in 1900, 141.94 out of every 10,000 adult males and 45.73 out of every 10,000 adult females suffered from venereal disease, whereas in the administrative district of Münster the comparable numbers were 4.76 and 1.44.

Conclusions about the moral quality of the population can also be derived from *divorce statistics.* In the year 1905 more than half of Prussia's total number of divorces took place in that state's twenty-eight big cities. The frequency of divorce in relation to the number of existing marriages was two-and-a-half times greater than in the totality of cities. According to the official statistical accounts of these facts, "the main reason for the increased frequency of divorce in the big cities is urban life, with its greater moral dangers, its relatively lax moral standards, and its multitude of bad influences on family life (lodgers, tenements)." Adultery was the particular ground for divorce in 40.7 percent of the cases in the countryside, in 52 percent of the cases in the cities, in 57.9 percent of the cases in the big cities, and in 65.9 percent of the cases in Berlin.

This sort of family life greatly increases the danger of *child neglect.* The fact that this danger is considerably greater in the big city than in the smaller cities and villages is indicated, among other ways, by the statistics pertaining to the numbers of children on welfare. Berlin has a disproportionately large share of these children—over a tenth of the total—and the other big cities with populations over 100,000 have another 25 percent, whereas the municipalities with fewer than 2,000 inhabitants account for only 19.3 percent.

At the same time *birth rates are falling off quite rapidly in the big cities.* According to Mombert, the average numbers of births per year per 1,000 married women in Prussia below the age of 50 during the period 1899–1902 were as follows:

In Berlin	152
In the other big cities	224
In the middle-sized cities	236
In the small cities	256
In the countryside	287

The figure for Berlin in 1876 was still 307; in 1881, 252; in 1891, 220; in 1901, 172. For all married women, without any age limitation, the fertility rates in Berlin in recent years were as follows: in 1901, 125.0; in 1902, 119.8; in 1903, 113.1; in 1904, 111.2; in 1905, 109.7. That is a drop of 12 percent in four years!

Finally, let us consider the *suicide statistics.* For every 100,000 inhabitants, there were the following numbers of suicides:

1903	Male	Female	Total
In Prussia	33.33	8.82	21.00
In Berlin	46.72	17.38	31.44
1904			
In Prussia	31.77	8.95	20.20
In Berlin	46.00	16.67	30.73
1905			
In Prussia	32.28	9.43	20.69
In Berlin	52.13	19.57	35.18

Such statistical comparisons certainly do not allow us to arrive at a favorable judgment concerning the moral quality of the big city.

The moral illness is not diminishing but rather getting worse. Our young people in particular seem to be increasingly corrupted by the influences of the big city. The frightfully sad fate which Gorki portrays in the novel discussed above is typical of what happens to thousands of big-city dwellers.

It is no surprise that the sort of deep *religiosity* that satisfies the heart and the spirit disappeared long ago in many sections of the big city. "People fear and hate the old faith of their fathers as if it were a ghost," and instead they frequently turn to foolish superstition. Just recently, in our intellectual metropolis, a special school for fortune-tellers was established; among other things it is supposed to teach "scientific palm-reading," or how to make prophecies from the lines of the hand, from coffee grounds, from lead, and from eggs, and there is no question but that this fortune-telling school is doing a good business. A highly regarded Berlin newspaper recently ascertained that no fewer than thirty fortune-tellers had advertised their services in another Berlin newspaper widely read by women.

On the other hand one hears the rejoinder that none of this really means very much in view of the fact that the big city is *the productive center of intellectual and artistic values.* In the big cities there are museums, theaters, and educational opportunities of all sorts. But if one examines the situation more carefully, one frequently discovers that the role that art and learning play in big-city life stems less from ideal inner motives than from the fact that intellectual commodities are purchased more readily in the big cities than elsewhere. The "ideal" can be turned into cash quite easily in the big city.

It has quite rightly been pointed out that one must begin with the monasteries rather than with the cities if one is seeking the origins of the new spiritual life which arose in the Middle Ages on the ruins of antiquity; moreover, at the same time that we recognize the importance of Rome and Paris in the history of the spiritual development of their nations, let us also recall that small cities such as Olympia and Weimar have attained a brilliant position in this regard. In addition, one must bear in mind that the great cultural centers numbered scarcely more than 100,000 inhabitants during their zenith. An increasing population was a sign not of cultural ascent but rather of cultural decline.

Besides, in the contemporary world we can see again and again that *great thinkers shun the tumult of the big cities,* and perhaps it is no accident that most of the leading intellectuals of recent decades were born either in the countryside or in small villages. Even the so-called "Bohemians," that special intellectual elite which is characteristic of many big cities, rebel periodically against the noise and the polluted air of the big city. The famous circle of young poets and thinkers that gathered around the Hart brothers in Berlin during the 1880s finally abandoned the tenements and the cafés of the big city so that they could carry on their free and easy life out of doors in Friedrichshagen, in farmhouses near the woods and the meadows.

And what about our *artists*? They have sought and found their stimulation in the villages and moors of East Frisia, in Worpswede, and in the mountains of Silesia and Bavaria. The fact that imprisonment within an urban jail sensitizes many people to the marvelous beauty in the unconfined world of divinely created nature can hardly be counted as a strong point of the big cities themselves.

Here and there we observe our artists and poets struggling against the corrupting influence of the big city. A number of years ago an appeal went out to the German princes to turn their courts into cultural centers, so that our poets and artists could withdraw from the spiritually unhealthy life of the big city, which was viewed as "the life of feeble and neurotic men." Here and there practical conclusions are being drawn from theoretical arguments. The Rhenish Friends of Art came into being as an association under the sponsorship of the Grand Duke of Hesse, who stated his primary objective as follows: "Native artistic energy should be bound to native soil and prevented from migrating into the big city, with its unworthy commercial competition and struggle."

Art which is at the same time *urban* and *genuinely German* seems to be a *contradictio in adjecto,* a contradiction in terms. Simplicity and modesty are inseparable from the German way. But do really *German* big cities still exist? The spirit of and a feeling for the homeland seem to have been irretrievably lost among an all too large segment of the big-city population. The sort of art that suits the big city is indicated by the ostentatious facades of the big tenement houses. Here as well as everywhere else the watchword is "sensation," and only those who advertise themselves are well regarded; there is no time to become really acquainted with people. Small wonder that everywhere appearances count for more than reality.

In the words of H. Müthesius, "People are nervously trying to gloss over natural relationships, to make themselves artificially refined, and to elevate themselves forcibly into a sham aristocracy. We seem to be ashamed of precisely what ought to be a source of pride, our middle class." The big city is witnessing a *"Fancy-dress parade of superficial modern culture,"* in which no genuine and deep art is able to thrive.

Sometime far in the future, perhaps even our *city plans* will make clear to the art historian the spiritual inferiority of our modern big-city culture. The great humorist Oberländer once compared the regular cities of modern times to inferior species of animals and the old irregular city to richly spiritualized forms of life. It is also well known that Field Marshal Moltke attributed less patriotism to cities with straight streets than he did to more complex cities. This observation contains a great deal of truth. City construction can indeed give evidence of an historical and aesthetic feeling for the homeland. But the "tragedy" in the modern big city is that traffic has frequently assumed such enormous dimensions in a relatively short time that good taste, joy in the homeland, and historical memories have to be sacrificed in order to make room for tyrannical "traffic." One feels how bitter this is and what far-reaching significance it must have when one wanders through the agreeable old streets of Heidelberg, Nuremberg, and Hildesheim and compares them with the cold structures of modern city-planning.

But *must one only talk about unpleasantness when one is discussing the cultural significance of the big city?*

Certainly not! We have already referred to the *economic* advantages of the big city, and fortunately there are only a few pessimists who insist on denying all cultural value to economic factors.

But we need not feel embarrassed even by these sharp-eyed critics. If they ask about the bright side of big-city development, I would refer in the first place to the brilliant progress that *"social hygiene"* has made in the big cities.

"Social hygiene"! What would an early nineteenth-century city-dweller say if he could see what is being accomplished today under the banner on which these words are inscribed? In his day, even during years that were free of epidemics, mortality frequently exceeded fertility. It was only in the era of the big cities—in large part thanks to the material and intellectual progress they brought about—that men dared to take up the "struggle against death," in which many brilliant victories have been won.

One need only think of several sorts of establishments that have been set up in big cities in order to appreciate the broad scope of the tasks assigned to social hygiene nowadays and by and large performed quite well: services for women in childbed and newly born children, pediatric hospitals, children's sanatoria, vacation camps, schools for the retarded, generous care for consumptives, convalescent homes, mental hospitals, treatment centers for alcoholics, public baths, public health offices, school doctors, doctors working for the city council, testing centers for detecting bacteria, and rescue stations in case of accidents or sudden illnesses. Sick people are cared for superbly in the big city. For example, in Berlin the splendid

Death Rates from Disease per 100,000 Inhabitants, 1903

Area	Cause of Death							
	Typhus	Diptheria and croup	Measles	Scarlet fever	Whooping-cough	Respiratory diseases	Digestive disorders
Germany	7.4	33.5	26.9	26.5	30.0	453.4	249.6
Berlin	3.3	12.8	17.7	17.2	22.7	406.9	111.2
Breslau	7.5	21.9	10.7	13.4	15.3	582.2	321.6
Munich	3.7	14.4	27.2	4.7	11.7	463.9	633.6
Dresden	5.1	15.3	24.2	11.0	25.4	401.9	126.6
Leipzig	3.7	32.4	10.7	28.5	—	391.5	345.9
Stuttgart	2.1	18.8	44.8	3.6	12.0	323.6	257.9
Hamburg	4.3	21.4	25.3	51.5	14.2	383.1	219.3

Rudolf Virchow Hospital has arisen on what used to be a virgin heath. It consists of sixty individual buildings, erected at a cost of 20 million marks, which cover 4,000 square meters. All the rooms for patients are exposed to the sun. One can look outdoors from every bed. The whole thing looks more like a special sort of suburban villa than like a hospital: one-story cottages, surrounded by hedges and shrubs, with friendly flowers greeting one from the windows. The sick urbanites can stroll in a lovely little park which is quite far removed from the commotion of the big city. And what about the *results of social hygiene* in the big cities? A few statistics provide the answer to this question.

The numbers of deaths from various illnesses per 100,000 inhabitants in the year 1903 were indicated on p. 80.

It is especially satisfying to note the success of efforts to combat tuberculosis in the big cities. According to the *Statistical Yearbook of German Cities,* between 1894 and 1906 the rate declined from 2.3 to 1.3 [deaths] per thousand inhabitants in Aachen, from 2.8 to 1.7 in Cologne, from 2.7 to 1.4 in Essen, from 2.4 to 1.1 in Kiel, from 3.9 to 2.3 in Nuremberg, from 2.4 to 1.8 in Leipzig, from 2.8 to 1.9 in Mannheim, from 3.1 to 2.1 in Posen, and so on. It is just as gratifying to note the falling rates of infant mortality: in the years 1891–1906 the rate declined in Munich from 30.9 to 19.6 [deaths of children under one year of age per 100 live births], in Düsseldorf from 28 to 19.5, in Cologne from 27.1 to 22.2, in Hamburg from 23.3 to 16.6, in Berlin from 24.9 to 17.7, and so on.

It was only a few decades ago that the economist Georg Hansen tried to prove that the city was inherently unhealthy, that it could not survive by itself, and that within two generations it would use up the human beings who had been delivered to it from the countryside. A pessimistic assessment of this sort is certainly no longer called for today. But it must be remembered nevertheless that the table presented [opposite] deals only with *mortality* and not with *health*. It is questionable whether the relatively favorable mortality statistics for the cities simultaneously provide proof of robust health and greater bodily vitality; moreover, it must not be forgotten that it is chefly the hardiest elements of the population that move from the countryside into the city, while the weaker ones remain behind. But such considerations are by no means serious enough to force us to modify our favorable judgment concerning the achievements of social hygiene in the big city.

Another bright spot in the life of the big city must also be considered. One can point with high hopes to the *hunger for education* felt by a considerable portion of the lower and middle levels of the big-city population. They acquire knowledge and try to deepen that knowledge, not because it is fashionable and not in order to make an ostentatious display, but rather because they sincerely wish to work at improving themselves, and this gives cause for rejoicing. At the very least, the *hope* remains intact that the great Humboldt was right when he said, "Along with knowledge comes thought, and with thought vigor and seriousness spread among the multitude." Even though the continual growth of popular education may have many unhealthy side-effects and may lead to the loss of much that ought to be preserved, if teachers and popular leaders seriously wish it, this development will help the population of the big city both spiritually and morally to attain a better future.

*   *   *

In a work that appeared a short while ago, W. F. Classen asked how our native breed of men will develop in the big city. He answered, "It has not yet been proved that the big city is a really fruitful source of healthy human energy. Thousands of dangerous demons are continually at work there, fraying our nerves and deadening our senses, and both the masses and the individual feel deeply in the soul how we have been cut loose from the sources of our strength." In another passage, he writes with regard to the working people of the big city, "Whoever enters into their life wholeheartedly certainly observes a great deal of big-city silliness and ridiculous conformity to fashion, but deep down healthy forces are at work and natural vitality continually blossoms forth."

I have already indicated in the first section that I would give a similar answer if someone asked me for my opinion concerning the big city and its future. My judgment is not too gloomy, and it would certainly be incorrect to condemn the big city totally. I have discussed big-city family life and dwellings, I have discussed the big-city worker's efforts to find employment and the problem of poverty, and I have depicted the tasks in the areas of popular education and social life which still await solution. Again and again I have had to point out things that are regrettable, but I have also indicated repeatedly that—even though they may be far away—there are means by which we can overcome the misery and hardship of the big city. But, as I have emphasized again and again, we shall not succeed in this endeavor simply by changing the external environment. Certainly a great deal can and must be done in this regard, but the most important thing is still to *reform men by transforming human character.* In any case, the big city poses extraordinarily important and difficult challenges for us, challenges that we must meet unless we are willing to see the culture we cherish give way gradually to a new kind of barbarism.

Lewis Mumford

PALEOTECHNIC PARADISE: COKETOWN

*Lewis Mumford has been writing about cities and related themes for over half a century. His work, which is marked by broad perspectives, great learning, and intense passion, has earned him a place as one of the most prominent American social thinkers of our time. The excerpts reprinted below, from his masterly survey of urban development in the western world from ancient times to the present—*The City in History *(1961)—focus on the industrial city of the nineteenth century. "Coketown," which in Mumford's eyes was the typical urban phenomenon of its time, appears to have been both a physical and a moral cesspool, degraded by brutality as well as filth. We have omitted the concluding parts of the chapter in which this selection originally appeared, parts dealing with attempts to improve living conditions in the cities. But even their inclusion would not have substantially brightened the dark picture of nineteenth-century cities which Mumford has painted.*

The Beginnings of Coketown

Up to the nineteenth century, there had been a rough balance of activities within the city. Though work and trade were always important, religion and art and play claimed their full share of the townsman's energies. But the tendency to concentrate on economic activities, and to regard as waste the time or effort spent on other functions, at least outside the home, had been growing steadily since

From *The City in History,* copyright 1961, by Lewis Mumford, pp. 446, 447, 451–454, 458–474. Reprinted by permission of Harcourt Brace Jovanovich, Inc.

the sixteenth century. If capitalism tended to expand the province of the marketplace and turn every part of the city into a negotiable commodity, the change from organized urban handicraft to large-scale factory production transformed the industrial towns into dark hives, busily puffing, clanking, screeching, smoking for twelve and fourteen hours a day, sometimes going around the clock. The slavish routine of the mines, whose labor was an intentional punishment for criminals, became the normal environment of the new industrial worker. None of these towns heeded the old saw, "All work and no play makes Jack a dull boy." Coketown specialized in producing dull boys. . . .

Between 1820 and 1900 the destruction and disorder within great cities is like that of a battlefield, proportionate to the very extent of their equipment and the strength of the forces employed. In the new provinces of city building, one must now keep one's eyes on the bankers, industrialists, and the mechanical inventors. They were responsible for most of what was good and almost all that was bad. In their own image, they created a new type of city: that which Dickens, in *Hard Times,* called Coketown. In a greater or lesser degree, every city in the Western world was stamped with the archetypal characteristics of Coketown. Industrialism, the main creative force of the nineteenth century, produced the most degraded urban environment the world had yet seen; for even the quarters of the ruling classes were befouled and overcrowded.

The political base of this new type of urban aggregation rested on three main pillars: the abolition of the guilds and the creation of a state of permanent insecurity for the working classes; the establishment of the competitive open market for labor and for the sale of goods; the maintenance of foreign dependencies as source of raw materials, necessary to new industries, and as a ready market to absorb the surplus of mechanized industry. Its economic foundations were the exploitation of the coal mine, the vastly increased production of iron, and the use of a steady, reliable—if highly inefficient—source of mechanical power: the steam engine. . . .

The process of un-building, as William Morton Wheeler pointed out, is not unknown in the world or organisms. In un-building, a more advanced form of life loses its complex character, bringing about an evolution downward, toward simpler and less finely integrated organisms. "There is," observed Wheeler, "an evolution by atrophy as well as by increasing complication, and both processes may be going on simultaneously and at varying rates in the same organism."

This held precisely true of nineteenth-century society: it showed itself clearly in the organization of urban communities. A process of up-building, with increasing differentiation, integration, and social accommodation of the individual parts in relation to the whole was going on: an articulation within an ever-widening environment was taking place within the factory, and indeed within the entire economic order. Food-chains and production-chains of a complicated nature were being formed throughout the planet: ice traveled from Boston to Calcutta and tea journeyed from China to Ireland, while machinery and cotton goods and cutlery from Birmingham and Manchester found their way to the remotest corners of the earth. A universal postal service, fast locomotion, and almost instantaneous communication by telegraph and cable synchronized the activities of vast masses of men who had hitherto lacked the most rudimentary facilities for coordinating their tasks. This was accompanied by a steady differentiation of crafts, trades, organizations, and associations: mostly self-governing bodies, often legally incorporated. This significant communal development was masked by the fashionable theory of atomic individualism: so it rarely achieved an urban structure.

But at the same time, an *Abbau,* or un-building, was taking place, often at an even more rapid rate, in other parts of the environment: forests were slaughtered, soils were mined, whole animal species, such as the beaver, the bison, the wild pigeon, were practically wiped out, while the sperm whales and right whales were seriously decimated. Therewith the natural balance of organisms within their ecological regions was upset, and a lower and simpler biological order—sometimes marked by the complete extermination of the prevalent forms of life—followed Western man's ruthless exploitation of nature for the sake of his temporary and socially limited profit economy.

Above all, as we shall see, this un-building took place in the urban environment.

The Postulates of Utilitarianism

Insofar as there was any conscious political regulation of the growth and development of cities during the paleotechnic period, it was done in accord with the postulates of utilitarianism. The most fundamental of these postulates was a notion that the utilitarians had taken over, in apparent innocence, from the theologians: the belief that a divine providence ruled over economic activity and ensured, so long as man did not presumptuously interfere, the maximum public good through the dispersed and unregulated efforts of every private, self-seeking individual. The nontheological name for this preordained harmony was laissez-faire.

To understand the uncouth disorder of the industrial town one must analyze the curious metaphysical preconceptions that dominated both the scientific and the practical life. "Without design" was a laudatory term in the Victorian period. As in the decadent period of Greece, Chance had been elevated into a deity that was supposedly in control not only of human destiny, but of all natural processes as well. "The gist of Darwin's theory," wrote Ernst Haeckel, the biologist, "is this simple idea: that the struggle for existence in nature evolves new species *without design,* just as well as man produces new varieties in cultivation with design." It was following what they presumed was nature's way that the industrialist and the municipal officer produced the new species of town, a blasted, denatured man-heap adapted, not to the needs of life, but to the mythic "struggle for existence"; an environment whose very deterioration bore witness to the ruthlessness and intensity of that struggle. There was no room for planning in the layout of these towns. Chaos does not have to be planned.

The historic justification for the laissez-faire reaction needs no demonstration now: it was an attempt to break through the network of stale privileges and franchises and trade regulations that the absolute State had imposed upon the decayed economic fabric and dwindling social morality of the medieval town. The new enterprisers had good reason to distrust the public spirit of a venal court or the social efficiency of the Circumlocution Offices of the growing taxation-bureaucracy. Hence the utilitarians sought to reduce governmental functions to a minimum: they wished to have a free hand in making investments, in building up industries, in buying land, in hiring and firing workers. Unfortunately, the preordained harmony of the economic order turned out to be a superstition: the scramble for power remained a sordid scramble, and individual competition for ever-greater profits led the more successful to the unscrupulous practice of monopoly at the public expense. But design did not emerge.

In practice, the political equality that was slowly introduced into the Western polities from 1789 onward, and the freedom of initiative that was demanded by the industrialists were contradictory claims. To achieve political equality and personal freedom, strong economic limitations and political restraints were necessary. In countries where the experiment of equality was made without attempting to rectify annually the effects of the law of rent, the result was a stultification of the original purpose. In the United States, for example, the free bestowal of land upon settlers in 160-acre tracts under the Homestead Law did not lay the basis of a free polity: within a generation the unequal properties of the soil, the unequal talents of the users, had resulted in gross social inequalities. Without systematically removing the fundamental disparities that grew out of the private monopoly of land, the inheritance of large fortunes, the monopoly of patents, the only effect of laissez faire was to supplement the old privileged classes with a new one.

The freedom demanded by the utilitarians was in reality freedom for unrestricted profits and private aggrandizement. Profits and rents were to be limited only by what the traffic would bear: decent customary rents and a just price were out of the question. Only hunger, distress, and poverty, Townsend observed in his commentary on the English Poor Laws, could prevail on the lower classes to accept the horrors of the sea and the battlefield; and only these same helpful stimuli would "spur and goad" them on to factory labor. The rulers, however, maintained an almost unbroken class front on any issue that concerned their pocketbooks as a class; and they never scrupled to act collectively when it was a question of beating down the working classes.

This theological belief in preordained harmony had, however, an important result upon the organization of the paleotechnic town. It created the natural expectation that the whole enterprise should be conducted by private individuals, with a minimum amount of interference on the part of local or national governments. The location of factories, the building of quarters for the workers, even the supply of water and the collection of garbage, should be done exclusively by private enterprise seeking for private profit. Free competition was supposed to choose the correct location, provide the correct time-sequence in development, and create out of a thousand uncoordinated efforts a coherent social pattern. Or rather, none of these needs was regarded as worthy of rational appraisal and deliberate achievement.

Laissez faire, even more than absolutism, destroyed the notion of a cooperative polity and a common plan. Did not the utilitarian expect the *effects* of rational design to appear from the unrestricted operation of conflicting random private interests? By giving rein to unrestricted competition, reason and cooperative order were to emerge: indeed rational planning, by preventing automatic adjustments, could, it was supposed, only interfere with the higher workings of a divine economic providence.

The main point to note now is that these doctrines undermined such municipal authority as had survived, and they discredited the city itself as anything more than a "fortuitous concourse of atoms"—as the physics of the time erroneously described the universe—held together temporarily by motives of self-seeking and private profit. Even in the eighteenth century, before either the French Revolution or the coal-and-iron revolution had been consummated, it had become the fashion to discredit municipal authorities and to sneer at local interests. In the newly organized states, even those based on republican principles, only matters of national moment, organized by political parties, counted in men's hopes or dreams. . . .

Factory, Railroad, and Slum

The main elements in the new urban complex were the factory, the railroad, and the slum. By themselves they constituted the industrial town: a word that described merely the fact that more than two thousand people were gathered in an area that could be designated with a proper name. Such urban clots could and did expand a hundred times without acquiring more than a shadow of the institutions that characterize a city in the mature sociological sense—that is, a place in which the social heritage is concentrated, and in which the possibilities of continuous social intercourse and interaction raise to a higher potential all the complex activities of men. Except in shrunken, residual forms, even the characteristic organs of the stone age city were lacking.

The factory became the nucleus of the new urban organism. Every other detail of life was subordinate to it. Even the utilities, such as the water supply, and the minimum of governmental offices that were necessary to a town's existence often, if they had not been built by an earlier generation, entered belatedly: an afterthought. It was not merely art and religion that were treated by the utilitarian as mere embellishments: intelligent political administration long remained in the same category. In the first scramble of exploitation, no provisions would be made for police and fire protection, water and food inspection, hospital care, or education.

The factory usually claimed the best sites: mainly, in the cotton industry, the chemical industries, and the iron industries, the sites near a waterfront; for large quantities of water were needed now in the processes of production, supplying the steam boilers, cooling hot surfaces, making the necessary chemical solutions and dyes. Above all, the river or canal had still another important function: it was the cheapest and most convenient dumping ground for all soluble or suspendable forms of waste. The transformation of the rivers into open sewers was a characteristic feat of the new economy. Result: poisoning of the aquatic life: destruction of food: befouling of water so it was unfit to bathe in.

For generations, the members of every "progressive" urban community were forced to pay for the sordid convenience of the manufacturer, who often, it happened, consigned his precious by-products to the river, for lack of scientific knowledge or the empirical skill to use them. If the river was a liquid dump, great mounds of ashes, slag, rubbish, rusty iron, and even garbage blocked the horizon with their vision of misplaced and unusable matter. The rapidity of production was in part matched by the rapidity of consumption, and before a conservative policy of scrap-metal utilization became profitable, the formless or deteriorated end-products were cast back over the surface of the landscape. In the Black Country of England, indeed, the huge slag heaps still look like geological formations: they decreased the available living space, cast a shadow on the land, and until recently presented an insoluble problem of either utilization or removal.

The testimony that substantiates this picture is voluminous; indeed, it is still open for inspection in the older industrial cities of the Western world, despite herculean efforts to cleanse the environment. Let me however quote from an early observer, Hugh Miller, the author of "Old Red Sandstone": a man thoroughly in harmony with his age, but not insensitive to the actual qualities of the new environment. He is speaking of Manchester in 1862.

> *Nothing seems more characteristic of the great manufacturing city, though disagreeably so, than the river Irwell, which runs through the place. . . . The hapless river—a pretty enough stream a few miles up, with trees overhanging its banks and fringes of green sedge set thick along its edges—loses caste as it gets among the mills and print works. There are myriads of dirty things given it to wash, and whole wagonloads of poisons from dye houses and bleachyards thrown into it to carry away; steam boilers discharge into it their seething contents, and drains and sewers their fetid impurities; till at length it rolls on—here between tall dingy walls, there under precipices of red sand-stone—considerably less a river than a flood of liquid manure.*

Note the environmental effect of the *massing* of industries that the new regime tended to make universal. A single factory chimney, a single blast furnace, a single dye works may easily have its effluvia absorbed by the surrounding landscape: twenty of them in a narrow area effectively pollute the air or water beyond remedy. So that the unavoidably dirty industries became through urban concentration far more formidable than they were when they had existed on a smaller scale and were more widely dispersed about the countryside. At the same time clean industries, such as the making of blankets, which still goes on at Witney, in England, with bleaching and shrinking conducted out in the open air of a charming countryside, became impossible under the old rural methods in the new centers. There chlorine took the place of sunlight, and for the healthful outdoor work that often accompanied the older processes of manufacture, with changes of scene as well as process to renew the spirit of the worker, came the dull drudgery of work within a dirty building hemmed in by other dirty buildings. Such losses cannot be measured in merely pecuniary terms. We have no calculus for figuring how much the gains in production were offset by the brutal sacrifice of life and a living environment.

While factories were usually set near the rivers, or the railroad lines that paralleled the rivers (except where a level terrain invited diffusion), no authority was exercised to concentrate factories in a particular area, to segregate the more noxious or noisy industries that should be placed far from human habitations, or to insulate for domestic purposes the appropriate adjacent areas. "Free competition" alone determined location, without thought of the possibility of functional planning: and the jumbling together of industrial, commercial, and domestic functions went on steadily in industrial cities.

In areas with a rough topography, such as the valleys of the Allegheny plateau, a certain amount of natural zoning might take place, since only the river bottoms would afford enough space for a big mill to spread—though this disposition ensured that the maximum amount of noxious effluvia would rise and spread over the homes on the hillsides above. Otherwise living quarters were often placed within the leftover spaces between the factories and sheds and the railroad yards. To pay attention to such matters as dirt, noise, vibration, was accounted an effeminate delicacy. Workers' houses, often those of the middle classes, too, would be built smack up against a steel works, a dye plant, a gas works, or a railroad cutting. They would be built, often enough, on land filled in with ashes and broken glass and rubbish, where even the grass could not take root; they might be on the edge of a dump or a vast permanent pile of coal and slag: day in and day out the stench of the refuse, the murky outpouring of chimneys, the noise of hammering or of whirring machinery, accompanied the household routine.

In this new scheme, the town itself consisted of the shattered fragments of land, with odd shapes and inconsequential streets and avenues, left over between the factories, the railroads, the freight yards and dump heaps. In lieu of any kind of overall municipal regulation or planning, the railroad itself was called upon to define the character and project the limits of the town. Except in certain parts of Europe where old-fashioned bureaucratic regulations happily kept the railroad stations at the outskirts of the historic city, the railroad was permitted, or rather, was invited to plunge into the very heart of the town and to create in the most precious central portions of the city a waste of freight yards and marshalling yards, economically justifiable only in the open country. These yards severed the town's natural arteries and created an impassable barrier between large urban segments: sometimes, as in Philadelphia, a veritable Chinese wall.

Thus the railroad carried into the heart of the city not merely noise and soot but the industrial plants and the debased housing that alone could thrive in the environment it produced. Only the hypnotism of a new invention, in an age uncritically enamored of new inventions, could have prompted this wanton immolation under the wheels of the puffing Juggernaut. Every mistake in urban design that could be made was made by the new railroad engineers, for whom the movement of trains was more important than the human objects achieved by that movement. The wastage of space by railroad yards in the heart of the city only furthered its more rapid extension outward; and this in turn, since it produced more railroad traffic, gave the extra sanction of profits to the misdemeanors so committed.

So widespread was this deterioration of environment, so hardened have people in big cities become to it in the course of a century, that even the richer classes, who could presumably afford the best, to this day often indifferently embrace the worst. As for housing itself, the alternatives were simple. In the industrial towns that grew up on older foundations, the workers were first accommodated by turning old one-family houses into rent barracks. In these made-over houses, each separate room would now enclose a whole family: from Dublin and Glasgow to Bombay, the standard of one room per family long held. Bed overcrowding, with three to eight people of different ages sleeping on the same pallet, often aggravated room overcrowding in such human sties. By the beginning of the nineteenth century, according to a Dr. Willan, who wrote a book on the diseases of London, it had produced an incredible state of physical defilement among the poor. The other type of dwelling offered to the working class was, essentially, a standardization of these degraded conditions; but it had this further defect, that the plans of the new houses and the materials of construction usually had none of the original decency of the older burgher houses: they were meanly built from the ground up.

In both the old and the new quarters a pitch of foulness and filth was reached that the lowest serf's cottage scarcely achieved in medieval Europe. It is almost impossible to enumerate objectively the bare details of this housing without being suspected of perverse exaggeration. But those who speak glibly of urban improvements during this period, or of the alleged rise in the standards of living, fight shy of the actual facts: they generously impute to the town as a whole benefits which only the more favored middle-class minority enjoyed; and they read into the original conditions those improvements which three generations of active legislation and massive sanitary engineering have finally brought about.

In England, to begin with, thousands of the new workers' dwellings, in towns like Birmingham and Bradford, were built back to back. (Many still exist.) Two rooms out of four on each floor therefore had no direct daylight or ventilation. There were no open spaces except the bare passages between these doubled rows. While in the sixteenth century it was an offense in many English towns to throw rubbish into the streets, in these early industrial towns this was the regular method of disposal. The rubbish remained there, no matter how vile and filthy, "until the accumulation induced someone to carry it away for manure." Of this there was naturally no lack in the crowded new quarters of the town. The privies, foul beyond description, were usually in the cellars; it was a common practice to have pigsties under the houses, too, and the pigs roamed the streets once more, as they had not done for centuries in the larger towns. There was even a dire lack of toilets: the *Report on the State of Large Towns and Populous Districts* (1845) states that "in one part of Manchester in 1843–44 the wants of upward 700 inhabitants were supplied by 33 necessaries only—that is, one toilet to every 212 people."

Even at such a low level of design, even with such foul accompaniments, not enough houses were built in many cities; and then far worse conditions prevailed. Cellars were used as dwelling places. In Liverpool, one-sixth of the population lived in "underground cellars," and most of the other port cities were not far behind: London and New York were close rivals to Liverpool: even in the nineteen-thirties, there were 20,000 basement dwellings in London medically marked as unfit for human occupation. This dirt and congestion, bad in themselves, brought other pests: the rats that carried bubonic plague, the bedbugs that infested the beds and tormented sleep, the lice that spread typhus, the flies that visited impartially the cellar privy and the infant's food. Moreover the combination of dark rooms and dark walls formed an almost ideal breeding medium for bacteria, especially since the overcrowded rooms afforded the maximum possibilities of transmission through breath and touch.

If the absence of plumbing and municipal sanitation created frightful stenches in these new urban quarters, and if the spread of exposed excrement, together with seepage into local wells, meant a corresponding spread of typhoid, the lack of water was even more sinister. It removed the very possibility of domestic cleanliness or personal hygiene. In the big capital cities, where some of the old municipal traditions still lingered, no adequate provision for water was made in many new areas. In 1809 when London's population was about a million, water was available over the greater part of the city only in the basements of houses. In some quarters, water could be turned on for only three days in a week. And though iron pipes made their appearance in 1746, they were not extensively used until a special act in England in 1817 required that all new mains be built of iron after ten years.

In the new industrial towns, the most elementary traditions of municipal service were absent. Whole quarters were sometimes without water even from local wells. On occasion, the poor would go from house to house in the middle-class sections, begging for water as they might beg for bread during a famine. With this lack of water for drinking and washing, it is no wonder that the filth accumulated. Open drains represented, despite their foulness, comparative municipal affluence. And if families were thus treated, one need scarcely turn to the documents to find out how the casual laborer fared. Deserted houses of uncertain title were used as lodging-houses, fifteen or twenty people in a single room. In Manchester, according to the police statistics of 1841, there were some 109 lodging-houses where people of both sexes slept indiscriminately; and there were 91 mendicant lodging-houses. "Playfair told the Health of Towns Commission in 1842 that in all Lancashire there was only one town, Preston, with a public park, and only one, Liverpool, with public baths."

This depression of living quarters was well-nigh universal among the workers in the new industrial towns, once the new industrial regime was fully established. Local conditions sometimes permitted an escape from the extreme of foulness I have been describing: the housing of the mill-workers at Manchester, New Hampshire, for example, was of a far superior order; and in the more rural industrial towns of America, particularly in the Middle West, there was at least a little free elbow room and garden space for the workers. But wherever one looks, the improvement was but one of degree: the *type* had definitely changed for the worse.

Not merely were the new cities as a whole bleak and ugly, environments hostile to human life even at its most elementary physiological level, but the standardized overcrowding of the poor was repeated in middle-class dwellings and in the barracks of the soldiers, classes that were not being directly exploited for the sake of profit. Mrs. Peel cites a sumptuous mid-Victorian mansion in which the kitchen, pantry, servants' hall, housekeeper's room, butler's and footmen's bedrooms were all placed in the cellar: two rooms in front and two rooms in the rear looked into a deep basement: all the others were "lighted" and "ventilated" by panes of glass high up in the inner walls. Corresponding forms of degraded housing were worked out in Berlin, Vienna, New York, and Paris during the middle of the nineteenth century. The new apartment houses of the middle classes backed upon deep, airless courts that had most of the characteristics of cellars even when they were technically above ground. Only "backward" towns escaped these infamies.

To judge by popular oratory, these defects were narrow in range, and, in any event, have been wiped out during the past century through the onward march of science and humanitarian legislation. Unfortunately, popular orators—and even historians and economists who supposedly deal with the same set of facts—have not formed the habit of making firsthand surveys of the environment: hence they ignore the existence of clots of degraded paleotechnic housing remaining in almost unmodified form throughout the Western world today: even back-to-back houses, tenements with airless courts, and cellar-lodgings. These clots not merely include most of the workers' dwellings built before 1900; they include a great part of what has been done since, though they show improvements in sanitation. The surviving mass of housing that was built between 1830 and 1910 did not represent even the hygienic standards of its own day; and it was far below a standard framed in terms of present-day knowledge of sanitation, hygiene, and child care—to say nothing of domestic felicity.

"Slum, semi-slum, and super-slum—to this has come the evolution of cities." Yes: these mordant words of Patrick Geddes apply inexorably to the new environment. Even the most revolutionary of contemporary critics lacked genuine standards of building and living: they had no notion how far the environment of the upper classes themselves had become impoverished. Thus Friedrich Engels, in order to promote the resentment needful for revolution, not merely opposed all "palliative" measures to provide better housing for the working classes: he seems to have held that the problem would be solved eventually for the proletariat by a revolutionary seizure of the commodious quarters occupied by the bourgeoisie. This notion was qualitatively inept and quantitatively ridiculous. Socially speaking, it merely urged as a revolutionary measure the miserable process that had actually gone on in the older towns as the richer classes moved out of their original quarters and divided them up for the working-class occupation. But above all the suggestion was naive because it did not perceive that the standards embodied even in the more pretentious new residences were often *below* those desirable for human life at any economic level.

In other words, even this revolutionary critic was apparently unaware of the fact that the upper-class quarters were, more often than not, intolerable super-slums. The necessity for increasing the amount of housing, for expanding the space, for multiplying the equipment, for providing communal facilities, was far more revolutionary in its demands than any trifling expropriation of the quarters occupied by the rich would be. The latter notion was merely an impotent gesture of revenge: the former demanded a thoroughgoing reconstruction of the entire social environment—such a reconstruction as the world is perhaps on the brink of today, though even advanced countries, like England and Sweden and The Netherlands, have not as yet grasped all the dimensions of this urban change.

Houses of Ill-Fame

Let us look more closely at these new houses of the working classes. Each country, each region, each population group had its own special pattern: tall tenements in Glasgow, Edinburgh, Paris, Berlin, Hamburg, Genoa, or two-story buildings, with four, five, sometimes six rooms in London, Brooklyn, Philadelphia, Chicago: vast wooden firetraps called three-deckers in New England, happily blessed with open-air porches, or narrow brick row houses, still clinging to an older Georgian row pattern, in Baltimore.

But in industrial housing there are certain common characteristics. Block after block repeats the same formation: there are the same dreary streets, the same shadowed, rubbish-filled alleys, the same absence of open spaces for children's play and gardens; the same lack of coherence and individuality to the local neighborhood. The windows are usually narrow; the interior light insufficient; no effort is made to orient the street pattern with respect to sunlight and winds. The painful grayish cleanliness of the more respectable quarters, where the better-paid artisans or clerks live, perhaps in a row, perhaps semi-detached, with a soiled pocket-handkerchief of grass before their houses, or a tree in a narrow courtyard in the rear—this respectability is almost as depressing as the outright slatternliness of the poorer quarters: more so indeed, because the latter often at least have a touch of color and life, a Punch-and-Judy show in the street, the chatter of the market stalls, the noisy camaraderie of the public house or bistro; in short, the more public and friendly life that is lived in the poorer streets.

The age of invention and mass production scarcely touched the worker's house or its utilities until the end of the nineteenth century. Iron piping came in; likewise the improved water closet; eventually the gas light and the gas stove, the stationary bathtub with attached water pipes and fixed outlets; a collective water system with running water available for every house, and a collective sewage system. All these improvements slowly became available to the middle and upper economic groups after 1830; within a generation of their introduction, they indeed became middle-class necessities. But at no point during the paleotechnic phase were these improvements made available to the mass of the population. The problem for the builder was to achieve a modicum of decency *without* these new expensive utilities.

This problem remained soluble only in terms of a primitive rural environment. Thus the original division of Muncie, Indiana, the "Middletown" of Robert Lynd's survey, had houses eight to a block, each on a lot sixty-two and a half feet wide and a hundred and twenty-five feet deep. This certainly provided better conditions for the poorer workers than what followed when rising land values crowded the houses and narrowed the garden space and the play space, and one out of four houses still lacked running water. In general the congestion of the industrial town increased the difficulties in the way of good housing, and added to the cost of overcoming these difficulties.

As for the furnishings of the interiors, Gaskell's picture of the housing of the working classes in England struck the lowest level; but the sordor continued, despite minor improvements, in the century that followed. The effects of pecuniary poverty were in fact aggravated by a general falling off in taste, which accentuated the impoverishment of the environment, by offering barbarous wall paper, meretricious bric-a-brac, framed oleograph pictures, and furniture derived from the worst examples of stuffy middle-class taste: the dregs of the dregs.

In China a friend of mine reports seeing a miner, grimy, bent with toil, tenderly fondling a stalk of delphinium as he walked along the road; but in the Western world, down to the twentieth century, when the allotment garden began to have its beneficent effect, the same instinct for fresh vital form was destined to feed on the deliberate monstrosities that the manufacturer offered to the working classes under the guise of fashion and art. Even religious relics, in Catholic communities, reached an esthetic level so low as to be almost a profanation. In time, the taste for ugliness became ingrained: the worker was not willing to move from his older quarters unless he could carry a little of its familiar filth, confusion, noise, and overcrowding with him. Every move toward a better environment encountered that resistance: a real obstacle to decentralization.

A few such houses, a few such lapses into filth and ugliness, would have been a blot; but perhaps every period could show a certain number of houses of this description. Now, however, whole quarters and cities, acres, square miles, provinces, were filled with such dwellings, which mocked every boast of material success that the "Century of Progress" uttered. In these new warrens, a race of defectives was created. Poverty and the environment of poverty produced organic modifications: rickets in children, due to the absence of sunlight, malformations of the bone structure and organs, defective functioning of the endocrines, through a vile diet; skin diseases for lack of the elementary hygiene of water; small pox, typhoid, scarlet fever, septic sore throat, through dirt and excrement; tuberculosis, encouraged by a combination of bad diet, lack of sunshine, and room overcrowding, to say nothing of the occupational diseases, also partly environmental.

Chlorine, ammonia, carbon monoxide, phosphoric acid, fluorine, methane, not to add a long list of some two hundred cancer-producing chemicals, pervaded the atmosphere and sapped vitality: often in stagnant lethal concentrations, increasing the incidence of bronchitis and pneumonia, causing widespread death. Presently the recruiting sergeant was not able to use the children of this regime even as cannon fodder: the medical discovery of England's mistreatment of her workers, during the Boer War and the First World War, did perhaps as much as any one other factor to promote better housing there.

The crude results of all these conditions may be followed in the mortality tables for adults, in the disease rates for urban workers compared with agricultural workers, in the expectations of life enjoyed by the various occupational classes. Above all, perhaps the most sensitive barometer of the fitness of the social environment for human life is the infant mortality tables.

Wherever the comparison was made between country and city, between middle-class quarters and poor quarters, between a low-density district and a high-density district, the higher rate of disease and death usually fell in the latter class. Had other factors stayed the same, urbanization by itself would have been sufficient to lop off part of the potential gains in vitality. Farm laborers, though they remained throughout the nineteenth century a depressed class in England, showed—and still show—a much longer expectation of life than the higher grades of town mechanics, even after municipal sanitation and medical care had been introduced. Indeed, it was only by a continual influx of new life from the country that the cities so hostile to life could survive at all. The new towns were established in the mass by immigrants. In 1851, out of 3,336,000 people of twenty years and upward inhabiting London and 61 other English and Welsh towns, only 1,337,000 had been born in the town of their residence.

Taking the infant-mortality rate, the record is even more disgraceful. In New York City, for example, the mortality rate for infants in 1810 was between 120 and 145 per thousand live births; it rose to 180 per thousand by 1850, 220 in 1860, and 240 in 1870. This was accompanied by a steady depression in living conditions: for after 1835, the overcrowding was standardized in the newly built tenement houses. These recent calculations corroborate what is known about the infant mortality rate in England during the same period: there the rise took place after 1820 and fell most heavily on the towns. There are doubtless other factors responsible for these retrograde tendencies; but the new towns, as an expression of the entire social complex, conditioning hygiene, diet, working conditions, wages, child care, education, had an important part to play in the result.

There has been much unwarranted congratulation over improvements in urban health under industrialism because those who believed that progress automatically occurred in every department of life during the nineteenth century refused to face the harsh facts. They did not let themselves make comparative studies between town and country, between the mechanized and the unmechanized; and they assisted further in creating confusion by using crude mortality tables, not corrected according to age and sex groups, and not therefore allowing for the heavier distribution of adults in the cities and the larger incidence of children and old people, more subject to disease and death, in the countryside.

These statistics made town mortality rates look more favorable than they really were on close actuarial analysis. To this day scarcely the beginnings have been made toward a satisfactory analysis of births and deaths, health and disease, in relation to environment. By lumping urban and rural rates together in a "national" figure the relatively poorer showings of the "prosperous" industrialized and urban areas have been concealed.

Similar misleading analyses, disguised as objective research, continue to be made. Thus Mabel Buer attempted to vindicate the Industrial Revolution from the charge of creating urban blight by making a study of the decrease in the death rate that took place before 1815— that is, before overcrowding, bad sanitation, and the general urbanization of the population had produced their characteristic devitalizing results. There is no need to cast doubt upon this earlier improvement any more than one need forget the steady *general* drop in the death rate throughout the nineteenth century. But it fails to wipe out the equally indisputable fact of later deterioration.

Instead of giving credit for the early advance to the mechanization of industry, one should give due credit to quite another department —the increase of the food supply, which provided a better diet and helped raise resistance to disease. Still another factor may have had a part: the wider use of soap, made possible by the increased amount of available fats. The use of soap in personal hygiene may have extended from the washing of the nipples of the nursing mother to the child in her care: finally it passed by example from the feminine to the masculine half of society. That increased use of soap is not easily measurable in trade schedules; for soap was originally a commercial monopoly, and as such, a luxury article: ordinary soap was mainly produced and consumed within the household. The spread of the soap-and-water habit might well account for the lowering of infant mortality rates before the nineteenth century; even as the dearth of water and soap might account in part for the deplorable infant death rates of the paleotechnic town.

In the main, hygienic poverty was widespread. Lack of sunlight, lack of pure water, lack of untainted air, lack of a mixed diet—these lacks were so common that they amounted to a chronic starvation among the greater part of the population. Even the more prosperous classes succumbed: sometimes even prided themselves on their vital deficiencies. Herbert Spencer, who was a nonconformist even to his own creed of utilitarianism, was forced to preach the gospel of play and physical relaxation to his contemporaries; and in his *Essays on Education* he went so far as to make a special plea to parents to permit their children to *eat fruit*.

A Close-up of Coketown

One may grant that at the tempo at which industrialism was introduced into the Western world, the problem of building adequate cities was almost insoluble. The premises which made these operations possible also limited their human success. How build a coherent city out of the efforts of a thousand competing individualists who knew no law but their own sweet will? How integrate new mechanical functions in a new type of plan that could be laid out and speedily developed—if the very essence of such integration depended upon the firm control of public authorities who often did not exist, or who, when they did exist, exercised no powers except those specifically granted by the state which put individual property rights at the top? How provide a multitude of new utilities and services for workers who could not afford to rent any but the most destitute types of shelter? How create a good physical plan for social functions that themselves remained abortive?

Cities that still contained vital residues of medieval tradition, like Ulm, sometimes managed, through the slow tempo of their growth and a bold policy of large-scale municipal land ownership, to effect the transition with relatively little loss. Where industry came in explosively, however, as in Nuremberg, the results were as vile as in towns that had no historic shell whatever. And in the New World, towns were built as late as 1906 (Gary, Indiana) with no regard for any physical features except the location of the industrial plant. As for still later industrial complexes like the motor car metropolis of Detroit, they learned nothing from the mistakes of the past: did not Henry Ford assert that history was bunk? So the plants they erected in accord with the most advanced engineering practice were set in the midst of an urban welter—classic models of municipal disorganization and technical incompetence. The very age that boasted its mechanical conquests and its scientific prescience left its social processes to chance, as if the scientific habit of mind had exhausted itself upon machines, and was not capable of coping with human realities. The torrent of energy that was tapped from the coal beds ran downhill with the least possible improvement of the environment: the mill-villages, the factory agglomerations, were socially more crude than the feudal villages of the Middle Ages.

The new urban emergent, the coal-agglomeration, which Patrick Geddes called the conurbation, was neither isolated in the country nor attached to an old historic core. It spread in a mass of relatively even density over scores and sometimes hundreds of square miles. There were no effective centers in this urban massing: no institutions capable of uniting its members into an active city life: no political organization capable of unifying its common activities. Only the sects, the fragments, the social debris of old institutions remained, left like the muddied debris scattered by a great river after the flood has subsided: a no-man's-land of social life. These new cities not merely failed for the most part to produce art, science, or culture: they failed at first even to import them from older centers. When a surplus was locally created it was promptly drained off elsewhere: the rentiers and financiers employed it upon personal luxuries, or upon philanthropies, like that of Carnegie's Music Hall in New York, which often benefited the capital cities long before any similar bequests were made to the region from which the riches were originally drawn.

Approach more closely the paleotechnic town: examine it with eye, ear, nose, touch. Present-day observers, because of the growing contrast with the emerging neotechnic environment, can at last see what only poets like Hugo or Ruskin or Morris saw a hundred years ago: a reality that the philistines, tangled in their utilitarian web of dreams, alternately denied as a sentimental exaggeration or greeted with enthusiasm as an indisputable mark of "progress."

Night spread over the coal-town: its prevailing color was black. Black clouds of smoke rolled out of the factory chimneys, and the railroad yards, which often cut clean into the town, mangling the very organism, spread soot and cinders everywhere. The invention of artificial illuminating gas was an indispensable aid to this spread: Murdock's invention dates back to the end of the eighteenth century, and during the next generation its use widened, first in factories, then in homes; first in big cities, later in small centers; for without its aid work would frequently have been stopped by smoke and fog. The manufacture of illuminating gas within the confines of the towns became a characteristic new feature: the huge gas tanks reared their bulk over the urban landscape, great structures, on the scale of a cathedral: indeed, their tracery of iron, against an occasional clear lemon-green sky at sunrise, was one of the most pleasant esthetic elements in the new order.

Such structures were not necessarily evil; indeed, with sufficient care in their segregation they might have been comely. What was atrocious was the fact that, like every other building in the new towns, they were dumped almost at random; the leakage of escaping gas scented the so-called gas-house districts, and not surprisingly these districts frequently became among the most degraded sections of the city. Towering above the town, polluting its air, the gas tanks symbolized the dominance of "practical" interests over life-needs.

The poisonous pall of smoke had already come into the pottery districts in the eighteenth century, through the use of cheap salt glazes; now it closed in everywhere, in Sheffield and Birmingham, in Pittsburgh, Essen, and Lille. In this new environment black clothes were only a protective coloration, not a form of mourning; the black stovepipe hat was almost a functional design—an assertive symbol of steam power. The black dyes of Leeds, for example, turned its river into a dark poisonous sewer; while the oil smudges of soft coal spat everywhere; even those who washed their hands left a rim of undissolved grease around the side of the washbowl. Add to these constant smudges on flesh and clothing the finely divided particles of iron from the grinding and sharpening operations, the unused chlorine from the soda works, later, the clouds of acrid dust from the cement plant, the various by-products of other chemical industries: these things smarted the eyes, rasped the throat and lungs, lowered the general tone, even when they did not produce on contact any definite disease. As for the reek of coal itself, it is perhaps not a disagreeable one: man with his long savage past has become fond of musty odors: so perhaps its chief misdemeanor was that it suppressed or made people insensitive to pleasanter smells.

Under such conditions, one must have all one's senses blunted in order to be happy; and first of all, one must lose one's taste. This loss of taste had an effect upon diet: even well-to-do people began to eat canned goods and stale foods, when fresh ones were available, because they could no longer tell the difference. The enfeeblement of elementary taste-discrimination extended to other departments than food: color-discrimination became feeble, too: the darker tones, the soberer colors, the dingier mixtures, were preferred to pure bright colors, and both the Pre-Raphaelites and the Impressionist painters were reviled by the bourgeoisie because their pure colors were thought "unnatural" and "inartistic." If an occasional touch of bright color was left, it was only in the signs on the hoardings—for Coleman's mustard or Reckitt's blue—paper surfaces that remained cheerful because they frequently had to be changed.

Dark, colorless, acrid, evil-smelling, this new environment was. All these qualities lowered human efficiency and required extra compensation in washing and bathing and sanitation—or at the last extreme, in medical treatment. The cash expenditure on cleaning alone was no small expenditure in the paleotechnic town, at least after the need for cleanliness itself was acknowledged. Take one item alone from a typical paleotechnic survival: Pittsburgh. Its smoke pollution began early, for a print in 1849 shows it in full blast. A generation ago the annual cost of keeping Pittsburgh cleaned was estimated at some $1.5 million for extra laundry work, $750,000 for extra general cleaning, and $60,000 for extra curtain cleaning. This estimate, about $2.31 million per year, did not count the losses due to the corrosion of buildings or the increased costs of painting woodwork, nor yet the extra costs of lighting during periods of smog.

Even after strenuous efforts to reduce smoke pollution, a single great steel plant in the heart of Pittsburgh still makes mock of these efforts at improvement—indeed, so heavy is the hold of paleotechnic tradition, that the municipal authorities only recently helpfully connived at the extension of this plant, instead of firmly demanding its removal. So much for pecuniary losses. But what of the incalculable losses through disease, through ill-health, through all the forms of psychological deterioration from apathy to outright neurosis? The fact such losses do not lend themselves to objective measurement does not make them nonexistent.

Indifference to these forms of devitalization during the paleotechnic period rested mainly on invincible ignorance. In "Technics and Civilization" I quoted the indignation and surprise of a leading apologist for this civilization, Andrew Ure, over the testimony offered by the astute physicians called before Sadler's Factory Investigation Committee. These physicians referred to the experiments made by Dr. Edwards of Paris upon the growth of tadpoles, proving that sunlight was essential to their development. From this they concluded—we now know with complete justification—that it was equally necessary to the growth of children. Ure's proud answer was that the gas lighting of the factories was a sufficient substitute for the sun. So contemptuous were these utilitarians of nature and well-tried human custom that they brought up more than one generation upon a devitalized diet, based purely on the consumption of calories. That diet has been improved during the last generation by a fresh budget of scientific knowledge, only to be debased once more by the spreading use of poisonous insecticides and pesticides, food preservatives and additives, to say nothing of equally fatal radioactive poisons like Strontium 90. As for the paleotechnic environment, it still widely resists correction, and casts its blight over tens of millions of people.

Next to dirt, the new towns boasted another distinction, equally appalling to the senses. The baneful effects of this blight have been recognized only in recent years, thanks to advances in technics not unconnected with that typical biotechnic invention, the telephone. I refer to noise. Let me quote an ear-witness account of Birmingham in the middle of the nineteenth century.

> In no town in the world are the mechanical arts more noisy: hammerings incessantly on the anvil; there is an unending clang of engines; flame rustles, water hisses, steam roars, and from time to time, hoarse and hollow, rises the thunder of the proofing house [where firearms are tested]. The people live in an atmosphere vibrating with clamor; and it would seem as if their amusement had caught the general tone, and become noisy, like their inventions.

The indifference to clang and racket was typical. Did not the manufacturers of England keep Watt from reducing the noise made by his reciprocating engine because they wanted auricular evidence of its power?

Today, numerous experiments have established the fact that noise can produce profound physiological changes: music can keep down the bacteria count in milk; and by the same token definite ailments, like stomach ulcers and high blood pressure, seem to be aggravated by the strain of living, say, within sound of a busy motorway or airport. The diminishment of working efficiency through noise has likewise been clearly established. Unfortunately, the paleotechnic environment seemed specially designed to create a maximum amount of noise: the early hoot of the factory whistle, the shriek of the locomotive, the clank and urge of the old-fashioned steam engine, the wheeze and screech of the shafts and belting, the click and whirr of the loom, the pounding of the drop hammer, the mutter and snuffle of the conveyor, the shouts of the workers who worked and "rested" amid this varied clamor—all these sounds abetted the general assault on the senses.

When reckoning up the vital efficiency of the country as compared with the city, or the medieval town as opposed to the paleotechnic town, one must not forget this important factor in health. Nor have recent improvements in certain departments, the use of rubber heels and rubber tires, for instance, lessened the strength of the indictment. The noise of the gasoline-driven motor cars and trucks in a busy city, as they start up, change gears, acquire speed, is a sign of their technical immaturity. Had the energy that has been put into styling car bodies gone into the design of a silent thermo-electric power unit, the modern city would not be as backward as its paleotechnic predecessor in the matter of noise and fumes. Instead, the "progressive" metropolises of motordom, like Los Angeles, exhibit, indeed magnify, all the urban evils of the paleotechnic period.

Experiments with sound made in the nineteen-thirties in Chicago show that if one grades noise by percentages up to 100 percent—which is the sound, like an artillery cannonade, that would drive one mad if continued over an extended period—the countryside has only from 8 to 10 percent noise, the suburbs 15, the residential districts of the city 25 percent, commercial districts 30 percent, and industrial districts 35. These broad lines would doubtless hold almost anywhere during the last century and a half, though perhaps the upper limits were higher. One must remember, too, that the paleotechnic towns made no effort to separate factories from workers' homes; so that in many towns noise was omnipresent, in the day and often in the night. The age of air transportation, whose noisy planes destroy the residential value of suburbs in the neighborhood of airports, now threatens to widen even further this assault on life and health.

Considering this new urban area on its lowest physical terms, without reference to its social facilities or its culture, it is plain that never before in recorded history had such vast masses of people lived in such a savagely deteriorated environment, ugly in form, debased in content. The galley slaves of the Orient, the wretched prisoners in the Athenian silver mines, the depressed proletariat in the insulae of Rome—these classes had known, no doubt, a comparable foulness; but never before had human blight so universally been accepted as normal: normal and inevitable.

H. J. Dyos and Michael Wolff

THE VICTORIAN CITY IN RETROSPECT

Although most current practitioners of urban history tend to avoid general qualitative statements about the nature of our urban past, H. J. Dyos and Michael Wolff concluded their massive collection of essays on nineteenth-century English towns with a finely nuanced appreciation of the Victorian city. Dyos, currently professor of urban history at the University of Leicester, has written widely on English cities and on the history of transportation. Wolff, formerly editor of Victorian Studies *and now professor of English and Victorian studies at the University of Massachusetts, heads the Research Society for Victorian Periodicals.*

To all appearances the Victorian city is now virtually a thing of the past. The actual city, the physical monument, that pile of solemn but exuberant shapes that has been for so long and for so many people the very emblem of urbanity is at last melting away. Those massive realities that once commanded the ground in such numbers are being furiously singled out as trophies by conservationists or reduced to rubble by property developers. The urban past has never had a very secure future. The ponderous and ever-accumulating mass that no Victorian generation could perceive as complete has remained intact, it now seems, for only the first two post-Victorian generations. Only now therefore can we be conscious of the whole cycle. We can even sense the shape of some of the things to come. The technologies that underpinned these first cities of the industrial era are being superseded by others with quite different implications, and the processes that built up such high densities in those cities may even be going into reverse. For the urban mass no longer generates forces of attraction directly proportionate to its density. Density, though susceptible to almost limitless engineering possibilities, is no longer a necessary condition of urban intercourse. No human settlement in Britain lies beyond the city's range. The perspective we get of the Victorian city from the ground is therefore a finite, tentative, historical one. In such respects it seems no longer contemporary.

From H. J. Dyos and Michael Wolff, "The Way We Live Now," in Dyos and Wolff, eds., *The Victorian City: Images and Realities* (London and Boston: Routledge and Kegan Paul, 1973), Vol. II, pp. 893-897. Reprinted by permission of the publisher.

Yet, if we look harder, what we see is something rather different. Our evolving cities are still governed by the ways in which earlier occupants of the ground divided their fields or settled their estates, and the centers of commercial gravity if not their circumferences are commonly still fixed where earlier convenience required. Inertia is part of the dynamic of urban change: the structures outlast the people who put them there, and impose constraints on those who have to adapt them later to their own use. The fact is that the framework of growth, however hastily devised, tends to become the permanent structure, and to be held fast by property titles and convenient routines that can seldom be undone at a stroke. Even urban clearways are making surprisingly clean-cut slices through the elaborate residues of nineteenth-century growth. Within that arena the relative standing of neighborhoods changes less than that of their salient as a whole, largely because housing produced in the mass must conform to standard specifications and be occupied by correspondingly uniform social groups. Then, as now, the social framework devised by developers, whether with eyes open or shut, becomes embodied in the structures themselves and is a bequest no less lightly given away than a more strictly entailed inheritance. Even when neighborhoods decay such covenants remain, for houses built for the servant-keeping classes decline inexorably into whole districts of one-roomed dwellings. The configuration of the ground, the prevailing wind, the means of locomotion, the location of the gas-works, the precise whereabouts of cemeteries, golf-courses, schools, hospitals, parks, sewage works, factories, railway sidings, and shopping centers—all amenities whose distribution tended to be settled at an early stage of urban growth—are ineradicable influences on subsequent patterns of urban life. To that extent what happened in the nineteenth century plainly matters still.

There is nevertheless a more fundamental reason for regarding the Victorian city as belonging to the present. The growth of cities in the nineteenth century not only marked the beginning of a period in which so many of the aches and aspirations of modernity were first felt but the beginnings of processes which have had since to be seen in unified global terms. It was then that the urbanization of the world first gathered momentum and a framework for the contemporary history of man became perceptible. It was then that the inherent characteristics of our present social condition became actual in comprehensive terms: the city as the environment of the social mass could be seen taking shape and its ultimate possibilities visualized. Britain was the first to complete this modern transformation, just as she had been the first to undergo the industrialization of her economy, and represents therefore the prototype of all industrializing, urbanizing, modernizing societies. Here, indeed, was a foretaste of the way we live now.

What unifies these Victorian and latterday phases of urbanization as a universal experience is, above all, the sharp awareness of multiplying numbers, of man by the million, of whole systems of growth points, of a prospect of cities without end, and of a political arithmetic that must embrace them all. The obsession with numbers which characterized the social investigations of the Victorians themselves was almost congenitally determined and the inevitable prefix to so many of their judgments, as to ours. For the unprecedented acceleration in the growth of the population gave to cities for the first time in six thousand years a totally new role. No longer dominated by the numbers and capacities of those living off the land, these new aggregates could generate their own energies, impose their own demands on the countryside, and develop a new culture. Though they first grew more by taking people off the land than by breeding them, British cities were, by the end of the nineteenth century, coming within reach of maintaining their numbers for themselves. That transition, presently followed by other European countries and their overseas settlements, was within a century being made throughout the world, under constraints not basically different from those prevailing in Victorian Britain. Once again the control of death preceded the control of birth, though with much more dramatic effect in our own time. Urbanization among the emerging countries in the third quarter of the twentieth century has become in consequence a simple function of population growth and the cities the decanters for agrarian poverty. Perhaps one-third of the world's population already live in urban places of some description and even the most halting extrapolations would bring this urban concentration to something like that of Britain in mid-nineteenth century before the end of the twentieth. Britain alone could be described as predominantly urbanized by the end of the nineteenth century; already the most advanced countries are comparably so; the rest are following behind.

The Victorian city is part of our culture in a still more general sense. The promise of modernity, however distant, is abundance and equality, the material and ideological products of the dual revolution in England and France in the late-eighteenth century, and the city is its exponent, if not its redeemer. Here, new opportunities for communication intersected, new patterns of human relationships began to form, new institutions sprang up, new values, sensations, conventions, and problems were expressed; while older perceptions, behavior, and limitations changed their pitch or disappeared altogether: everywhere a flickering failure of absolutes in ideas and attitudes, a stumbling advance towards free association between people, a more democratized urbanity. The humanization of mankind became for the first time a momentarily imaginable possibility, even if the petty realities of individual lives too often remained stubbornly gross and seemingly hopeless. In the modern world, we contend, the path of progress has been an urban one. The very existence of the city has been a demonstration of the capacity, however uneven, to lift human effort beyond subsistence and a preoccupation with the brute facts of mere existence; and the urbanization of the whole population is an index, however crude, of rising standards of material welfare. Here is a measure of our civilization.

What is so conspicuous in the city is the gathering of vast crowds of ordinary people for everyday purposes, something hitherto impossible. It has by the last quarter of the twentieth century become such a routine of urban life that deserted streets betoken something wrong. Perhaps nothing illustrates better than our joint numerosity the affinities we have with the first modern city-dwellers of Victorian Britain and the differences that exist between us both and the generations that went before. Modern man is essentially thick on the ground. On the lower and darker side of pre-Victorian respectability what we see is a vast ignorable pit of shadows from which few ever emerged to make any distinguishable mark of personal achievement. The traditional urban mob was personified only by its ringleaders and remained essentially anonymous and undifferentiated. The modern aspect of the crowd militant as we see it developing early in the nineteenth century included implicit disciplining, the dawning of a new sense which the urban working classes began to have of themselves, and the heightened sensitity felt by the ruling classes towards popular unrest. What also began to happen at the same time, though barely perceptibly, was something that can only be described as a process of faces appearing in the crowd.

In conditions of urbanization, a dominant culture is always faced by new groups of people previously thought of as beneath consideration. The close juxtaposition of rich and poor, of the mercantile and servile elements in urban society, which had persisted since ancient times, only began to break down in England during the eighteenth century and it was not until the nineteenth that this disintegration became at all marked. Before this time the allocation of social space was determined more than anything by the divisions between crafts and between townsmen and aliens, though the accumulation of private property, the award of public honors, and the expanding scope for conspicuous consumption had also helped to draw such groups apart. The analogue to this process was the suburb, at one time a no-man's-land for all that was disreputable—dungheaps, gallows, stinking trades, bloodsports, low taverns, prostitutes, thieves, and the mob—and at another the means for keeping such things at a safe distance. It represented at once a glint of mutual perception between the middle and working classes and a blindfolding of their social relations wherever it happened at least during the nineteenth century. This mutual recognition and distancing has supplied many of the images and realities probed in this book [*The Victorian City*]. To that extent they are symptoms of the Victorian city as a phenomenon of modernity, of the capacity for sustained awareness of other societies or cultures. What the Victorian city began to do by way of opening up the possibilities of the dual revolution was to permit this sustained awareness of differences in social conditions to take place. Here, almost for the first time, was some visible prospect of the advancement of whole classes but, more than that, a stirring consciousness among the lower ranks of society of the removable differences in the quality of human life. It was the city which enabled such things to be seen.

It was not an ennobling experience through and through. For the working classes had been thought of as subhuman for so long that it was almost natural for them to display, or for their superiors to see them as displaying, their reputation for animality—brute strength, brute instincts, brute deserts. The faces in the crowd were as often as not seen to be marked by strong drink, violent passions, degraded character. The great unwashed were socially unclean, too, and the typical attitudes first expressed to this emergent group by those above them were also stereotyped—a blend of contempt, fear, hate, and physical revulsion. Threaded into such attitudes was a mixture of awe and envy derived from general knowledge of the profligacy of the working classes, itself partly dependent on the common, if not first-hand, observation that prostitutes, like prize-fighters, ordinarily came from the lower orders. The pornography of the period assumed that all servants, shop girls, and laborers were inexhaustibly libidinous. To the respectable classes such things spoke of an almost totally unregenerative condition redeemable in very few instances and then only by acts of grace and forgiveness. They remained deeply gloomy about the lower reaches of the Victorian city and conceived the notion of a residuum to cover the unknowable poor. Slum missionaries brought back their tales of horror and pathos from this nether world as if they had been journeying in darkest Africa. They were for the most part, as it seems now, both deaf and dumb, incapable of hearing the authentic tongue of the voiceless or of telling the prisoners how to escape. The poor man was in truth a long way from paradise and the rich man from longing for his touch, but the gulf between them was no longer fixed and the city itself was capable of closing it in other ways.

The Victorian city was essentially a great leveler, even though it began, like the railway, by hardening the categories of those using it and directing them into socially segregated compartments. To be sure, its population was distributed more explicitly in this regard by night than it was by day, and there were always incongruous pockets of privilege and understood affiliations. Urban society developed diversity, too, so that the range of its modes of behavior and particular attributes became almost a function of size. Yet the city was above all the province of anonymity and the nondescript. In it the individual's identity tended to be smudged and made less distinguishable; he could lose himself in the crowd, become part of the common multiple, disappear. This is precisely what he could never do in village society. There, understood roles, systems of deference, and clear lines of demarcation designating ground to be covered or avoided, still expressed the animus of feudalism. The difference between the city and the village was not so well established everywhere, especially in the nascent industrial cities, where the lords of the loom and the mine were creating conditions in which individuals could be marked men and their lives could be molded to new forms of serfdom. The general tendency was altogether less idiosyncratic and more organizational. The urban masses were in truth composed, not of social atoms, but of individual human beings. Yet for purposes of social action, as for mutual perception, it was the extrafamilial grouping, the collective label, more generalized identification of ordinary needs, more abstract reference to people as such, that now began to pass into common parlance about the city. Inhospitable to the stranger, unyielding even to its own, the city was nevertheless a great force towards equalizing its inhabitants.

III THE URBAN MIDDLE CLASSES

Wolfgang Köllmann

THE MERCHANTS AND MANUFACTURERS OF BARMEN

Wolfgang Köllmann, whose general essay on German urbanization is reprinted above, has written one of the finest case studies of a nineteenth-century city available in any language, a social history of Barmen. Located on the Wupper River, just east of Düsseldorf in the area of the Ruhr Valley, Barmen became an early center of the German textile industry, growing from 16,289 to 169,214 inhabitants between 1810 and 1910. (In the 1920s, Barmen, Elberfeld, and several other communities were combined to form the city of Wuppertal.) Entrepreneurs—merchants and manufacturers—formed the backbone of Barmen's middle-class elite. The selection from Köllmann's book reprinted below portrays their style of life and their outlook on the world as they evolved from generation to generation over the course of the century.

The upper class in Barmen at the beginning of the nineteenth century had been formed as the economy developed. The elite of the class consisted of several long-established families, who had already achieved status and influence through the yarn trade. At the beginning of the eighteenth century, families such as Bredt, Wichelhaus, and Keuchen already belonged to this circle; a little later, they were joined by the Engels, Schuchard, Barthels, Wuppermann, and Wulfing families; others, such as the von Eynern family, were included in the closing decades of the century. In this way a tightly closed elite emerged which, as a result of Napoleonic administrative reform, acquired legal recognition of the position in public life which it had already possessed de facto for a long time. The representatives of the group were called upon to govern the city in the city council, after having already participated in public affairs through the parish councils of the churches. Starting in 1826, they were able, owing to a favorable suffrage law, to select the delegate to the provincial house of representatives; starting in 1831, the members of the chamber of commerce came from their ranks.

This group provides a classic example of a class of notables [*Honoratiorenschaft*]. Traditional social prestige accompanied by economic independence and willingness and the time to perform

From Wolfgang Köllmann, *Sozialgeschichte der Stadt Barmen im 19. Jahrhundert* (Tübingen: J. C. B. Mohr [Paul Siebeck], 1960), pp. 108–123. Reprinted by permission of the publisher. Translated by the editors.

public service gave them an undisputed position of leadership in the public life of the city. They stepped forward as city councillors, as church elders, as members of boards of trustees, the chamber of commerce, and the commercial court, as representatives in the county and the provincial houses of representatives, and as leaders of associations, often holding a number of offices and positions simultaneously. Only a very few of these men were able to support themselves without working for a living; most of them were active from day to day in business, and consequently their readiness to serve stemmed not only from their favorable economic situation but also from their sense of responsibility for the good of the community.

This willingness was closely linked to the world view of the entrepreneurs, in which the Protestant ethic and the capitalist spirit had been welded together. "We come together today in the name of God, for whose blessing on our efforts we pray, in order that our association may provide many benefits for our community," said Johann Wilhelm Fischer in 1816 as he greeted those who had assembled to form a Grain Association for the purpose of warding off the threat of famine. This view of "the world as duty," according to which public service and work in one's own business were tasks imposed by God, demanded that one contribute one's personal efforts and material resources unstintingly. Men such as Johann Wilhelm Fischer used the assets of their own firms in order to secure public loans, and sometimes they neglected their own business when the well-being of the community required their attention. "From September of 1816 until the end of 1818," i.e., during one of the worst periods of crisis, "I have devoted my time exclusively to the Barmen Grain Association, with the most intense patriotism, out of brotherly and Christian feeling and a conscientious sense of duty, at personal sacrifice and with enormous effort," Fischer later wrote about his performance.

The notables regarded such fulfillment of their duty as evidence that they were moral men. They felt that success was "confirmation of being in a state of grace" and that their property was "a gift of God, which they were to administer and use in His honor." The Calvinist doctrine of predestination persisted in this form in their consciousness. To be sure, only a fraction . . . of the families belonged to the Reformed faith, whereas the others . . . were Lutheran, but the influence of the Reformed spirit even in the Lutheran parishes was such that hardly any differences were apparent. Consequently, meeting the demands that arose in public life and in business led to an unshakable self-assurance and self-satisfaction, such as Johann Wilhelm Fischer displayed when he reported about his successes with the Grain Association:

> *What was my reward? Answer: Several polite letters from the royal government; quiet recognition by the better elements of the citizenry, but above all else a* clear conscience *and the* glorious feeling *of having helped to protect Barmen from want and hunger during hard times. The* sweet feelings of self-satisfaction *make me happy; I do not need anything more! Because of the* simplicity of my character, *the* modesty of my disposition, *and my contempt for everything which even suggests* presumption, *I gladly go without any public recognition.*

If this was true of public activity, it was expressed even more clearly in business activity. The expression "Soli deo Gloria,"[1] which appeared on the covers of company books, was not an empty formula for these men; instead, it showed that as far as they were concerned their work in their vocations amounted in the end to "divine service." Fulfillment in life lay in work itself, and the certainty of being one of the "elect" grew not only out of faith in God's grace but also out of success in business. To be sure, such an attitude toward life often led to a rigid self-righteousness, but it also contributed to the early upsurge of the economy of Wuppertal and the tough endurance displayed during crises. The speculator and the fortune-hunter were entirely lacking among these thrifty, sober, and self-willed entrepreneurs. But at the same time they possessed exact knowledge of the world economy and the vision and daring necessary in order to turn the remote agricultural area on the Wupper into a thriving commercial and industrial area, given the fact that this expansion depended almost exclusively on exports. Their daring was proved in the 1820s by the founding of the Rhenish West Indies Company and the German-American Mining Association, which were efforts to gain a foothold in Latin America, and also by the establishment of the firm of Engels and Engels in Manchester, one of the centers of English competition. Certainly many were distrustful of innovations—for instance, the Barmen delegate Schuchard, one of the outstanding representatives of his generation, vigorously opposed plans in the Rhenish provincial house of representatives for a railroad—but in general people knew how to recognize and use the possibilities of technological development at the appropriate time.

---

[1] "Glory to the one God."—Eds.

The education of the young merchant was designed to meet vocational demands. Primary school and attendance at a boarding school, usually without any study at a gymnasium, preceded the period of commercial training, which frequently was completed abroad. There was special emphasis on learning foreign languages and commercial mathematics; the location where the training was to take place (usually in the firm of a business friend) was carefully selected. Then the young merchant entered his father's business or the firm of a friend, in order gradually to work his way toward a partnership. During his time as an employee, he undertook extended travels in foreign countries on matters of business. Four trips each year to Holland, France, and England were not unheard of even before the means of transportation improved through the spread of the railroads. In this way the young merchant acquired the knowledge of the world he needed. For the most part he married at an early age, choosing his bride from the families of notables and clergymen. For those merchants who had migrated to the city, such a marriage indicated recognition by and acceptance into this group, whose members were related to each other by blood and marriage in a multitude of ways. Family feeling was especially pronounced among Barmen's merchants.

The style of life was simple and unpretentious. The woman of the house ran the household just as economically as her husband ran his factory. But people still knew how, when the occasion demanded it, to put on a show which befitted their wealth and reputation. The local middle-class house of the period, with its clearly articulated design and its simple and austere rooms and furniture, characterized the middle-class life-style, which was not showy and did not make any claims unless they were justified by character and accomplishment. At the same time, this life-style gave expression to their sense of their own worth and to their sense of personal achievement.

The Puritan tendency toward an "inner asceticism" also prevailed in private life. Business and church affairs evoked "the liveliest . . . interest." Theological, geographical, and historical books filled the libraries. In some cases the classics were read, but in general the reading of belletristic literature was regarded as a "waste of time," and the theater was shunned on principle. Only love of music enlivened the cultural scene. Musical events took place in almost every house. There were even several organs in homes. The Barmen merchants' association, Concordia, set up a big concert organ in their hall that was the first of its kind on the Continent outside a church. Naturally, religious music predominated, but the "modern" classics and the romantics were also performed.

Cultural life was closely linked to church life. The clergymen were the only social group that ranked equally with the merchants and manufacturers. Many manufacturers' wives came from clergymen's families, and many a manufacturer's daughter married a young clergyman. The highly regarded vocation of the preacher outweighed the lack of wealth in the eyes of these people, for whom property implied neither merit nor claims but rather tasks and duties.

The relationship of the entrepreneur to his employees was patriarchal in nature. As at home, so too in his factory the manufacturer conducted his affairs strictly but firmly, demanding of his employees the same attitude toward work that he himself displayed. Such an attitude explains the long hours and the hard working conditions. But it must not be forgotten that this patriarchal management was accompanied by patriarchal social services. While the manufacturer made heavy demands, he was also deeply interested in the personal well-being of his workers, and he was supported in this area by his wife. Not only did he know the individual domestic or factory worker personally, but he also felt obligated to protect him from hardship. His workers responded to this attitude with unreserved recognition of the "sovereign authority" of the local notables and with unshakable devotion to their work, which can be documented with many examples. The domestic workers, who often were employed by the same firm for their whole lives, felt especially strong personal ties to the family of the manufacturer.

This patriarchal relationship accounts for many measures which were undertaken in public affairs. It gave rise to the early factory-based health insurance plans and to other relief funds, to participation in the "labor courts," and to the extension of the "Elberfeld system" of welfare work (the prototype of which had been developed in church parishes), which institutionalized patriarchal social concern and leadership. Schuchard's successful struggle against child labor, like opposition to other abuses of the early industrial period (such as the truck system and unpaid preparatory labor), was based on a sense of responsibility for his subordinates. The patriarchal structure of society was evident even in the appearance of individual areas of the city: the church and the factory-owner's house formed the core of a residential area, around which were grouped the houses of domestic workers and other laborers.

The members of the elite socialized in tightly-knit merchants' clubs, of which the Concordia, founded in 1801, was the oldest and most important. Membership in this club counted as proof that one belonged to the upper crust. Then in 1827 there arose in Wupperfeld the Association for Art and Industry, whose primary task was the advancement of industrial education, and, in Lower Barmen, an association known as "Union," which never equaled Concordia in rank and importance. Concordia became the focal point of the city's social, intellectual, cultural, and political life. City receptions, such as the ones on the occasion of the crown prince's visit in 1833 and of the king's visit in 1842, took place in its rooms, demonstrating the amalgamation of the economic elite and the government of the city.

All the merchants of this generation possessed the same basic traits. But this did not mean that they constituted a homogeneous stratum, since the character traits which we have protrayed tended precisely toward the development of self-reliant and independent personalities. Frequently blunt and intractable and often stubborn and self-willed, the individual doggedly stood up for his views and pursued his own course of action with iron tenacity. It was the great achievement of this generation that it produced a large number of independent personalities, all of whom lived by the same basic code and were animated by the same spirit.

The next generation, which moved into the positions of leadership during the period of early industrialization, was different. The attitudinal change which the middle class experienced as a result of the Industrial Revolution was clearly evident among Barmen's entrepreneurs. It became clearer and clearer as the religious revival of the 1830s petered out and involvement in church affairs declined, with some individuals becoming quite indifferent to religion. Ernst von Eynern, whose father was vestryman of the Wupperfeld congregation for several years, made the following observation concerning his confirmation in his autobiography:

> *I followed the rules set down by inflexible orthodoxy in order to pass the examination with honor. But I do not remember any of the hundreds of bible verses and hymns which I learned by heart. Religious questions have never excited my interest. I shall make my way through life, for better or worse, without holding onto particular beliefs which do not affect me in my innermost being.*

The transition of the young Frederick Engels from pietism to communism indicated that for many young people this development was preceded by an earnest and often painful struggle over religion with their parents and teachers. The circle around the *Barmer Zeitung,* which struggled for greater intellectual freedom, had an important influence, as did Ferdinand Freiligrath,[2] who worked from 1837 to 1839 as a bookkeeper for the von Eynern firm and made friends among the young businessmen. This generation of entrepreneurs was a generation of transition and ferment, which attempted to grasp a changed world with new viewpoints and new methods. In general this generation was more open to cultural concerns than were their fathers. Concordia became the breeding ground for various middle-class cultural associations that arose in the 1860s, placing its rooms at their disposal. To be sure, the self-assured liberality displayed by personalities such as August Freiherr von der Heydt (an Elberfeld banker and later a minister in the Prussian government) or David Hansemann[3] was rare, but men acquired broader perspectives and became more open to the world nonetheless.

The belief persisted that one had duties to perform in the world, but this outlook was no longer based on religion. It was based on the ethical belief that "in my favorable situation in life I have been extremely fortunate and I must prove myself deserving of this good fortune by dedicating my feeble energies to the service of others." An honorably and conscientiously conducted life provided self-justification. This was the case not only in private and business life but also in public life, where the claim to a position of leadership was based on the view that "every good citizen has the duty to dedicate his energies not only to his family and his business but also to the state and to the city." Like their fathers, the sons were active in city offices, as city councillors or representatives, even though their preeminence was no longer accepted without question after the social structure of the city had been transformed by the rise of the working class and its emergence as a politically independent force. Of course, the local electoral law, which made the vote dependent on the amount of taxes one paid, protected their dominant position in city hall, but they could no longer prevail in elections for the Reichstag.[4]

As the structure of business enterprise changed, the close patriarchal ties between entrepreneurs and their workers were loosened.

[2] A politically radical poet.—Eds.
[3] A merchant and leader of the liberal forces in the Rhineland who served in the Prussian government in 1848.—Eds.
[4] There was universal manhood suffrage in elections for the Reichstag.—Eds.

To be sure, in the case of the domestic workers the old relationship of familiarity and trust persisted. Workers' jubilees were celebrated, there were outings for workers' families, and most of the factory-owners spoke the familiar local dialect with their workers; but in general the social distance increased, especially in those firms where office-workers came between the manufacturers and the manual workers.

Starting in the 1840s a new sort of entrepreneur began to displace the notables. It is characteristic that complaints about bad conditions were first raised by dyers and spinners, i.e., in precisely the trades where the transition from a situation characterized by master craftsmen working at home to one characterized by wage-laborers and factory-owners had begun earliest. The new entrepreneurs, having originally been domestic masters themselves, frequently became ruthless "factory lords," displaying "the ugly, hard, materialistic side of entrepreneurship" which advanced capitalism brought to the fore. . . . Hard work and self-denial had enabled them to rise in life, and they ruthlessly demanded the utmost in performance from their employees. Many of them lacked any feeling of moral obligation toward their workers, and intolerable working conditions were the rule in these factories. In some cases the citizenry supported the complaining workers and attacked these abuses of the industrial system, especially in the spinning industry, but this did not prevent the intensification of the workers' struggle, starting in the 1860s.

The differences among the entrepreneurs that became apparent during these years were paralleled by the social differentiation among the businessmen's clubs: whereas Concordia, whose preeminence remained unchallenged, generally was restricted to notables, the Union consisted of businessmen whose fathers had established their firms, and the Association for Art and Industry consisted largely of upwardly mobile first-generation businessmen. In addition, during the 1860s Christians joined together to found the Evangelical Citizens' Association and the Christian Association of Young Businessmen.

This differentiation indicated a growing exclusiveness within the economic elite, which was to intensify during the Wilhelmine period.[5] An article in the *Barmer Zeitung* of December 1, 1873, already complained about the "self-satisfaction displayed by native elements to-

[5] 1888–1918.—Eds.

ward intruders" and the "intolerance" of these social groups, which were beginning to turn themselves into castes by limiting their contacts almost exclusively to a small circle of socially equal families. As in the past, the old families of notables still constituted the elite of the merchant class during the Wilhelmine period, even though they were beginning to be displaced and new names appeared increasingly among the big entrepreneurs. In any case the new men frequently married daughters of old families, so that the members of the upper stratum were extensively related to one another by marriage.

The displacement of the old elite, which began during this period, intensified as a result of the economic changes brought about by World War I, and was completed during the inflation,[6] was caused by several factors. In the first place the long-established entrepreneurs were tradition-bound and adhered much longer to the putting-out system, because the transition to their own factory seemed to them to involve too great a risk, especially during the early 1870s. Capital that had been laboriously accumulated would have had to be invested in the new establishment, and one's own business would have borne the brunt of fluctuations in demand, whereas earlier the domestic workers had borne this burden. As a result, young entrepreneurs, who had risen during the period of economic expansion between the middle of the century and 1873, enjoyed a head-start which many of the older businessmen were never able to overcome. Moreover, inasmuch as they were not bound to tradition they were more flexible, and adapted production to changes in demand more quickly. The newly developed branches of industry offered opportunities that were exploited by these newer forces, while many of the older firms were displaced. The decline of the trade in Turkish-red yarn and the diminished importance of middlemen in the yarn trade after the big firms started buying their raw materials themselves hit the old firms especially hard. Consequently, many families, such as the Bredts, the Siebels, the Keuchens, the Engels, the Schuchards, the Wuppermanns, and the von Eynerns, lost their leading economic positions. In some cases, owing to the lack of possibilities for expansion, businesses moved away from the city; for instance, the management of the firm of Engels moved in 1885 from Barmen to Engelskirchen, the location of the main factory, after a railroad connection had been established there.

---

[6] During the early 1920s.—Eds.

At the same time the old notables lost ground economically as they came increasingly to hold state offices and to live off their investments. Statistics showed what a large portion of the economic elite depended upon unearned income. Moreover, this trend frequently resulted in a move to a resort city, such as Godesberg or Wiesbaden. The sons, whose education away from home had frequently alienated them from the one-sided and demanding work patterns of the city, devoted themselves to their studies and became lawyers, doctors, academics, officers, or land-holders. The middle class, beyond its economic accomplishments, thus provided essential personnel for the leadership of the state, but these people were lost to the economy itself.

The young entrepreneurs who overtook the older businesses were vigorous men who dedicated themselves totally to their work, which was the focal point of their lives and claimed all their energies. Their efforts were oriented solely toward success in business, to which everything else was subordinated. They were proud of the fact that they were working for "progress" and that their constantly improving business techniques enabled them to produce their goods better and more cheaply. Labor power was now totally subordinated to the newly developed system of machines, and ruthless severity toward the workers often accompanied the rationalization of work. One certainly cannot say that labor power was ruthlessly exploited in all cases. Many workers indicated that they preferred to work in the factories of rising young entrepreneurs than for the older businessmen. Whereas the latter had no practical experience as laborers and often were totally unable to comprehend the newer sort of industrial worker, the work experiences of the former better enabled them to understand the mentality of their subordinates and their attitude toward their work. Moreover, the rationalization of business permitted higher wages for higher output. Consciously or unconsciously, however, the fear that setbacks might take away what one had gained, quite natural after the economic crisis of the early 1870s, resulted in severity toward oneself and toward the workers. In place of the view of "the world as duty" there appeared a relentless pursuit of profits, which now became the entrepreneur's basic motive. Of course this was not always the case. A considerable portion both of the older and of the rising manufacturers remained devoted to the religious tradition. Their working ethos was still closely linked to their religious convictions, and in their eyes success in business confirmed that they had been "elected" by God and that they were morally worthy. In their factories the demands placed upon the workers were often especially heavy; indeed, some of them even refused to give their workers Saturday afternoon off, because they feared that too much free time might tempt the workers to drink liquor or engage in some other worldly activity. They told the workers to "abstain from earthly things," and this advocacy of the ideal of poverty was not really hypocritical, inasmuch as they did not look at themselves as being personally rich but rather as God's stewards. The Christian self-justification by the industrial "exploiter" expressed in this attitude was rooted in the beliefs of Calvinist Puritanism. In any case the hardships in such factories were counterbalanced in many respects by the fact that the entrepreneur felt himself to be personally responsible to God for his subordinates and therefore worried about them a good deal. The traditional patriarchal direction and concern lived on in such factories, even though their number grew ever smaller.

Those who were no longer motivated by religious faith still conformed to the religious customs of the older generation. Young men who were just starting out in business joined the Christian associations, especially the Christian Association of Young Businessmen, in which, as in the educational associations, they sought to make social contact with the families of the notables. In this way the church sphere often became an important way-station on the path toward social recognition.

In their places of business, the young as well as the older entrepreneurs did their utmost to maintain religious traditions, inasmuch as they, like the clergy, regarded religion as the only means of combating the influences of social democracy among the workers. In any case the workers knew clearly when the Christianity of their employers survived only as a formality and did not permeate the basic attitude toward life.

These exceptions notwithstanding, the old religious spirit of the Barmen entrepreneurs faded more and more. It gradually died from within, without there being any declarations of war or freethinking of the sort still displayed by individual representatives of the liberal elite around the middle of the century. No one declared himself openly to be an enemy of the church, but the newly rich felt superior to the "little people" and either turned away from or were indifferent to the frequently pious sectarianism of the established church.

This spiritual change underlay the change in attitudes and life-style which characterized the businessmen around the turn of the century. Three interdependent processes revealed their changed position in the industrial big city: their concentration on the functions of economic and business leadership, their gradual abandonment of public tasks, and their adoption of the mode of life of upper bourgeois Wilhelmine society.

As the account of the development of the economic structure and of the young entrepreneurs has already made clear, the industrial world placed new demands on those businessmen who wished to succeed. Technological change, with which one had to keep pace, demanded the factory, with all its innovations. The various work processes, from preparatory work to the finished product, all overlapped in the same area. In the decades before World War I, there arose planned factories, huge and elaborate, whose workrooms bore hardly any resemblance to the first small "establishments" of the period of early industrialization. This development contributed to the transformation of the work force. The wage-laborer—frequently, like the old domestic worker, a highly qualified skilled worker—had become the typical worker in Barmen. Because of the large numbers of new workers, the patriarchal relationship generally could no longer be maintained. This raised anew the question of leadership and social services. People found a new answer in the expanded social arrangements of the factories and in the effort to provide healthier and more attractive places in which to work. In addition, the old contacts did not break down completely: the factory-owner, who spoke with his workers in the local dialect and read aloud the work-rules, almost always succeeded in creating an atmosphere of trust and respect and a good human relationship. The fact that many of the younger businessmen had begun as domestic workers or artisans and that they possessed an exact knowledge of the individual work processes and of the mentality of the workers had a favorable influence on the climate of the factory, whereas the old patriarchal sense of obligation persisted most strongly among those who maintained close ties to the church.

Not only the transformation of the structure of the factory, but also the unforeseen development of the world economy and of world commerce required more intensive activity and accomplishment by the entrepreneurs. The need for quick decisions, the possibility of daily communication with almost all areas of the world, the constant danger of crises or changes of fashion, and the hard competitive struggle meant that business activity required much more time and energy than before. To be sure, the executive office, which came between the factory-owner and the workers, lightened his load, but it did not relieve him of the responsibility for making decisions. Only if he successfully met these demands could he securely maintain his factory, which now more than ever before filled his life. . . . The old conception of "the world as duty" lived on—secularized and diminished, to be sure—in this attitude toward work as "a responsibility and a duty" and provided the underpinning for the work ethos of this generation, too.

The greater demands imposed by the factory reduced the readiness of the businessman to perform public service and caused him gradually to withdraw from public and church offices. In addition, as a result of social changes at the time associated with the gradual onset of democratization, other groups—such as the lower middle class and the workers—now sought recognition, so that the notables would no longer have been able to maintain their claims to sovereign authority even if they had wished to. It is also important to remember that public administration, like the administration of the factory, became more extensive and specialized, so that civil servants had to take on tasks that formerly had been performed by honorary officials; the diminished participation in the administration of church affairs stemmed for the most part from changes in spiritual and religious attitudes. On the other hand, a new area of public activity opened up in the boards of various economic associations, although here too only a small elite (usually the owners of the larger businesses) participated actively, so that again a few people monopolized a number of these positions. This did not mean that men had totally lost interest in the development of the city, but they tended to further it by contributing money rather than their own labor. The city parks, funded exclusively by the contributions of leading citizens, are the most beautiful example of their generous promotion of the public welfare, providing a distinctive and splendid monument to this generation.

The economic elite also withdrew physically from the industrial city. They moved out of the city into their own suburbs, set apart from the other residential areas, where tenements were becoming more and more widespread. People acquired their own land outside the city and frequently spent their later years in the retirement cities, in Godesberg and Wiesbaden. The rising exclusiveness of the economic elite, which was already apparent in social life during the 1870s and 1880s, widened this gap.

This phenomenon brings us to the changed life-style of this generation, which began to take pleasure in and to enjoy its prosperity. People began to adopt the upper-bourgeois customs of the Wilhelmine period, which were closer to those of courtly society and the nobility than to the strict simplicity of their ancestors. The new villas were no longer constructed in the austere style of the earlier houses of factory-owners; instead, they were modeled after ostentatious country houses, palaces, and castles. The same was true of their interior decoration: valuable collections of art were assembled. Here was a sort of patronage that could be extremely generous and frequently was of benefit to the public in the form of monuments and gifts to the city museum. People became accustomed to celebrating holidays and to enjoying life, and people participated in everything available which was of cultural value. The pride and joy of ownership expressed the exultation over industrial progress, which also was the basis for their claim of social equality with the nobility. The first marriage ties were established with the nobility during this period, and their life-style was imitated more and more. A thorough secondary and higher education became the rule for their sons and daughters. Training in business often came first. Most of the sons became reserve officers, which confirmed their social position, while their fathers received the middle-class titles of "commercial councillor" or "privy commercial councillor."

The focal point of society was still the Concordia, which had developed completely into an association of big merchants and entrepreneurs. Its rooms were the scene of receptions and festivities, dinners, celebrations of Sedan Day, balls, meetings of army officers, and so on, in which wealth and tradition asserted themselves. People felt links both to the Prussian-German elite and to the state, which had played an important role in encouraging and maintaining economic progress. Whereas at mid-century largely liberal—and in some cases "progressive"—tendencies had marked the political stance of the businessmen, the generation of the turn of the century was thoroughly conservative. This outlook was characterized by veneration of Bismarck and loyalty to the Kaiser, symbolized by the "Hall of Fame," which was both a monument in the *Jugendstil* style to the historical achievements of the Hohenzollerns and a museum.

Nonetheless, even during this period, when money was plentiful in Barmen and everywhere else in Germany, most of the merchants and manufacturers preserved a thrifty business outlook. Certainly their living standards rose, but only a few succumbed to the danger of extravagance and living beyond their means. This danger was generally greater for the newer business families than for the older ones, in which the spirit of austere simplicity, which had characterized the notables, lived on. New names appeared and disappeared along with their businesses after two or three generations, and only their costly burial places in the cemeteries preserved their memory. Whoever failed to keep pace with the working rhythm of industry could not maintain his position in the city. Therefore, despite their wealth, modesty and simplicity characterized the daily life of the families of the elite. In this way the old spirit, the influence of their ancestors' strict religious attitude toward life, to which only a few still felt themselves bound, survived. These few, however, still had such a strong impact that they were widely regarded as typical of the Barmen businessmen, indicating the impressive strength of this life-style.

This generation, like its predecessors, did not possess distinguished individual personalities. The social structure of Barmen differed in this respect from the big industrial cities of the Ruhr area, in which a few outstanding entrepreneurs and their families dominated the scene. As a result of the economic situation, which favored the development of middle-sized businesses, the elite remained fairly broad, and a larger stratum of basically secure middle-level manufacturers and merchants was able to develop. Barmen's entrepreneurial class consisted of a large number of basically similar people. It changed somewhat from generation to generation, but one basic characteristic hardly changed at all: the spirit of the merchants and the entrepreneur, which continued to assert itself in performance, fulfillment of duty, and awareness of responsibility.

Adeline Daumard

THE PARISIAN BOURGEOISIE, 1815–1848

Adeline Daumard, Professor of History at the University of Amiens, has written a pioneering social history of the Parisian bourgeoisie in the first half of the nineteenth century. Her work combines a statistical study of wealth and social stratification with an analysis of the mentality of the middle classes. She treats the members of the bourgeoisie both as family men and as citizens, showing the private as well as the public faces of social relations. In this selection she describes the process by which the upwardly mobile entered the bourgeoisie and the attitudes of these independent men toward their wealth and their social inferiors.

The New Men

Between 1815 and 1848 the Parisians who became part of the various strata of the bourgeoisie were to a great extent new men. Their geographic origins and their family ancestry visibly transformed the Parisian bourgeoisie.

A majority of these new men were immigrants, generally former salary-earners, almost all of whom worked in Paris in subordinate positions before setting up their own businesses. In the group as a whole those from the country predominated. Without wealth and coming from a modest background, they learned a manual trade and succeeded in becoming heads of businesses, often helped by their wives' capital, skills, or connections. They could be found at all levels of the economy but were most numerous among the shopkeepers. Although many succeeded in building considerable fortunes and stable businesses, there were just as many who lacked adequate capital and sometimes commercial skills and went bankrupt, especially when crises dried up credit. City-dwellers from the provinces also succeeded in becoming part of the Parisian bourgeoisie, but they usually belonged to higher social groups. Some had no wealth, others had modest amounts of capital; some were gentlemen's sons or the sons of old and influential provincial families attracted by the opportunities offered by the capital. While some created an independent

From Adeline Daumard, *Les bourgeois de Paris au xixe siècle* (© Flammarion Paris, 1970; an abridged edition of *La Bourgeoisie parisienne de 1815 à 1848* [Paris, 1963]); pp. 215-220, 271-278, 281-285. Reprinted by permission of the publisher. Translated by the editors.

position for themselves at the start, most of them, like the rural immigrants, served a time as subordinates. They began working as salary-earners in a commercial firm or in an office. The provincial, whether he came from the countryside or a town, had to serve a period of apprenticeship before entering the Parisian bourgeoisie.

The upward social mobility of the Paris-born was much more limited. To be sure, many families who before 1789 belonged to the lower middle class profited from opportunities opened up by the Revolution and the Empire to improve their condition, and increases in wealth from one generation to the other were obvious. But the proportion of native Parisians who rose noticeably on the social scale from father to son or from their marriage to their death was smaller than that of immigrants. Besides, even though representatives of old Parisian families became locally influential, they seldom rose to the elite of the bourgeoisie. The renewal of the Parisian middle class took place above all from outside. The rich maintained or set up links with the provinces.

Whether immigrants or natives, almost all the upwardly mobile succeeded by applying their talents to business. Only during the Revolution and the Empire were people from modest backgrounds able to make brilliant careers in the military or in the civil service. ... Formal education and "merit" were only very weak factors in upward social mobility after 1815. First of all, education was not widespread among the lower classes. Then there were only a few opportunities for those with education or an advanced degree. Therefore, careers that demanded a liberal education had only a limited attraction for the children of the Parisian bourgeoisie. They did not despise them; some sons and sons-in-law, especially in large families, went into public service or chose a liberal profession. But entry into these jobs was not viewed as a rise in status, relative to a position in business or industry. The opportunities for men whose trade was to think or to perform administrative tasks were too narrow, at least at the beginning. . . . Parisian society offered more opportunities to those who wished to found a business and join the ranks of management.

From 1815 to 1848 the recruitment of the bourgeoisie changed. At the time of the Restoration, the Parisian middle classes were the heirs of the Revolution and the Empire. Every social group had been transformed: the growing wealth of men of property, the decline of the most influential families of the prerevolutionary bourgeoisie, and the influx of immigrants and men descended from quite modest families all helped to transform every social group, from the moderately well-to-do to the most humble. The Parisian bourgeoisie after 1815 sprang from political revolutions and their economic and social consequences.

In the next generation [1830–1848] this movement did not slow down, but its scope contracted. Looked at as a whole, the bourgeoisie remained open. The middle class grew, as did the whole Parisian population. It expanded by drawing on lower social groups. . . . Similarly, the top level of the Parisian bourgeoisie tended in effect to close ranks at the same time as a new aristocracy asserted its power and independence under the July Monarchy.[1]

A new society was being built. . . . Occupation and income tended to fix one's social position, but the Parisian bourgeoisie split into stratified groups which comprised representatives of several occupations and a wide range of fortunes. One point, however, is quite clear. The bourgeois aristocracy in Paris ignored professional men. Not that it repudiated their culture—quite the contrary—but it valued action more highly and recruited businessmen and civil servants. Perhaps this situation was temporary, but it existed during the reign of Louis Philippe.

Apart from the financial aristocracy, the shifts from one group to another were many. Must it be said that social mobility characterized society at that time? No. In the first place, this renewal of the bourgeoisie, which one cannot stress too much, says nothing about the great bulk of society. It is a question of percentages. The bourgeoisie, even defined quite broadly, represented only a tiny proportion of the Parisian population. Despite the importance of the influx from below in relation to this tiny group, what matters is that for the mass of the Parisian lower classes the prospects for social mobility were very limited. Besides, the belief in social mobility implied that only the most deserving kept their privileged position. But the signs of downward mobility were rare in families ensconced in the Parisian bourgeoisie for one or more generations, particularly among the richest groups. The privileges of wealth and birth were therefore maintained. Bourgeois society was open, but the success of those lower on the social scale implied a continued increase in the numbers of the upper classes, since very few places became vacant.

[1] The reign of Louis Philippe, 1830–1848.—Eds.

Inasmuch as there were still only a few salaried jobs open to men of ability, and jobs in business were the principal opportunities open to ambitious young men, the stability of the social system rested on economic expansion.

Turned toward the future because of its recruitment, denying its old reverence for occupations smacking of the aristocratic life or based on the liberal arts and accepting the preeminence of economic careers, the Parisian bourgeoisie still kept some traditions, or more exactly, it created some.

Their culture and their mentality were traditional. The rule of life accepted by all was the fundamentally humanist code of the upright man [*honnête homme*] in which a few traces of Christianity remained. All of this contributed to forming the individual, but nothing in his development attached the young man to a group.

But the son of a Parisian bourgeois was integrated into the social milieu of his parents. He generally remained there through the moment of choosing his occupation. In the middle class, children only rarely succeeded their fathers, but fathers and sons were generally of the same social rank. At the somewhat higher levels of the bourgeoisie, the inheritance of businesses was much more frequent. It was the rule in the bourgeois aristocracy, and often all the children, sons-in-law included, participated in the family business.

After attaining a certain level of comfort and wealth, parents made little effort to have their children change their social status. Was it because they denied the ideal of social mobility, despite the fact that public opinion still valued it highly? Did they feel that they could advance without changing status, by developing existing businesses and by working to reinforce the prestige and influence associated with the specifically bourgeois occupations, notably in business? In any event, this seemed to be the view of the higher social groups, since nothing would have hindered the heirs of large fortunes from turning to occupations of their choice or from living off their annuities.

A new tradition was being born. The desire to work in order to create something lasting and profitable was superimposed upon the old ideal of a leisured life and free and disinterested cultivation. A passionate quest for monetary wealth? Not merely. The bourgeoisie believed in the value of work, of individual effort. But concern for social mobility and success was also present. The Parisian bourgeois wanted to advance throughout his life. He wanted to undertake new things, and he shaped his destiny through his own efforts. Relatively young parents did not turn over their businesses to their children: to retire would be to admit powerlessness. Thus the bourgeois worked, preaching individual effort and an entrepreneurial spirit, but they believed in the value of acquired experience. They remained active as long as possible, the curve of their life ascended until the end. In this regard they differed from the lower classes, notably the workers, who declined at an early age as a result of the rapid decrease of their physical abilities. The wealthy groups were those in which individuals wanted to and were able to work the longest. This was especially noticeable in the financial aristocracy. In contrast, the lower middle class had more taste for retirement. The upper bourgeoisie best realized the ideal of the middle class since it more than any other group was the symbol of success and of continued success. To the extent that the higher social groups closed their ranks, this ideal became more difficult to realize and thus became an element of disequilibrium in the social order.

Bourgeois life rested then on a certain number of beliefs. A tradition developed: it was a modern tradition, but one that gave experience a large place. In what measure had the new men and their sons, the most active elements of all ranks of the bourgeoisie, become aware of it? Inasmuch as an essential aspect of this tradition was the belief in social mobility, to what extent did they wish to maintain the existing economic and social structure? To what extent did they wish for advancement? Was the newly created tradition a sign of hardening or a basis for new developments? The behavior of men is at issue. . . .

The Psychology of the Property-Owner

It was axiomatic for contemporaries who based their opinion on the conditions of life at the time and their experience of human beings that all Parisians wanted to become rich.

Many examples underline the efforts Parisians without wealth made to amass capital. When very young, Scribe[2] worked hard at increasing his income by using an important part of the profits he earned by writing to purchase state annuities. In the material and moral balance sheet he drew up every year, he listed his purchases.

[2] Augustin Eugène Scribe (1791–1861), famous French playwrite.—Eds.

He also wanted to possess real property: he had bought a house in Paris under the Restoration, he owned land and a country house. In 1835 he decided to acquire the Séricourt property in Seine et Marne, "a pretty piece of land, a pretty house which will have cost me a lot," he writes in 1837, "almost 300,000 francs for 5,000–6,000 francs in income, but it is a retreat far from Paris, it is a port, a shelter after the storm. And I will retire there in a few years, after the catcalls of the public have disgraced me." He lived from then on with the thought of increasing his estate, the symbol of his success. Similarly, he always wanted to increase his income and every year he bought state bonds.

In spite of his conspicuous expenditures, Scribe was very cautious. He reconciled his taste for ostentation with concern for preserving the future. Many middle-class Parisians who lacked comparable financial opportunities were less prudent. The aim of those who had not inherited much was to create a substantial fortune in order finally to enjoy a secure income. The typical thing to do, notably among the numerous shopkeepers, was to acquire a house in Paris even at the cost of considerable debt. The property was bought, but it was only paid for with mortgages. Moreover, several years later the house was often mortgaged beyond its purchase price without the initial sum having been repaid. Often this system ended in catastrophe. Often, too, the rise in rents and of business profits permitted the shopkeeper to meet his obligations and to carry out his plans. What we do not know about, but what one can imagine, are the continual efforts, the privations undertaken in order to meet the heavy payments that were added to the obligations to pay off commercial debts. It was characteristic of the middle ranks of the Parisian bourgeoisie to possess only a little and to risk it all in order to build a fortune, while basing all their hopes on capital gains and even more on profits derived from frantic work.

Debts contracted by the wealthy did not have the same character. As a general rule, when their position was established, merchants, industrialists, and financiers asked for credit; they did not go into debt. Outside the business world the debts of rich Parisians were usually rather small. It is particularly significant that their real estate was rarely mortgaged.

The rich bourgeoisie of Paris under the Constitutional Monarchy[3]

[3] The reign of Louis Philippe (1830–1848).—Eds.

did not try to increase their wealth indefinitely. To be sure, they grew rich from the rising value of their capital and from the profits from their businesses. Some even increased their wealth by investing a part of their income. But to buy without having the necessary capital to discharge the debt, to pledge a large part of one's assets in order to undertake new businesses or to meet current obligations while anticipating eventual profit, this was the attitude of those who considered their position transitory. . . . Rich Parisians, the bourgeois aristocracy, were not extravagant. In the nineteenth century the desire to get rich was general, but it was limited by the concern to maintain acquired status.

Napoleon and the Bourbons imposed primogeniture on the newly promoted nobility so that part of their property would be put aside for the profit of the family. The bourgeoisie ignored the practice of primogeniture, which, favoring the eldest son to the detriment of younger brothers, was contrary to their egalitarian idea of the family, but they understood the practice of putting assets aside. Indeed, the real estate bought by middle-class Parisians of all ranks was rarely sold voluntarily by its owners, even to meet an exceptional situation. Houses in Paris frequently changed hands, but chiefly in cases of absolute necessity. When they were not forced by necessity, the children of a Parisian bourgeois kept the real estate inherited from their father, whereas newcomers from the earlier generation did not hesitate to get rid of the few acres of land they had inherited from their ancestors. Once past the difficult initial process of getting settled, Parisians bought; they did not sell. It is more difficult to follow financial as opposed to real property, but the basic elements of portfolios were just as stable in one case as in the other. . . . Loans to individuals were extended when due or, when repaid, re-lent to others. The second main component consisted of state bonds, also bought to be kept. Here, Scribe's evidence is definitive. He bought state bonds to build an assured income and not for capital appreciation. Thus he paradoxically welcomed a falling market and regretted a rising one, since he had no intention of selling the appreciated bonds.

The rich owned almost all of the shares of the Bank of France. These shares represented an important part of the wealth of certain families. For a long time the bank shares were considered as a patrimony which one scarcely touched. Transfers of stock were much more numerous after 1840; however, they remained limited.

A major preoccupation of Parisians was therefore to conserve their inherited or acquired patrimony. Is this to say that they refused to speculate? The fever of playing the market was unanimously denounced during the entire Constitutional Monarchy by the representatives of every viewpoint: speculation in French and foreign government bonds, speculation in Parisian land and houses, especially at the end of the Restoration, an infatuation aroused by the stocks of all sorts of fantastic companies formed after the July revolution; finally, after 1844, "greatly increased speculation in railroad shares."

But there were two types of Parisian speculators. Some were occasional speculators: speculation for them was only a means to improve their social position, often modest at the beginning. Others, much less numerous and generally rich, had a taste for financial manipulations; they were guided above all by an entrepreneurial spirit, by a taste for risk, which, even when they were not in trade, connected them to big businessmen and to the great financiers.

The majority of the Parisian bourgeoisie, when they decided that they had made it, were not speculators. . . . Annuitants, who belonged to every class of Parisian society, had bought bonds for a guaranteed income and not to speculate. Is it necessary to conclude that the Parisian bourgeoisie was not interested in the stock market? In truth, Parisians, desirous of keeping intact the fortune which very often they had amassed themselves with much trouble, devoted only a tiny part of their property to playing the market. The Parisian bourgeoisie wanted to get richer, but they also wanted to stay wealthy. The taste for gambling, for occasionally adventurous speculation, corresponded to the first need. The building of a capital reserve, inherited or acquired, which was increased if possible but not sold, is explained by the second need. These two tendencies corresponded to two stages of the life cycle. In the first stage, one who wanted to get into a higher social group put everything he had to work in order to become a part of the group he wished to join. At that point the Parisian did not hesitate to risk all that he had, for only the future interested him. In contrast, during the second stage the bourgeois, satisfied with his position, feared to compromise it. To get richer, even to rise into a higher social stratum, was a luxury to which he was able to dedicate some capital, but not if it meant sacrificing what he had acquired. Almost all Parisians belonging to the middle ranks of the bourgeoisie passed through these two phases, for they had felt the need to assert their social position. In higher social strata, the first stage was generally dispensed with. The desire to get rich existed, but it was held in check by the reluctance to risk acquired status. The entrepreneurial spirit had not lessened, for a greater degree of security produced more assurance, more lucidity, but the existence of a substantial nestegg created a psychological barrier between the upper and lower middle class.

For the Parisian bourgeoisie wealth was not an end but a means. To possess wealth was to have influence; political influence, first of all, thanks to the property qualification for voting. As the future prefect of the department of the Seine, Rambuteau, said early in 1833, to own property was to belong to "that class which, by means of the electoral system, the jury, and the national guard protected, judged, administered and governed the country." But thanks to the press, the Parisian bourgeoisie was clearly aware of this.

Did Parisians seek equally to exercise their influence in the economic realm? The middle class, taken as a whole, assigned only a limited role to industrial investment, and this type of investment proceeded specifically from the desire to save and not from a wish to participate in the economic development of the country. The richest social groups, especially those with their roots in trade, took a close interest in their investments. Through the force of circumstances they had influence to exercise, but their impact on the economic life of the country was the result of their wealth; nothing leads to the conclusion that the upper classes systematically used their capital to take over essential positions in the French economy. In any case they were neither clearly aware nor proud of this role. The use of wealth and the influence it brought remained in the area of strictly personal business affairs.

In reality, for the Parisian bourgeois of every rank, to possess wealth was above all to have the feeling of and the means of being independent. The lower middle class and those in the middle ranks wanted to amass capital for their old age; for Scribe, for example, this was a genuine obsession from his youth. To get rich was a sign of foresight. But besides, whoever had capital sufficient to permit him and his family to live modestly had an intense feeling of liberty. He was able to rebuff pressures from outside and to keep his dignity while refusing those compromises and collaborations which, without means, he would have had to consider. For example, it was helpful if one was applying for a post in the magistracy or a notary's commission to make a point of one's wealth, since affluence was a guarantee of impartiality and independence. The Parisian bourgeoisie tried to get rich, but they were motivated less by the taste for money as such than by the concern to win a position that would permit them to enjoy fully their condition as independent, responsible, and free men. This explains why the need to get rich made itself felt more frenetically in the lower ranks of society, in the lower middle class, and among those who had not yet won a place in the social group they wished to join.

Landlords, annuitants, capitalists, the whole middle class hoarded. They also knew how to spend, and the taste for comfort in the middle class and for luxury among the rich contributed considerably to the prosperity of Paris. But these expenses scarcely cut into their capital. Therefore, a reserve which was one of the elements of the power of the bourgeoisie was amassed. Considerable wealth was spread throughout all sections of the bourgeoisie. To be sure, many bourgeois were in debt, but they thought of this position as being transitory. And so it was: some paid off their debts, and those who failed were often relegated to the edge of the lower class. The Parisians who were ultimately successful, those who had definitely become integrated into the bourgeoisie at different levels, genuinely owned property. Holders of small annuities, landlords, capitalists, all were independent men, aware and proud of being so. No matter how modest his position, the middle-class Parisian was a man who believed his future was secure. This gave him a feeling of satisfaction, of tranquility, providing an element of social cohesion at the core of the Parisian bourgeoisie.

The composition of fortunes revealed differences among social groups. On the one hand the bourgeois aristocracy moved out from the capital to invest in the entire country, while the interests of the mass of the bourgeoisie remained narrowly linked to local business. In this there was a seed of misunderstanding and discontent. On the other hand the most profitable speculations tended more and more to be reserved for the rich capitalists; under Louis Philippe they were primarily stock market transactions in which the outsider was lost. The real estate business under the Restoration appeared to be open to all comers, even though in fact only rich capitalists had benefitted from the land speculations of 1825. Fortunes based on increased stock values were reserved for the privileged few who were capable of acquiring sound and profitable securities. The advance of economic life and of finance had opened up a chasm between the various strata of bourgeois society in Paris.

Relations with the Lower Classes

. . . A barrier was raised between the lower classes and the ranks of the middle class. Workers were conscious of belonging to a special world, and the well-to-do kept their distance from the lower classes. Although formal courtesy was in fashion in Paris, customs underlined class differences. An etiquette book pointed out for example that if it rained, whoever did not have an umbrella might ask a passerby for shelter, and that a truly polite person ought to offer these services himself. But in so doing "it was necessary to note whether differences of age, sex, and dress did not get in the way; it would be out of place to address people of a very low social class; but if one of them demanded it, it was necessary to receive him graciously." Moreover, in other than material areas the working class was ranked much lower than the entrepreneurs. When the arbitration councils were being created in Paris, it was decided to give more places to representatives of the employers than to those of the workers, for "if masters are not perfect, workers are much less so."

Ordinarily relations between the common people and the upper social groups were based on condescension or contempt. The workers perceived the barrier that separated the bourgeoisie from the lower classes; the bourgeoisie built it with all the more perseverance the closer they were to those with whom they did not wish to be confused.

The workers and the bourgeoisie belonged to two separate worlds, but bourgeois opinion was not able to ignore the condition of the mass of the people. Official initiatives would have been sufficient to open everyone's eyes. The legal arrangement which exempted those who paid low rents from the tax on personal property underlined the fact that many heads of families were permanently in a state of such need that the community had to assume part of their financial burden. The usefulness of this measure, which caused the city to go heavily into debt, was never questioned. This indicated a recognition that Paris included the poor and the indigent, whose numbers almost matched those of the workers rooted in Paris and whose condition warranted special concern.

These attitudes crystallized on the occasion of the revolution of 1830. After a brief period of euphoria, the *Journal des Débats* put the middle class on guard by comparing the rise of the proletarians in modern society to that of the barbarians in the Roman Empire. This article made a big splash; therefore, without changing its views, the newspaper was led some months later to amplify them:

> *Workers are outside of the political community, outside the city. These are the barbarians of modern societies, barbarians as full of courage and energy as their predecessors, who ought to bring their vigor and life to our society to strengthen it. . . . The problem to resolve is how to maintain the present society by improving the lot of the lower classes.*

The dominant tendency under the Restoration was to assume that misery was an unfortunate necessity inherent in the human condition and one that charity ought to alleviate. But according to Tocqueville there was more and more thought of replacing "private alms" by "direct and legal charity, based on the resources collected by the public administration for relieving, regularly and administratively, different forms of hardship" and by a "legal indirect charity which consists of giving to the poor the means of extricating themselves from need."

The desire to aid the unfortunate took many forms, for the most part inherited from the past. Individual charity in life or after death had existed in every epoch; group philanthropic activity was a legacy of the last years of the old regime, and the philanthropic impulse received new momentum at the start of the Restoration. Welfare work, done individually, became obligatory for people of high status, an attribute of the influential without being the property of one social class. To practice it was to assure one's reputation.

There was an element of egotism in this direct action. The rich were aware of their charitable acts. Some certainly were driven by the spirit of evangelical charity; but a spirit of pride accompanied the charity.

The avowed objectives of philanthropy pointed up the differences which, in the eyes of contemporaries, separated the rich from the poor, the bourgeois from a person of the lower classes. Members of most philanthropic associations limited themselves to the execution of these material tasks, but in so doing they thought they ought to exercise moral guardianship over the lower classes. Even when their virtues were being exalted, it seemed necessary "to spread healthy ideas among the people of the lowest class, who, lacking the leisure time to think, receive from enlightened men the stimuli which ought to direct them." The exercise of charity did not lower the barrier separating social classes; to the contrary. The bourgeoisie was aware of its superiority, and the desire to maintain the social order directed their action as much as compassion.

All of this activity had only limited results, which were not commensurate with the efforts expended. The charitable were interested too exclusively in those who lived near their houses. The rich generally lived far from the poor; thus, the most deprived were the least aided. Attempts to ease misery were scattered in a multitude of efforts; there was a waste of energy with the result that the fundamental problem was neglected and the lower classes were left in their debased condition.

The basic problem was to integrate the mass of the population into the community. One part of the bourgeoisie was aware of this. In 1846, Leon Faucher wrote:

The middle class occupies today the same positions that the nobility did formerly; it holds them only on the condition of raising little by little the lower classes, of working for the education and the emancipation of the mass of the people. If it is not the instrument of progress, it fails to fulfill its destined purpose; it will have to contend with another 1789.

The elite of the Parisian bourgeoisie in the nineteenth century sought to give the lower classes the means of working by themselves to improve their condition. For example (in the opinion of their promoters) saving societies ought to have permitted their depositors to build up a modest stake, intended to become one element of their emancipation. The fate of the lower classes was put back into their hands; they were urged to adopt a mode of life based upon an ideal of personal independence which was adapted to the condition of the bourgeoisie, but the handicap derived from the workers' material situation and from the moral degredation which chronic misery and constant uncertainty about the future frequently brought about was not eliminated.

The cultured middle class of all ranks strove to encourage the development of education among the Parisian lower class: free public education for adults, gifts of money to found schools, time given to young girls by women of good will. But what goals did these efforts satisfy? The wish to encourage the advancement of men, but also shabbier considerations came to light. It was necessary to spread instruction and moral education in order to combat corruption, to teach the people their duties, to stop them from surrendering to the hatred which the ignorant felt toward society, and at the same time to encourage industrial development by supplying industry with intelligent capable workers. The results were tangible: young men old enough to do military service almost all knew how to read and write.

But were the popular classes better integrated thereafter into the city than in the past? Education was quite elementary, of such a sort that nothing prepared the son of a worker to rise into another social group. The moral instruction and the code of conduct recommended to children attending primary school were rudimentary: the love of work, honesty, temperance, charity, all seasoned with assorted religious principles, but nothing which prepared the future worker to rise above his individual obligations and to participate in the beliefs and collective responsibilities of the upper classes.

Both before and after the law of 1833, the education given to the masses was only suited to a man who was supposed to remain in an inferior social position, to a man without a city or a country. More or less consciously, well-to-do Parisians, if they interested themselves in their social inferiors, built up a barrier between the bourgeoisie and the lower classes.

Francis Sheppard

LIVING IN LONDON, 1808–1870

The selection reprinted below is drawn from a general history of early and mid-nineteenth-century London. A London resident and editor of the multivolume Survey of London, *Francis Sheppard has spent most of his professional life studying the architecture and the history of the English capital. His treatment of the social world of London's middle class moves from their homes to their shops to their entertainments. The richness of London's urban culture emerges clearly from his descriptions of the city's theaters, parks, and organizations. As Dr. Johnson noted, "He who is tired of London is tired of life."*

Behind the impassive brick or stuccoed fronts of countless Victorian terraces and villas, within the privacy of lace curtains and a plethora of heavy mahogany furniture, middle-class domestic life in London differed little from its counterpart in numerous provincial towns. There was more of it, of course, in terms of numbers, and after the flight from the overcrowded conditions of City residence had begun, the scale of living was more often grand and luxurious. But in general the pattern of home life in London was much the same as elsewhere. In many households there were family prayers, dutifully attended by the servants, and family meals when the children had outgrown the nursery; there was the governess or the spinster's private schoolroom round the corner; there was sewing and dressmaking to be done, afternoon calls to be paid and visiting cards to be left, and annual visits to the country or the seaside to be arranged. The rooms were often filled with either the vacuous gossip of women with time on their hands, or with the pompous pronouncements of masculine outward preeminence; and always there were the servants, servants scrubbing, polishing and dusting, servants with cans of hot water and pails of bedroom slop, servants carrying up the coals for the fires whose smoke enveloped the air with grime and fog, servants endlessly trudging up and down the stairs.

There was, to be sure, an almost infinite range of minute gradations in both the style and the scale of living, for anyone with an

From Francis Sheppard, *London, 1808–1870: The Infernal Wen* (Berkeley and Los Angeles: University of California Press, 1971), pp. 353–362. Reprinted by permission of The Regents of the University of California and Martin Secker and Warburg Ltd.

146

annual income of upwards of £150 probably regarded himself as middle class. But despite this variety there was also a more potent underlying homogeneity of outlook, which was most clearly to be seen in times of crisis such as the great Chartist assemblies of 1848; in more normal times it manifested itself in the domestic orderliness and the formality and reserve of even the closest family relationships which prevailed in so many well-to-do Victorian households, and which seldom failed to catch the notice of foreign observers.

Within the citadels of the home the garrisons of London lived, in fact, the same sort of life as they might have lived in many other places. Even in the great metropolis entertaining still took place in the home, for only a very few restaurants had yet appeared in London, and apart from a few small hotels in the West End, such as Long's in Clifford Street, where Sir Walter Scott stayed in 1815, chop-houses, coffee-houses or coaching inns—all unsuitable for ladies—were the only places where one could eat out. It was not until the building of large hotels at some of the principal railway termini, and of the Langham Hotel at the south end of Portland Place in the 1860s, followed around 1870 by the slow discovery of the gastronomic delights of Soho, that this depressing state of affairs began to change.

But outside the home, London had much to offer—shopping boulevards and bazaars of unrivaled splendor, parks and pleasure gardens, galleries and museums, concerts and theaters, all in a profusion unknown in any other English town and all contributing to that sense of being at the center of affairs which citizens of any great capital city always possess, and which citizens of provincial towns often find so exasperating. And if the enjoyment of these amenities required respectable people to leave the refuge of their homes and expose themselves to the scenes of vice and depravity in the streets which foreigners often remarked upon—"however rigid English prudery may be in the home circle, it is shocked by nothing in the street, where licentiousness runs riot," was Monsieur Wey's comment—Londoners themselves seem to have been oblivious of the contrast.

Shoppers had never hitherto been so well served as they were in the mid-nineteenth century. Shops were still small and independent, owned and run by the shopkeeper, who kept his door open to all hours, allowed credit and was always ready to deliver. He had to provide keen service in order to stay in business, for he found formidable competition from the street hawkers—13,000 of them, according to Mayhew—and in the food trade, from the retail markets, today almost extinguished by the supposedly more important requirements of motor traffic, but enjoying their heyday in mid-Victorian times. Bakers' shops were not so common as they were later to become, for bread was still often baked at home; fruit and vegetables were usually bought in the markets, and milk and dairy produce were delivered by the roundsman, who called twice daily. But still, food shops were the most numerous, followed by the haberdashers and linen drapers, whose trade in materials rather than in finished articles shows the importance of domestic sewing and needlework in the days before the mass-production of ready-made garments. Only in the tailors' and shoemakers' shops were the traditional direct contacts between maker and purchaser still to some extent maintained.

But change was coming, reflecting the vast increase in the population of London. The drapers had led the way in the more intensive use of capital, concentrating on low profits and a quick turnover; it was they, for instance, who had in the 1820s first used price labels on the goods exhibited in their windows. The center of gravity of their fashionable trade was moving from the City and Fleet Street to the West End, particularly to Oxford Street and Regent Street, where there was space for larger shops like Swan and Edgar's, equipped with the great plate-glass windows first used by Francis Place at his tailor's shop at Charing Cross, and now brilliantly illuminated by gaslight. Henry Colman thought that one of the most beautiful sights he had seen in London had been "on a ride down Regent Street, on the box-seat of an omnibus, in the evening, when the streets are crowded with people elegantly dressed, and the shops in long ranges, with their illuminated windows of immense length, and their interior, exhibiting an almost indefinite perspective, are in all their glory."

In the second half of the century the pace of change increased. Bigger shops and more pushing business methods produced great armies of shop assistants and very long hours of work. A few West End drapers again led the way by enlarging their shops into department stores offering a very wide range of goods, Debenham's, Swan and Edgar's and Dickins and Jones being pioneers in this field. But this process was not restricted to the West End, for prosperous suburbs were generating new shopping centers of their own in such places as High Street Kensington and Knightsbridge, where Barker's and Harrod's quickly rose from small beginnings to departmental status. Harrod's was originally a grocer's, and it was chiefly the grocers who were to initiate another revolution in retailing by the introduction of multiple shops, the leader here being John Sainsbury, who opened his first shop in 1869 in Drury Lane. By the 1880s John Barker of Kensington was combining grocery and drapery, and he already employed 400 hands. He closed at between 6:30 p.m. and 8 p.m., depending on the time of year, but some shops nearby stayed open until 10 p.m. or even midnight on Saturdays, and many shop assistants worked 80 or 90 hours a week.

But almost all shops—except those kept by the Jews—did shut on Sundays, and Sunday was therefore the most popular day for a family excursion to the parks. The royal parks open to wheeled traffic—Kensington Gardens, Hyde Park and Regent's Park—were the most popular, and the Green Park and St. James's were convenient for the West End. Many people often came to these oases from a considerable distance, for elsewhere in London many traditional open spaces such as Spa Fields had recently been covered with bricks and mortar, and the municipal authorities had not yet started to establish new parks. The only new parks formed in London before the establishment of the Metropolitan Board of Works in 1855 were therefore formed by the government, acting through the Commissioners of Woods and Forests. Besides Regent's Park there were Victoria Park, Hackney, opened in 1845, and Battersea Park (1858), where the marshy nature of the ground had required the deposit of a million cubic feet of earth excavated during the building of the Victoria Docks at Blackwall. In 1852 Kennington Common, where the Chartists had held their last great rally in 1848, was emparked, but on the commons at Blackheath, Clapham and Wandsworth building encroachment continued until the Metropolitan Commons Act of 1866 forbade any further enclosures within a radius of fourteen miles of Charing Cross. Ultimately the remains of these and other once wide expanses of common land were vested in public ownership of one kind or another. By the 1870s the Metropolitan Board of Works was beginning to take an interest in the matter, Finsbury Park (opened in 1869) being its first important achievement, followed by the acquisition of Hampstead Heath in 1872.

The lack of public open spaces in many parts of mid-nineteenth-century London helps to explain the continuing popularity of the

privately owned pleasure gardens to be found in many of the suburbs. The pleasure garden, with its pavilions and its groves of trees
for polite promenading to the soft sound of the music of a string
band, was an essentially eighteenth-century form of diversion. In the
first half of the nineteenth century many of these resorts were engulfed in the outward march of the suburban frontier, particularly in
the 1840s and 1850s, when Bagnigge Wells, Islington Spa, White
Conduit House and Copenhagen House all closed their doors, the
last in 1852 to make way for the new Metropolitan Cattle Market. Yet
elsewhere new gardens were opening, often in the grounds of a
popular tavern, and the successful adaptation of old traditions gave
this form of recreation a new lease of life which enabled it to survive
into the late 1870s. Sadler's Wells, indeed, where the theater built in
the original pleasure garden became first a music hall and then after
rebuilding a home for opera and ballet, survives to this day.

The nineteenth-century pleasure gardens ceased to have any pre-
tensions to fashion and catered instead for the less sophisticated
tastes of a middle-class clientele. This was so even at Vauxhall, the
most famous of the eighteenth-century resorts, which survived until
1859, and where in 1833 as many as 27,000 people crowded in on a
single day. Everywhere the formality of the traditional eighteenth-
century fare was supplemented by new attractions—by fireworks, by
displays of juggling, conjuring or acrobatics, by dioramas or balloon
ascents, or indeed by any novelty which would draw custom. At the
Red House, Battersea, there were pigeon-shooting matches and boat
races, while on the outskirts of north and east London wrestling,
dog-fights and rat-killing were favorite sports. But everywhere the
soot and grime of the smoke-laden atmosphere—hard even to imagine in the mid-twentieth century—was slowly moving all these diversions indoors, to improvised saloons and halls and theaters like
the Grecian Saloon in the City Road, the offspring of the garden at
the Eagle tavern, or the Surrey Music Hall, built in the grounds of the
Surrey Zoological Gardens at Walworth.

The most famous of the nineteenth-century resorts was Cremorne
Gardens, which occupied twelve acres of ground in Chelsea between
the river and the King's Road. For some years after its opening in
1832 Cremorne had flourished as a private sports club with facilities
for archery and golf, but in the mid-1840s a new owner opened the
grounds to the public (subject to payment for admission, of course)
and after a flamboyant advertising campaign he drew large crowds to

a miscellany of diversions which included balloon ascents and a mock tournament. The gardens and the dancing were the main attractions for the students and shop girls, soldiers and civilians, dissipated young bloods, paterfamilias with their better halves, schoolboys and children's nurses who patronized Cremorne, but in the course of time the proprietor's endless search for novelty produced little more than a vulgar pastiche and a great deal of noise. The Chelsea Vestry and the residents of the new streets which had been built around the grounds protested at the rowdyism and the drunkenness, the prosperity of the place declined, and within a year or two of its closure in 1877 most of the site was covered with houses—the inevitable ultimate fate of almost all the London pleasure gardens. The urban *al fresco* tradition of the eighteenth-century gardens was indeed dead at last.

But indoors it was already branching out into a new form of entertainment, the music hall, as essentially Victorian as the pleasure gardens had previously been so characteristically Georgian. With the inexorable outward advance of the built-up area the pleasure gardens had retreated beyond convenient walking-distance of central London, and so to meet the demand there for eating, drinking, light music and popular entertainment, numerous song and supper rooms had arisen in the 1840s and 1850s. The first and most famous of these were in or near Covent Garden, at Evans's in King Street, at the Coal Hole in the Strand and the Cider Cellars in Maiden Lane. But with the decline of the pleasure gardens the song and supper rooms had soon spread to such suburbs as Whitechapel, Hoxton and Lambeth. The proprietors were usually licensed victualers, whose principal source of revenue was the sale of drink. At first the singing and entertainment was provided by the customers themselves, but soon professionals were hired, a platform at one end of the hall was constructed for them, and a small entrance fee of perhaps sixpence was levied. From there it was only a short step to the full-blown music halls. Among the earliest were the Canterbury Hall in Upper Marsh, Lambeth (1852) and the Oxford Music Hall in Oxford Street (1861). The former was built on the site of a skittle alley at the back of the Canterbury Arms tavern, the latter in the yard of an old coaching inn. Sites such as these provided a home for many of the forty-odd music halls which existed in London by 1868, many of them in the suburbs, but including also such famous West End names as the London Pavilion and the Alhambra.

Besides the pleasure gardens and the music halls there was an extraordinary variety of other entertainments to be had in mid-nineteenth-century London. There was a circus at Astley's Amphi-theater, Westminster Bridge Road, a short-lived race course out at Notting Hill, a menagerie at Exeter Hall in the Strand and the gardens of the Zoological Society in Regent's Park. The wide desire for knowledge, as well as mere human curiosity, probably accounts for the immense popularity of exhibitions of all kinds. Madame Tus-saud's waxworks were already famous, all the wonders of the world seemed to find their way to the displays at the Egyptian Hall in Piccadilly, and John Ruskin thought that the educational value of the beautifully painted panoramas exhibited at Burford's in Cranbourn Street was so great that the government ought to make a grant for the support of the place in its declining years in the 1860s. Until its destruction by fire in 1865 Savile House, a capacious old mansion in Leicester Square, became a favorite venue for innumerable exhibi-tions and lectures as well as other less respectable diversions, and for ten years Wyld's Great Globe, a gigantic model of the earth, was permitted to occupy the greater part of the open ground within the Square itself. The area round Piccadilly Circus and Leicester Square was in fact already becoming the acknowledged center of London's entertainment world long before the building of half-a-dozen theaters nearby in Shaftesbury Avenue at the close of the century.

The London theater as a whole was not enjoying one of its great periods during the first three-quarters of the nineteenth century. Until 1843 the two great theaters of Drury Lane and Covent Garden still in theory enjoyed the dual monopoly of theatrical rights which had been conferred upon Thomas Killigrew and Sir William Davenant and their heirs by royal letters patent in 1662–63. At the opening of the nineteenth century both these theaters were of enormous size; in-deed they had to be in order to justify their claim that they could still meet the theatrical demands of the already vast population of Lon-don. But in 1808–1809 both the patent theaters had been destroyed by fire. After rebuilding they were still uneconomically large and they entered on their new careers burdened with very heavy capital debts. They now found themselves beset by the competition of a rapidly growing number of minor theaters whose presentation of "burlettas," or quasi-musical entertainments, successfully disguised the system-atic evasion of the restrictions imposed by the royal patents of 1662–63. Whereas in 1800 there were fewer than half-a-dozen such rivals, including the Haymarket Theater and the King's Theater or Opera House, also in the Haymarket and both licensed by the Lord Chamberlain, by 1843 nearly forty new minor theaters had been established all over London. Many of these newcomers were very short-lived, but a few survive to this day, notably the Adelphi and the Royal Coburg (now known as the Old Vic). The fiction of monopoly could no longer be maintained, and in 1843 it was finally abolished.

During these troubled years the London theater was no longer fashionable. The aristocratic patrons who subscribed for the rebuilding of Drury Lane in 1810-12 soon lost interest; the behavior of the audiences in the two patent theaters was sometimes riotous and debased and in the minor theaters coarse and disorderly. Only attendance at the opera retained any significance in the social season. By the 1820s, too, the evangelical moral code was already beginning to cast its baleful influence over the stage. The great writers of the time—even those such as Byron, Keats or Dickens, who were unaffected by this influence—devoted little or no time to writing for the stage, and although there were many great actors the size and bad acoustics of the two patent theaters forced them to vulgarize their techniques and encouraged excessive expenditure on splendid scenic spectacles. The star performers commanded such high fees for their services that there was little left for the playwrights, and apart from their frequent productions of Shakespeare the indifferent melodramas and extravaganzas which were so popular at this time were often unworthy of such great actors as Macready, the Keans or the Kembles.

There were, however, some hopeful signs. The introduction in some theaters of stall seats in place of the old disorderly pit, and of reserved seats, reduced rowdyism, and the use of gas light on the stage opened up a whole new field of scenic effect. The gradual removal of proscenium doors and of the stage apron was perhaps not so fortunate in the long run, for it divided the audience from the action and led on to the total separation imposed by the modern picture-frame proscenium. But in those days of insensitive audience behavior this was perhaps a necessary phase of theatrical evolution, and no doubt contributed to the gradual emergence in the 1840s of a new playgoing public. In the early years of her reign Queen Victoria's frequent visits to the theater encouraged quieter behavior there, while less fortunate people whose recreational needs required an opportunity to make a noise as well as merely to listen tended to go to the new music halls. After the Act of 1843 ending the monopoly of the patent houses hardly any new theaters were built in London for over twenty years, and when another surge began in the mid-1860s even Drury Lane and Covent Garden (the latter rebuilt again in 1856–58 after another fire) were enjoying some share in the general rise of national prosperity. Railways and omnibuses were making the theater accessible to a far larger public than ever before. Ranting histrionics were giving place to more naturalistic acting, and under such new leaders as Squire Bancroft and W. S. Gilbert the modern director in charge of the whole production was superseding the confused and ill-rehearsed performances hitherto often prevalent.

Music, or at any rate indigenous music, was at a low ebb after the great days of Handel and Arne. Despite the foundation of the (Royal) Philharmonic Society in 1813 London had no adequate concert hall until the building of the St. James's Hall in Piccadilly in 1858, and at the King's Theater in the Haymarket (renamed Her Majesty's in 1837) the management of opera was bedeviled by personal squabbles and by interminable legal and financial difficulties. Eventually the headquarters of opera in London was transferred to its modern home at Covent Garden Theater in 1847, and twenty years later the destruction of Her Majesty's by fire proved the death knell of opera there. There were no English composers of note, and few native performers either, and all of the musical distinction of the period was imported from abroad in performances of opera by Mozart, Rossini and Donizetti, and in ballet, in the exquisite romantic dancing of Marie Taglioni.

Painting and learning were beginning to be objects of public patronage and encouragement. This was the age of the foundation of the National Gallery in 1824 (in Pall Mall, until its removal to Trafalgar Square in 1837), of the National Portrait Gallery in 1856 and of the South Kensington Museum in 1857, from which later developed the Science Museum and the Victoria and Albert Museum. In 1867 the Royal Academy obtained possession of Burlington House and subsequently built extensive galleries on the site of the garden to the north. The British Museum was entirely rebuilt, its collections were greatly enlarged, notably by the acquisition of the King's Library, the Grenville Library and the Elgin Marbles, and the number of annual visitors leaped from about 13,000 in 1808 to nearly 900,000 forty years later. Yet few if any of these places were open on Sundays—the British Museum, for instance, not until 1896—and their use was therefore restricted to persons of leisure, or (to quote the regulations of the British Museum in 1810) to "persons of decent appearance." At the more popular level, the ratepayers of the City voted twice, in 1855 and 1861, against the adoption of the Free Libraries Act, and although the Corporation eventually, in 1870–72, erected the building still used to house the splendid Guildhall Library, no progress was yet being made elsewhere in London in the provision of public libraries.

But whatever its shortcomings and limitations might be, London was indisputably the cultural and intellectual capital of the nation. It was here that almost all of the societies which proliferated at this time had their origins and their headquarters—learned societies, professional societies, religious societies, philanthropic societies, well over a hundred of them dating from between 1810 and 1870, and many of them, such as the Howard League for Penal Reform or the Royal Society for the Prevention of Cruelty to Animals, now household names. In the world of the theater London's preeminence was absolute. The residence there for substantial periods of many of the greatest writers, including Keats, Byron, Coleridge, Lamb, Carlyle, Thackeray, Browning, George Eliot, Macaulay and, of course, Dickens, demonstrates the capital's ascendancy in the field of letters. Many even of those writers who never lived there, such as Jane Austen or the Brontë sisters, nevertheless had business dealings with their publishers there, for only Edinburgh could rival London in the book trade. For the painters the position was, it is true, rather different, for London had nothing of visual interest for them in the age of the romantic revival. Yet despite frequent absences on provincial or foreign tours, most artists who exhibited at the Royal Academy had at least a *pied-à-terre* in London and often a studio or a house as well, usually in St. Marylebone, or from about 1850 onwards, in South Kensington or Chelsea. The Pre-Raphaelites all had their headquarters in London, and even Constable spent many years there. Two of the very greatest painters of the time, Blake and Turner, were both Londoners by birth, and made their homes there throughout most of their lives.

IV THE URBAN LOWER CLASSES

Louis Chevalier

CRIME AND SOCIAL PATHOLOGY AMONG THE PARISIAN LOWER CLASSES

Louis Chevalier's study of the Parisian lower classes during the first half of the nineteenth century, published in 1958, is a major work in European social history. His view that urban growth and demographic pressures pushed the workers of the French capital into pathological forms of behavior—such as crime, prostitution, and suicide—has been both controversial and influential. Chevalier, a professor at the College de France and at the Institut d'Études Politiques, was trained both as an historian and as a demographer. His books on the history of Paris remain an indispensable source for any investigation of French cities in the nineteenth century.

The Problem of Crime: Its Importance

The writers who have dealt with the economic, social and political history of Paris in the first half of the nineteenth century have gone astray by ignoring the problem of the socially dangerous classes and the vast mass of documentation on it, as if crime were merely a secondary, virtually negligible aspect of urban development and the description of crime merely a passing literary fashion of dubious historical value.

Yet crime was one of the major themes in all writing in Paris and on Paris during the period running from the last years of the Bourbon Restoration to the early years of the Second Empire, when there arose amid the debris of the older city a new Paris, monumental and spacious, with its government and business quarters, a Paris fit for human habitation, a city far more like the one in which we live today than the Paris of the past, racked and branded as it was by the Ancien Régime. About no other city, even London, except for a few in our own time—Chicago between the two world wars, for example—has so much been written. From the most famous novels and the most important philosophical and sociological treatise to the most insignificant pamphlet, from works of imagination to pedestrian surveys, this writing has dwelled insistently on every aspect of crime, as if the proliferation of the criminal classes really was, over the

From Louis Chevalier, *Laboring Classes and Dangerous Classes in Paris during the First Half of the Nineteenth Century*, trans. Frank Jellinek (New York: Howard Fertig, Inc., 1973), pp. 1–3, 269–270, 275–292, 471–472. Reprinted by permission.

years, one of the major facts of daily life in Paris, one of the main
problems of city management, one of the principal matters of general
concern, one of the essential forms of the social malaise. No matter
what groups we take, whether the bourgeois, apparently secure behind their triple bars and bolts, or the lower classes, menacing and
menaced; no matter what trend we study in the events, whether
social or political, however artificially divorced from such sordid
considerations, this documentation and this weight of testimony
loom on the threshold as we enter the Paris of the period and
present us inescapably with a sanguinary preview of it. However
repugnant it may be, we simply cannot burke the sight of a city in
which crime assumed an importance and an implication which we
can hardly appreciate today, living as we do in a capital where crime
is of interest only as a minor news item, except when it happens to
bring to mind certain ancient terrors and some recollection of an
earlier age not unlike the period we shall be dealing with in this
study.

"Criminal" is the key word for the Paris of the first half of the
nineteenth century; first of all, because of the increase in the number
of crimes committed, as recorded in the crime statistics, but brought
out even more strikingly in other documents such as the economic
and demographic statistics. For even though these are not directly
concerned with crime, yet when they are correlated with the crime
statistics proper, they enable us to pierce through the criminality
reflected simply in the number of arrests and convictions to criminality in its broadest sense, the only form of criminality that really
counts.

"Criminal," secondly, because of the imprint of crime upon the
whole urban landscape. No part of the contemporary Paris was un-
shadowed by crime. At the old gates and on the outer boulevards,
the barrières, where, until the railroads were built, highwaymen carried on the traditions of the Ancien Régime and, as the lower classes
drank and danced nearby, forgathered in the shadows with criminals
of a new type spawned by the recent outward sprawl of the city. And
in the central quarters themselves, where the capital's complex and
disordered growth had engendered a tangle of lanes, passageways,
courts and blind alleys and had ranged cheek by jowl sunny street
and cesspool, the affluent mansion and the slum, areas of light and
shade in a landscape we can now barely make out, and had almost
everywhere left nooks and corners ideally suited to robbery with

violence by day or night—and, indeed, in some places day hardly differed from night. For risk to life, or at best, to purse, our Parisian had no need to linger in the purlieus of the place Maubert or the Cité, or to push on as far as the sinister boulevards bordering on the faubourg Saint-Jacques or the faubourg Saint-Marcel; for every route running from the Temple to the Seine, from the Palais-Royal to the place des Vosges, through the huddle of houses barely threaded by the rue Saint-Denis and the rue Saint-Martin, must at some point pass through a district far from secure, brush by some thieves' kitchen, or worse.

"Criminal," above all, because of the citizens' overwhelming preoccupation with crime as one of their normal daily worries. Crime was an abiding cause of fear, a fear which reached heights of terror in certain winters of cold and destitution. Deadly fear and terror were the theme of police reports and newspaper reports alike in the winter of 1826–27, when the crime rate and the death rate rose in parallel; and, too, in the last years of the July Monarchy, when every form of urban poverty was aggravated, accumulated and intermingled. "We are back in the palmy days of the Middle Ages, when the streets were dark and deserted," the vicomte de Launay wrote in his *Lettres parisiennes* on December 21, 1843:

> *For the past month the sole topic of conversation has been the nightly assaults, hold-ups, daring robberies. . . . What is so terrifying about these nocturnal assaults is the assailants' noble impartiality. They attack rich and poor alike. . . . They kill at sight, though they may get the wrong man; but little do they care. At one time the advantage of being poor was that at least you were safe; it is so no longer. Paris is much perturbed by these sinister occurrences. A concern for self-defense greatly troubles family gatherings especially. Evening parties all end like the beginning of the fourth act of* Les Huguenots, *with the blessing of the daggers. Friends and relatives are not allowed to go home without a regular arms inspection. . . .*

More important than the fear of crime, however, was the interest in crime and everything connected with it. Besides the persistent daily murmur nourished by the ordinary crimes and the small change of minor brawls which the Parisians could tot up each morning, there was the mighty reverberation of the great crimes, inspissated with horrid gloom and haloed, as it were, with a somber glory, occurrences in the social history of the Paris of this period at least as important as the major events in foreign and domestic policy. . . .

Destitution in Paris during the first half of the nineteenth century provides a monstrous experience of the physical and moral destitution secreted by great cities in every age. The study of the dark Paris of that period is relevant to the study of modern Paris, just as modern urban sociology illuminates many aspects of the old Paris. For our purposes, crime is simply an expression of a biological determinism, which we are here concerned with singling out and examining.

Our study is concerned less with crime itself than with one of the major aspects and probabilities of working-class life in the Paris of the period, summed up by crime. For crime reveals the downward course of working-class life at that period and throws light on the major factors involved. We are not concerned with crime in itself, save to the extent that it was for some, was likely to be for many and was considered by most to be the final possibility, the last act in an existence which everything combined to drive in that, rather than any other, direction. The problem of crime is important because it was the major problem of working-class life in this period. Proudhon summed this up in 1851 in his *Idée générale de la Révolution:*

> And just as if evil, like good, must have its sanction, so pauperism, thus foreseen, prepared and organized by economic anarchy, has found its own sanction in the crime statistics. . . . When the worker has been stupefied by the fragmentary division of labor, by serving machines, by obscurantist education; when he has been discouraged by low wages, demoralized by unemployment and starved by monopoly; when he finally has neither bread nor cake, neither farthing nor groat, neither hearth nor home, then he begs, he filches, he cheats, he robs, he murders. After passing through the hands of the exploiters, he falls into the hands of justice. Is that clear?

The advantage of taking crime as our theme is that it sums up the problem of the course of working-class life in an extreme form and reduces it to its simplest and most striking expression. It supplies a basis for studying social deterioration in the working classes during this period—a fundamental aspect of the general study of social mobility in an urban environment—which may be almost as precise as the study being carried out today in the great modern metropolises. It is true that modern research has a number of advantages, such as a fuller, more varied and more readily renewable quantitative documentation; the permanent accessibility of experimentation of every sort; and the results of the general advances in psychology and biology. Nevertheless, and apart from any question of the precision of the study, the demographic conditions of social mobility in an urban environment emphasize the fact that the phenomenon of social deterioration was more evident in the first half of the nineteenth century than it is today, and is therefore easier to study, even though the quantitative documentation of social deterioration itself may be less abundant.

This phenomenon was more evident then than now because the evolution of the population has driven it in opposite directions in the two periods: in modern times toward success, during the first half of the nineteenth century toward failure. Of this irresistible, simplifying and determinant demographic drive we have to examine both the mechanics and the major aspects. Part of the Paris population was doomed to failure. Firstly, because of the way in which it had assembled—no matter whether we look at the overrapid and overlarge immigration, which kept the part of the population concerned on the fringes of the city by its weight alone, or whether we take the fertility rate, the proportion of illegitimacy within it enabling us to calculate how large the criminal classes were likely to become. Secondly, it was doomed to failure by its living conditions and by its mode of life, as expressed and summed up in the statistics of mortality. . . .

Social Deterioration: The Phenomena

. . . Despite the lack of detailed documentation, social deterioration is easier to trace during the first half of the nineteenth century than it is today and therefore easier to examine. This is so, to begin with, because the phenomena summed up in social deterioration are more sharply delimited today. Each of them exists independently and has specific characteristics instead of blending, as they did in the first half of the nineteenth century, with the major phenomena of urban life; they are truly exceptional and abnormal, not commonplace, normal and social in the full sense of the word. To take only the extreme forms of urban pathology, this is true of infanticide, prostitution and madness, which in the earlier period were closely bound up with the general conditions of working-class existence and fully representative of it, though we do not find so many examples or such adequate statistical documentation for them as for the major phenomena. The city's poverty, more particularly that of the working classes, shows up strongly in such basic statistics as the general or exceptional death rate and the illegitimate birth rate. But it is equally accessible in other statistics, those for crime, infanticide, prostitution and mental disorders, which, though they embrace fewer units, are nonetheless meaningful for that and were used by contemporary statisticians on a par with the general statistics. They are not marginal statistics concerning merely exceptional and abnormal phenomena, since they reproduce, though in miniature, the occupational and economic correlations which can be derived from the general statistics.

The General Significance of Certain Limited Phenomena

Infanticide: In Paris during the first half of the nineteenth century the correlation between infanticide and the general increase in the population was close and indubitable.

This correlation was reflected first of all in the facts: in the extent of infanticide, as measured by the number of indictments and convictions, and (noted in the reports of the Board of Health) as a form of criminality expressed in the definite correlation both between the increase in infanticide and in population and between this type of crime and economic, political and biological crises. It was reflected, secondly, in the distribution by occupation and locality, where the highest proportionate figures are found in the working-class districts and in the lower-class groups. And finally, it was reflected in the many accounts indicating that the practice was far more widespread than appears from the judicial and other statistics and was a very common form of behavior in certain social environments. The abolition in 1838 of the *tours*[1] doubled the cases of infanticide registered by the Morgue. This Parisian practice had been reported from the earliest times; under the Ancien Régime the Commissioners of the court of justice known as the Châtelet used to collect numbers of corpses of newborn babies from the sewers every day. Furthermore, infanticide was freely practiced in most large towns: "At Lyon infanticide is a common practice," we find in a report to the Board of Health of the Rhône department. . . .

Prostitution: There are other phenomena, too, which while they

---

[1] Tower-like structures at foundling homes for the deposition of deserted infants.—Eds.

cannot be regarded as significant of the general social development, undoubtedly bear some relation to it. Prostitution is probably one of them.

Prostitution was a basic phenomenon of urban life, more particularly of working-class life, during the first half of the nineteenth century. The general importance and significance of prostitution were plain enough in Parent-Duchatelet's description of it and in the rough but adequate correlations he established between the number of prostitutes and the size of the Paris population; between the prostitutes' and the inhabitants' provincial origins; between the prostitutes' occupational origins and the occupational distribution of the lower groups in the working class; and between the economic situation and the increase or decrease in prostitution. Its social importance is brought out even more clearly by general phenomena which Parent-Duchatelet was unable to perceive: the relations we are going on to establish between working-class cohabitation, illegitimacy and prostitution, and the description we shall have to try to construct of the workers' general behavior and, indeed, of their general morality, manners and customs, of which prostitution is simply one aspect. . . .

Madness: When we note the number of cases during this period of workers arrested as mentally deranged by the gendarmerie of the department of the Seine or by the municipal police on day or night patrol, we cannot but ask ourselves whether madness too may not be regarded as a phenomenon just as characteristic of urban pathology as these we have already mentioned and whether it does not differ in some respects from mental disorder today.

It must be acknowledged that the documents, though numerous and couched in statistical terms, are of little help. This should not be surprising in the light of the modern difficulties involved in attempting a quantitative study of insanity. The definition of madness differed from one contemporary alienist to another, like the definition and list of the causes, which they regarded as either physical or mental. The most eminent appear more concerned to derive confirmation of their preconceived ideas from the statistics than to use them for a description and explanation of the facts. Writers like Esquirol and Brière de Boismont, for example, convinced beforehand of the influence of what they call moral causes, had no trouble in establishing a correlation between political disturbances and the evolution of madness. "In 1830," Esquirol wrote in his *Histoire et statistique de Charenton, social apprehensions and social disturbances exercised a certain influence upon madness. This conclusion confirms what we first published in 1805, namely, that the ideas prevailing in every century, the state of society and the political upheavals exercise a great influence upon the incidence and nature of insanity. I could compile the history of our country between 1789 and our own time from an observation of mentally deranged persons who attributed the cause or nature of their madness to some outstanding political event during this long period of our history. And if I had to account for the large number of suicides noted in 1834 and the reasons for their frequency, I would simply refer to a well-conceived history of the mental and moral state of society in France. We should see that the disease was long-seated, but aggravated by new circumstances.*

Brière de Boismont, noting in his study, *L'influence de la civilisation sur le développement de la folie,* the relation between the main crises in the first half of the century and the growth of madness, had no difficulty in finding confirmation of his thesis in the figures. Almost anything up to a visit to Paris by the Pope, according to him, would bring on a vast access of religious mania. "In his report on the insane," he wrote, "Desportes notes that 3,222 persons were committed to the Salpêtrière and Bicêtre between 1831 and 1833, one-sixth more than in previous years; this was due to the Revolution and the epidemic." Some—like Moreau de Jonès—classified destitution as a physical cause; others as a mental cause. In any case, what was destitution, *la misère?* "To cite destitution as a cause of madness is to use a very vague term," a contributor to the *Annales d'Hygiène* objected against Jonès. "In my opinion, it means the worry caused by privation and the anxieties attaching to poverty. *La misère* is, I believe, a mental, not a physical, cause."

To add to this confusion there was a belief in a part-madness for which at the beginning of the century Esquirol coined the lasting name "monomania," the term being used to designate states in which the patient retained the use of almost all his faculties and was insane only on one subject or a few subjects, but otherwise felt, acted and reasoned as he had before he fell sick. "Everybody knows what monomania is; you are seized with a desire to kill or rob. It overpowers you, but that does not mean that you are a dangerous criminal. The patient needs cold baths, plenty of cold baths," declares Simon, the doctor in *Le Monomane,* a melodrama by Charles Duveyrier first performed at the Porte Saint-Martin Theater on April 13, 1835. Monomania was invoked time after time by lawyers defending hopeless cases, quoting Pinel, Esquirol, Gall, Foderé, Marc and Georget, and relying on Article 64 of the Criminal Code, which laid down that an act is not a crime or felony if the accused was of unsound mind at the time. So did novelists; Sue represented the Slasher's urge to kill and the erotic mania of the notary Ferrand as cases of monomania. Indeed, the *Annales d'Hygiène* was much read by Sue; it carried many articles on erotic monomania, and we find traces of these in Sue's novel, as well as of the crime news from the press.

The statistical study of madness, particularly madness among the workers in Paris during the period, is inevitably obscured by this cloud of beliefs exploiting rather than using the statistics, falling upon them in rather the same way as destitution fell upon the poor. Such a study would, however, be feasible. Its findings would be of great interest, even if they proved negative; but even more interesting would be the intriguing methodological problem of using a relatively small body of statistical material for quantitative history. While one can easily see what history can derive from massive statistics such as the censuses or the figures for births and deaths, even if they are only approximate, it is a fascinating question whether it is equally able to use statistics covering only a few cases for the study of such phenomena as madness. The accuracy of the statistics is of no great importance in measuring the major and normal phenomena, for the errors cancel out; it is quite easy to apply a refined technique to deduce what is impossible and what is certain in the doubtful statistics for backward countries or distant ages. But is this true of abnormal phenomena which are not precisely defined, where measurements must be meticulously exact just because they record only a few cases?

We shall reserve such methodic analysis for another problem, that of workers' suicides. We take the opportunity to note here that in the specific case of madness a statistical study itself is not as important as the two facts on which some light is thrown by even approximate statistics, namely, the occupations of the workers afflicted with mental disorders and the districts in which they lived.

The occupations are, as a general rule, the lowest, the hardest and the most despised, those, in fact, in which there was the heaviest death rate from cholera. "The dockers at the port at Bercy," Parent-Duchatelet wrote, *are particularly prone to mental disorders and insanity: eight dockers there were stricken in 1827. Why there and not at other ports? While in some yards they drink red wine and spirits to excess, the workmen at Bercy are exceptional in that they drink nothing but white wine, 5 to 6 liters a day. Almost all these white wines come from Anjou and are often blended with perry to give them extra strength and bite. Since these wines are the headiest known, we should not be at all surprised if they were the cause of the disease. But why the difference? It is solely due to the municipal duty on wines, which makes for great variations in the price of wines and leads to innumerable adulterations, themselves varying with the competition and the location of the retailers' shops.*

In the files of the Paris police and the gendarmerie of the department of the Seine and in articles in the *Annales médico-psychologiques* there are, however, many more cases of the insanity of day-laborers and workers described as "itinerants" or "nomads." Most of them were from the provinces and were arrested at the barrières or in the central districts where these lower-class groups were densest, such as the Cité, the Hôtel-de-Ville and the market districts. This seems to confirm the correlation between mental disorders and the failure to adjust to the urban environment which was to be studied in detail by later sociologists. There is good reason to believe that madness among the workers was, like the other phenomena we have examined, a fundamental element in the pathology of the Paris of the period.

This is also true of workers' suicides. But here we must stress even more strongly than we have in connection with madness the difficulties involved in attempting any historical examination of the abnormal facts, because the relevant statistical material is so scanty.

An Example: Workers' Suicides

The assertion of the fact: One assertion found constantly throughout the descriptions of the Paris population in the first half of the nineteenth century is that the suicides of proletarians accounted for the general increase in suicides and that they were a reflection of the misery of the working class. We must start with this belief before we go on to discuss its validity and significance. Even if we later find that it does not square with the truth, it is nevertheless significant that the belief did exist as a fact of opinion throughout the period, quite patent in the most diverse documents, but most notably in the picturesque literature we have already discussed, which here as in other ways carried on the tradition of Mercier.

As early as 1782 Mercier wrote:

Why have so many people killed themselves in Paris during the past twenty-five years? What is the reason for so many suicides when one hardly ever heard of them in the old days? People have tried to blame modern philosophy for what I venture to say is simply the work of the Government. Those who kill themselves when they have no notion how they are to survive next day are anything but philosophers; they are the indigent, the wearied, those worn out by life because merely to subsist has become so difficult, nay, sometimes impossible. The number of suicides in Paris may amount in the calendar year to 150, or about one-third of their present number. The police take care to ensure that the public hears nothing of these suicides. When someone kills himself, a superintendent of police presents himself in plain clothes, draws up a report without more ado and compels the priest to bury the body hugger-mugger. Those who used to be prosecuted after their death under an absurd statute are no longer carted to the scaffold. Indeed, that was a horrible and disgusting spectacle calculated to have dangerous consequences in a city teeming with pregnant women. This kind of death is nowhere recorded on paper, and those who compile history from such papers a thousand years hence may well cast doubt on what I am advancing. But it is all too true that suicide is commoner in Paris today than in any other city in the known world.

There are many similar allusions to workers' suicides in the *Tableaux de Paris* under the Empire and the Restoration. "Every day one hears talk of suicides and murders among the people and the petty bourgoisie," wrote Reichardt in *Un hiver à Paris* in 1802.

We find the most definite assertion, however, in Lachaise's *Topographie médicale* (1822), and the most important, because it was based upon the many and varied daily observations of a Paris doctor and because he used the earliest quantitative research on the subject and in this work reflected what we described in an earlier chapter as the statistical revelation. In Lachaise's description, as in the *Recherches statistiques sur Paris,* the figures for suicide were part of the normal statistical material and the study of suicide an indispensable feature of urban demography. . . .

Lachaise believed that there were more suicides than were recorded in the statistics:

One of the reflections that strike us when we examine the mortality tables for the two sexes, and one which deserves more thought, is the suicide rate. Many unfortunates in Paris despair of happiness, devise their own destruction and lay violent hands upon themselves. The average arrived at by sifting the recorded deaths is between 300 and 350; in 1817, it was 351, 235 men and 116 women; in 1819, 376, 250 men and 126 women. This number, though alarming as it stands, may, however, be thought to fall far short of the true average, for two reasons. The first is that the relatives of some suicides try, and in many cases succeed, to have deaths of this kind recorded as the outcome of delirious fever and accordingly to have the phrase "while of unsound mind" substituted for "suicide" on the death certificate in order to avoid the stain on the family honor. The second is that the death registers carry no mention of the many persons who had not the resolution to consummate their deed or cases where the deliberate attempt to put an end to themselves was frustrated by prompt and unexpected rescue.

As to the distribution of suicide, "Experience shows," says Lachaise, "that it is by far the most frequent in Paris among the class of proletarians. . . ."

The further one goes into the nineteenth century, the more numerous the assertions about the frequency of workers' suicides. There were a great many in the principal descriptions of the manners and customs of the period, though the chief emphasis was placed on political and literary suicides, and less on poverty than on the fashion mentioned by Balzac: "Suicide was all the rage in Paris at the time." In his lectures on literature, *Du suicide et de la haine de la vie,* Saint-Marc-Girandin said in 1843: "If the very craftsmen are now, alas, infected with the malady of suicide, the reason is that their minds are constantly irritated and soured by modern science and civilization." Perhaps; but the real point is "the very craftsmen are . . . infected with the malady of suicide." We have only to look at the number of craftsmen's suicides in the descriptive and social literature, not to speak of the works actually devoted to the subject which became very common during the last ten years of the July Monarchy.

Suicide was on the increase, more in Paris than elsewhere and among the working class more than among other classes. This assertion we find in the medical literature, the moralist literature, the picturesque literature and—during and after the last ten years of the July Monarchy—the working-class literature, including the working class press, the popular novels and the writings of the social reformers.

The nature of public opinion: This aspect of public opinion must be examined as such, being itself a fact. The belief in the large number of workers' suicides must inevitably have been a factor in their increase, just as opinion concerning suicide in general contributed to the general increase in suicides. It seems very probable that the many sensational suicides during the Revolution and the Empire familiarized people with the idea of self-slaughter. The contagious effects of suicide were often noted. Suicide had its own favored spots in the city, and popular belief soon came to decide that they attracted suicides; not necessarily heights—the towers of Notre-Dame very seldom, but the July Column and the Vendôme Column, which had to be equipped with a balustrade in 1843. Different spots were preferred at the end of the nineteenth century and in the twentieth. "The newspapers," the *Annales d'Hygiène* wrote in 1829, "ought to refrain from reporting any suicides whatever. We have good reason to believe that such publicity has on more than one occasion decided people already in a desperate frame of mind to hasten the ending of their lives."

It is likely that the workers were just as much affected by the influence of the contemporary fashionable despair, for which material circumstances do not adequately account. The influence of literature on bourgeois suicides was often noted. "If I seek the source of these extravagant ideas, is it not to be found in Romanticism, in these antisocial books, in these plays which lead the imagination astray?" cried the defender of Dr. Bancal, to whom the double suicide of Indiana and Ralph in George Sand's novel had suggested the idea of killing himself together with his mistress. There were even queerer cases, such as that reported by Jules Janin of the Courbevoie hairdresser, named Molard, whose head had been turned by the Preface to [Hugo's] *Cromwell.* He gassed himself, leaving this note: "Farewell, my friends in politics and literature. . . . Farewell, all my good neighbors. . . . Down with *The Sicilian Vespers* and hurrah for *Cromwell!*" We could find many documents to show, if we had not already suspected it, that the workers were just as subject to these influences as the other classes. We have only to look at the novels of Sue or Frédéric Soulié, the Porte Saint-Martin melodramas and the street ballads. We have, too, only to read the crime news in the papers, or, even more to the point, the suicides' letters used by Guerry in his *Statistique morale de France,* some of which were published in the press. These reveal how the contagion worked. They contain references to recent suicides and friendly and affectionate messages, as if, on the point of quitting a society in which he no longer can, or no longer wishes to, live, the suicide, rejecting the solitude in which he is living, and even denouncing and denying the apparent solitude to which death dooms him, were taking refuge in another society in the Beyond, whose existence he asserts and indeed proposes to prove by his act itself. It is a classless society, as we can see from the case of the worker who, on the point of flinging himself from his garret under the eaves of a tall house in the rue Saint-Denis, mentions the suicide of a peer of the realm in his farewell letter. A species of fraternity of suicides grew up, similar to the fraternity of the guillotined imagined by Hugo in the *Dernier jour d'un condamné,* with its stress on the fatal attraction of the Grève:

> *More than one who goes there for my sake will go there for his own. For these doomed beings there is a certain place on the place de Grève, a fatal spot, a pole of attraction, a snare. They linger around it until they are caught. . . . It may well be, too, that on a certain date the dead of the Grève may gather on black winter nights on the square that is theirs. It will be a livid and bleeding crowd, and I shall not fail to be among them. There will be no moon and the talk will be low. The Hôtel-de-Ville will be there, and its clock, which once struck pitilessly for all of them.*

A kindred society of suicides takes form in these letters and in the popular literature, in which the street ballads have pride of place.

The fact itself: Although there is a good deal to be said for observing this evidence as revealed in opinion concerning the frequency of workers' suicides, we still have to see how far this belief was justified by the facts. The problem is whether the number of suicides in general did increase, more especially among the lower classes, and whether the increase can be regarded, like the increases in prostitution, madness and crime, as expressing pathological conditions of urban living. Death by suicide was only a small component of the general death rate.[2] Is its significance comparable to that of

[2] The number of attempted or successful suicides in Paris from 1817 to 1826 and from 1839 to 1848 was as follows:

1817	351	1822	317	1839	670	1844	715
1818	330	1823	390	1840	748	1845	745
1819	376	1824	371	1841	712	1846	713
1820	325	1825	396	1842	670	1847	918
1821	348	1826	511	1843	681	1848	698

the general rate, or is it merely a sum of individual cases, each differing from the other, each due to different causes and to a long private history irrelevant to the kind of history we are concerned with here?

A problem for sociology rather than history. The suicide statistics and the comments on them—both at this period by Quételet in particular and later by Durkheim in particular—seem to show that while suicide was commoner in Paris than elsewhere and while it was perhaps more frequent in the first half of the nineteenth century than at any earlier or later period, it is a phenomenon whose interest is not confined merely to Paris and to the particular period. It concerns other great cities besides Paris and a study of it is thus far more relevant to the description of urban civilizations in general than to one of Paris alone. It is relevant, too, to the general development of societies up to the present day as well as specifically in the first half of the nineteenth century. It is, basically, a social rather than a historical phenomenon, material for sociology rather than history, since it can be studied in itself, and not necessarily as it developed chronologically.

The increase in the figures for suicide is constant and regular in all countries for which statistics are available all through the nineteenth century and beyond it, as if there were a constant and stable correlation between the course of suicide and the course of other demographic, economic and social phenomena.[3]

Moreover, this increase is greatest in the cities, both in Paris and in the other European capitals for which statistics are available.

The stability of the other characteristics is even more patent and even more surprising; the demographic characteristics to begin with. A similar distribution by sex is observable almost everywhere. "The tables show over ten years," the *Annales d'Hygiène* stated in 1829, "that women are able to bear the vicissitudes of life better than men,

---

[3] For France alone, the increase was:

	Annual average	No. of suicides per 100,000 inhabitants	Increase in number of suicides (1826–30 = 100)
1826–1830	1,827	50	100
1831–1835	2,119	60	130
1836–1840	2,574	70	148
1841–1845	2,931	80	170
1846–1850	3,446	90	199
1886–1887	8,194	210	471

since they account for barely one-third of the suicides." Distribution by age is similar. "Suicides in France," wrote Quételet, "are infrequent at an early age; their number increases with age and the rule applies in practically the same way to men and to women. But rather more women commit suicide before twenty or twenty-five, presumably for the same reasons as they commit infanticide." He noted, too, that the distribution in Paris was much the same as that in Geneva, Berlin and London, and that there were more unmarried than married suicides.

The distribution by season, day of the week and time of day is equally general and equally surprising. Spring and summer seem to be the periods in which most suicides occur, while they are least frequent in winter and autumn. "Summer," Quételet noted, "has a greater influence on the number of suicides than the other seasons, as it has on the number of cases of mental disorder and crimes against the person." And Esquirol noted the effects of a very hot summer followed by a wet autumn in his articles on suicide in the *Grand Dictionnaire des Sciences médicales.*

Most suicides occur early in the week and early in the morning. The methods of suicide are also just as stable and general. Concluding a statistical study of suicide in Paris, Guerry wrote:

> *Nothing would seem more arbitrary and to leave a wider freedom of choice than the method of killing oneself. But this choice is unconsciously influenced by age, sex, social status and a variety of other circumstances often very hard to assess. Chance has no more to do with it than with the distribution of crime or any other statistical fact; and, provided that enough observations are made, certain well-tested criteria can be used to work out some of the other factors. One remarkable example is that man chooses a particular method of killing himself at each age; in youth he takes to hanging, but soon drops this for firearms. As his strength declines, he goes back to the earlier method; and an old man putting an end to his life usually resorts to hanging.*

Factors other than occupation have a determining influence. As Legoyt demonstrated, Esquirol's assertion that suicides as a general rule prefer the tools they use in their trade was mistaken, though it was actually true of laundrymen and especially washerwomen, who took poison, or rather substances containing poison, such as Prussian blue for whitening laundry. . . .

. . . Durkheim held that suicide varied in inverse proportion to the degree of integration with religious society—religion is a protection—in inverse proportion to the degree of integration with domestic society—marriage is a protection—and in inverse proportion to the degree of integration in political society—the city is a protection. Although he corrected and supplemented Quételet,[4] Durkheim lifted suicide out of the diversity of historical facts and set it in the context of the immutability of sociological space just as much as Quételet did.

So the suicide statistics, and such analyses of them as Quételet's and Durkheim's, relate to a pathological phenomenon less relevant to our study than those we have already examined. The statistics establish a constant relation between suicide and population and its demographic characteristics, and great stability and uniformity in the methods of suicide throughout the entire course of a century and in most of the great cities in which a quantitative study can be made. Unlike the other pathological phenomena—which are specifically Parisian and specifically of the Paris of the period, and reveal the unhealthy state of the city even when broken down into the detail of district, occupation and year—suicide seems to have had much the same characteristics in Paris as it had elsewhere. The tragic situation was no more typical of Paris than any other city nor of our period than of any other period. It was one factor in Paris, just as it was in similar or even quite different cities. In any quantitative description of Paris or any statistical quest for it, the material to be derived from an examination of suicide is meager indeed for the purposes of description or, for that matter, of history in general.

The same could be said of Quételet's and Durkheim's interpretations. Their analysis of suicide takes it into a realm with which we are not concerned. Their conclusions cannot be used for a description of Paris during a single restricted period in its development.

But this is only apparently so. This sociological description, especially Durkheim's, is in fact relevant to our form of social history both where it is incontrovertible and where it is inadequate.

The sociology and history of suicide. Though Durkheim moved his study of suicide outside our area and period, his basic conclusion is relevant: that there are no individual suicides and that personal motives, such as poverty, sickness or frustrated love, are significant only insofar as they are related to collective pressures or prohibitions. However unfortunate individuals might be, suicide would not

---

[4] Adolphe Quételet, a nineteenth-century Belgian statistician.—Eds.

be endemic in a society strongly integrated in respect of politics, economics, religion and the family. The thing to be noted is the degree of a society's integration, not the individual factors.

The term "social integration" was new, but not the idea. We find that the conclusion which Durkheim reached at the close of lengthy surveys was similar to that reached by all who dealt with suicide throughout the nineteenth century, moralists and churchmen, alienists and criminologists alike. "If a man has not fortified his soul, education aiding, with religious ideas," Esquirol wrote in *Maladies mentales* (1839),

> *with the precepts of morality and with orderly habits and regular conduct, if he has not learned to obey the law, to fulfill his duties to society and to bear the vicissitudes of life, if he has learned to despise his fellow men, to disdain the parents who bore him and to give full rein to his desires and whims, it is certain that, other things being equal, he will be more prone than others to put an end to his life as soon as he meets with disappointment or adversity. Man needs an authority to direct his passions and govern his actions. Left to his own weakness, he falls into indifference and then into doubt; he has nothing to bolster up his courage, he is defenseless against the sufferings of life's mental anguish.*

The fact remains that the advantage of the new term coined by the sociologists is that it defines a concept used very vaguely and inconsistently in the nineteenth-century studies. Adopting both the concept and the terminology, we may say that the weaker the material and moral integration, the higher the number of suicides. It is very high, therefore, in large cities, "which often entail the torments of passion **and** interest," as Esquirol wrote in his article on suicide; and this was especially so in Paris during the first half of the nineteenth century when, as we have already pointed out, the increase in its population relegated part of its working class to the margin of the material and human environment.

Though sociological analysis does point to social nonintegration as an important factor in the increase in suicide, and though this generalized conclusion does throw a certain amount of light even on a study narrowly bounded in space and time, it does not satisfactorily account for the particularized aspects of suicide at one specific place and in one specific period.

The reasons for this inadequacy are statistical. The prerequisite for a statistical study of suicide is a numerical count of the facts; it must be extremely precise, simply because death by suicide is far less frequent than death in general. A statistical study of the general death rate need not be absolutely accurate in detail, but a study of suicide must be, since only a few cases more or a few less may throw the conclusions completely out of kilter. Lachaise, it will be recalled, warned that doctors ascribed many cases of suicide to illness or accident in order to spare the family's honor. As to attempted suicide, Esquirol wrote: "Not 40 of 100 attempted suicides are successful." And hundreds of attempted suicides were never recorded. It hardly seems feasible, therefore, to compile statistics of suicide by age, sex and cause.

We can, however, set this objection aside. A constant relation may be assumed between suicides recorded and suicides concealed; since the number of recorded suicides remained fairly constant, the total number of attempted and successful suicides very probably remained constant too.

Our main criticism is directed not so much to this point as to the notion of some sort of constant or invariable rate of suicide. This idea will do well enough when applied over long periods of time in which the peaks and discontinuities level out. But while both the sociologist and the historian deal in averages, the historian is bound, once the averages have been established, to look more closely at the annual totals from which these averages are derived, but which they conceal. Admittedly, the rate levels out over a period of a hundred or even fifty years; but from year to year the differences come to the fore. It is here that there emerges in the background to the series for suicide in general, about which there is no disagreement, a particular kind of suicide, or rather kinds of suicide, as evidenced in a particular city, in particular districts, in particular methods, for particular reasons, in particular social groups and in particular years. And it is here that the history of suicide parts company with the sociology of suicide.

First, it becomes clear that the increase in suicide is greater than the increase in the population. To take only suicides consummated in death, these rose from 285 in 1817 to 357 in 1826 and 477 in 1835; the number of suicides in 1835 was 250 percent above that of 1817 and 350 percent above the average annual rate for the period 1794–1804. "This increase," a criminologist wrote in 1836, "cannot be due to the population increase, since it did not multiply by three in forty years."

Secondly, it is clear that there were many more suicides at particular periods and even in particular years. The peaks did not occur at the time of the great revolutionary upheavals; in 1830, suicides in Paris fell by 13 percent, as compared with 1829, from 307 to 269; in 1848, by 32 percent, as compared with 1847, from 698 to 481. "The great social disturbances," said Durkheim, "stimulate the sense of community and promote integration with society; people come closer to each other; the individual thinks less of himself than of the common weal." But suicides increased in the years of gross poverty preceding and preparing the final political upheavals before, as it were, finding an outlet in them, as in the last years of the Restoration, notably 1826, and in 1840 and 1841 and the last years of the July Monarchy.

In these years, too, suicides increased at the same rate as other acts of violence, notably homicide. Guerry observed in 1833 that there were twice as many crimes against the person in the southern provinces as in the northern, whereas the reverse held good as regards suicide. He concluded that to some extent suicide did not parallel homicide, and here he was followed by the principal Italian criminologists of the second half of the nineteenth century, who held that since suicide and homicide were two manifestations of the same state, they would express themselves now in one form, now in the other. Lombroso believed that the psychological constitution predisposing to one or the other form of violence was likely to be an identical decay of the organism which put the person at a disadvantage in the struggle of life. Both the murderer and the suicide accordingly were degenerate and impotent; equally unable to play a useful part in society, they were consequently doomed to defeat. The only difference between them was that one person killed other people and another killed himself, depending on the social environment and the period. In actual fact, there were periods in Paris in which there was a great deal of murder and an equal amount of self-slaughter; in the last years of the Restoration and between 1840 and 1850, suicide and homicide ran parallel. In this respect, suicide was clearly one of the forms of urban pathology.

The cause was identical: poverty. It is true that, without nonintegration with the city, poverty would not in itself have been sufficient to cause suicide, since at other places and in other periods poverty acted as a protection against suicide. But actually, in Paris and at this period, it was poverty that caused a large proportion of the suicides shown in the statistics, whatever category we take. All the commentators agree on this. "Since the beginning of this summer," the *Journal des Débats* wrote on July 9, 1847,

> *suicides have been increasing at an alarming rate, not only in Paris but in the neighboring communes too. Within the space of a month and a half there have been eight in the commune of Batignolles. The reports from the criminal courts show that the number of suicides is on the increase, but never before at this year's rate. Why? You can easily account for it if you look at the ever-growing poverty of the working classes.*

The working classes were mainly affected. But which in particular? In the last decades of the century the official statistics for France divided suicides into ten occupational categories, the last headed "Persons without occupation or occupation unknown"; the highest proportion of suicides fell into this category. Commenting on these statistics, but extending his conclusions to cover the whole century, Legoyt wrote in 1881: "Persons with no known occupation and therefore with a very precarious social position account for by far the most suicides. We might well call this category that of the *misérables.*"

The *misérables:* the term conjures up a myriad memories and throws a flood of light on the history of suicide. Let us look at our statistics once again, especially those of the Morgue, which were very accurate. Not all suicides went to the Morgue, only those who died on the public highway or in places of public resort; deaths by drowning account for about two-thirds of them. Whereas at the end of the nineteenth century only a very small proportion of the suicides laid out at the Morgue remained unknown and unidentified by their family, between 1830 and 1835 almost two-thirds of them were not claimed or identified—an anonymous mass, without civil status in death as in life. The rest, whose identity and residence were known, had had the worst jobs and had come from districts with the largest nomadic population.

Michael Anderson

FAMILY STRUCTURE IN NINETEENTH-CENTURY LANCASHIRE

In order to assess the impact of industrialization upon urban kinship net-works, Michael Anderson, a sociologist teaching at the University of Edin-burgh, studied the family structure of an English cotton-manufacturing town in the first half of the nineteenth century. His work treats Preston, a Lanca-shire city having about 70,000 inhabitants in 1851. Making detailed use of the 1851 census and of descriptions by contemporaries of working-class households, Anderson challenges the view that workers' family life disinte-grated under the harsh and unfamiliar disciplines of city and factory.

In this chapter I turn to a consideration of selected aspects of rela-tionships within the urban nuclear family. I concentrate in particular on those aspects which have implications for the main question under review in other chapters — why should people have wanted to maintain relationships with parents and other kin, and what influenced the quality of those relationships?

I tried to show in the last chapter that most young people before and after marriage maintained some relationships with their parents and I argued that the evidence suggested that these relationships were seen as useful and important. I also showed that some people broke off relationships with parents and I suggested that many more who maintained relationships yet adopted a calculative instrumental orientation to them.

One possible interpretation of these patterns would point to un-satisfying relationships of younger children with their families of orientation as the cause of such orientations and behavior. It would begin with the observations of a mass of middle-class contem-poraries to the effect that the nuclear family was disintegrating and that child neglect, drunkenness, and even infanticide were wide-spread. It would then argue that in consequence lack of respect for parents, desertion of parents by children when in need, and a gener-ally instrumental attitude were only to be expected. Such an interpre-tation would also, of course, lend support to a simple "industrializa-

From Michael Anderson, *Family Structure in Nineteenth-Century Lancashire* (Cam-bridge, Eng. and New York: Cambridge University Press, 1971), pp. 68-78. Reprinted by permission of the publisher.

tion leads to disruption" thesis; indeed such data have often been used by polemicists for precisely this purpose. In this chapter I try, as far as the data allow, to assess the extent to which behavior of this to us extreme kind did in fact occur and the validity of an interpretation which perceives this as a cause of family disruption. I shall argue that such an interpretation is not wholly supported by the generality of the data. I shall suggest further that it ignores the total context of which such behavior was a part and, by doing so, ignores the actors' perceptions of their situations and, in particular, certain factors which can be seen as counterbalancing the "neglect" which occurred.

Firstly, then, what was the attitude of parents to their children? Middle-class writers often argued that many of the working class did not want to have their children, saw them as a burden, frequently allowed them to die, deserted them, or even more or less killed them for the sake of the money they would receive from a burial club, and that in the cotton towns affection within the family was almost entirely lacking.

It is undoubtedly true that, as the size of their families grew, many mothers did view further additions to their families with some reservations. It is, however, naive to assume without further inquiry that when the children arrived they were not treated with as much care and affection as the family could afford to, and knew how to give them.

Similarly, the allegation that working-class people "often appear to be very indifferent at the death of their children, and sometimes express satisfaction at it, saying that they ought to be thankful to God for taking away a child when they have so many to provide for..." shows little about the strength of family bonds. Firstly, it seems highly probable that, as a result of its far greater frequency, death was viewed with greater equanimity by the Victorian working class than it is today or was by middle-class contemporaries. Moreover, the rationalization that it was best for parents and children for the new baby to die sooner rather than suffer on and probably die later had at least some justification and certainly would have helped to reconcile the parents to the loss.

There is anyway at least as much evidence to suggest that, except in a minority of cases, parents usually grieved heavily at the loss even of very small children. Thus there are recorded the "gentle sorrow" of a father at the death of his child, and the "deeply distressed state" of a joiner who "just before the boy died . . . had caught him up in his arms in an agony of sorrow and kissed him several times." In spite of the dangers, real or imaginary, not one case where a sick person was deserted in sickness by a member of his or her nuclear family has been found in the literature searched.

Then again, allegations are frequently found to the effect that, because their parents were so often drunk, many children suffered severely from neglect and ill-treatment. To some extent, indeed, these allegations have some truth and, where this was so, this factor does appear to have operated to an important degree in weakening the bonds between children and their parents. The nineteenth-century working-class world was, however, a harsh one, and much of the treatment which may seem cruel to us, and even did so to the Victorian middle classes, was almost certainly defined as much less harsh by those who administered and received it. It must also be remembered that in many cases of alleged neglect (for example, parents who gave their children no food to take to work during the day), the parents were often quite literally unable to afford the food because of their large families and low wages. Similarly, the ragged clothes and insanitary state of the young urchins of the towns were as much due to ignorance and poverty as to neglect.

It is of course true that examples of extreme behavior do occur. For example, a boy and his brother were taken to a nearby canal and thrown in by their father, with, it was alleged, the express intention of drowning them. Their stepmother was said to have "locked them up in the house, tied them up to the bedposts, and 'clemmed' (starved) them shamefully." "A boy driven to idleness by the strike was turned out of doors by the father, who was nevertheless, able to keep two cows," and other cases are noted where children were "'turned out of doors' the moment they ceased to contribute to family income."

It is, moreover, also true that in many of these cases of cruelty and neglect, drink was involved. A drunken husband beating his wife until her face was "one mass of bruises," and pawning all the furniture, can hardly have encouraged the children to have much affection for him. Nor can the behavior of those men who, it was alleged, spent all their earnings in the alehouse and left their children to starve. The misery caused by this type of behavior is clear from this statement from the son of a molder who, though he earned 36s. per week, "called at the alehouse on Saturday night, and spent half his money before he came home; my mother would sit crying, not knowing how the shop bill would be paid. About twelve o'clock my father would come home as drunk as a pig; he would clap down about eighteen shillings, and with that they might have done well, but he kept on wanting drink all the week." Some mothers, too, were frequently drunk, and it was alleged that children were killed by being overlaid by mothers in their drunken stupor.

Certainly, in the nineteenth century, drinking was widespread among the working classes. In 1846 Lancashire magistrates tried over 25,000 cases where men and women were charged with offenses in which drink had probably been involved. The intensive study suggests that there was a beershop or public house in nearly every street. Rowntree found at the end of the century in York that the average working-class family spent "not less than 6s. per week" on drink, which was about one-sixth of income or about 31 pints of beer (or alcohol equivalent). Clay claims that a strike involving 4,000 people over 18 led to a fall in consumption of beer and spirits worth £1,000 per week which, even allowing for the downward multiplier effect on community aggregate demand, does suggest a very considerable rate of consumption, since five shillings would buy about 32 pints of beer (or alcohol equivalent). Some, but a minority, of members of all SEG's[1] were involved in heavy drinking, though some commentators believed that the better class of cotton operative drank less, and some artisan groups more.

In sum, there is no doubt that heavy drinking did lead to some serious neglect of children and some brutality. Against this, however, must be set the fact that some degree of drinking by fathers was undoubtedly an accepted part of daily life and part of a child's expectations. It is also probable that brutality by fathers had the effect of increasing affective bonds between children, and between children and their mothers. And it does at least seem very likely that middle-class commentators tended to exaggerate both the degree of drinking that was general, and its effects, from too great emphasis on isolated cases and on misleading averages. It undoubtedly influenced the attitudes of some children to their fathers. It can hardly have been the only factor involved for the majority.

A further set of allegations that surrounded the working-class family and the mother in particular was that the long hours worked by many

[1] Social-Economic Groups.—Eds.

women and the neglect of home and family that ensued (with husband and children driven to the beer shop by the unwelcoming domestic scene) were a further source of the disintegration which many imagined existed. These allegations and the other supposed detrimental effects on the healthy development of the children have been fully documented by Margaret Hewitt, and so only a brief discussion is necessary here.

Women had always worked in England, but their work had usually been domestic or agricultural but seasonal and had therefore allowed them to give at least casual attention to home and children for at least part of the day. This domestic employment for married women was still common in the 1850s. Women "in certain branches of business at home render important services; such as wives of farmers, of small shopkeepers, innkeepers, shoemakers, butchers." Many families had their earnings increased by wives running a little provision shop or a beer-house. Well over a third of all working wives in Preston in 1851 were employed in nonfactory occupations. Many others also worked irregularly or part-time in such occupations, but were not so recorded.

Mill work, however, was very different. Here women were employed all day, away from home, in a situation where they could not usually take their children with them and where the needs of children and home had to a great extent to go unmet, or be provided by some other person.

In all, in the Preston sample 26 percent of all wives living with their husbands worked. The effects of this work on the family, however, were considerably less than they might have been, both because many women (particularly those with children) worked at home, and because it was above all the younger wives and those with few or no children who were in employment at all. This is clear from Table 1.

There is evidence from the intensive study and from descriptive data to confirm that these trends away from work and away from factory occupations as the family moved over the life-cycle were the results of more than a mere quirk in cross-sectional data or of a once-and-for-all shift in behavior patterns. Nevertheless, nearly a quarter (23 percent) of all wives with children worked (20 percent of those with children under 10), and probably (if some account is taken of "weavers") about 15 percent of all wives with children worked away from home for most of the day. In all, 23 percent of children

TABLE 1
Employment and Type of Employment of Wives Co-residing with their Husbands, by Life-cycle Stage, Preston Sample, 1851

LCS[a]	Of all wives, proportion working %	All wives N(100%)	Of working wives, proportion in factory occupations[b] %	All working wives N(100%)
1	44	159	72	92
2	38	59		
3	28	388	52	134
4	23	122		
5	15	234	19	52
6	16	106		
All with children	23	822	52	185
All	26	1,068	52	278

[a] LCS means life-cycle stage. A family's LCS depends upon its composition and the ages and employment of its members. Anderson defines the stages as follows: (1) wife under age 45, no children; (2) wife under 45, one child under age 1; (3) children over age 1 at home, none employed; (4) children at home, some but under half employed; (5) children at home, half or over half employed; (6) wife 45 or over, no children or only one, over age 20, at home.—Eds.
[b] These figures should be seen as minima as they exclude "weavers," who made up 11 percent of working wives in LCS's 1 and 2, 13 percent in 3 and 4, and 25 percent in 5 and 6. Only some of these, and almost certainly a smaller proportion in the later LCS's, would have been factory weavers.

under 10 who had a co-residing father had working mothers; almost exactly half of these mothers worked in factory occupations.

These data, taken alone, do at first sight seem to provide some basis for the proposition that many of the children suffered neglect because their mothers worked, though many of the examples of neglect given in the literature were undoubtedly isolated and exaggerated. Before charges of neglect can be substantiated, however, two further questions must be asked:

1. Did the mothers work because they were callous, or because they had to to improve the life chances (quite literally) of the family as a whole? In other words, is this one more example of the crucial role played by direst poverty in determining the family relational patterns of large sections of the population under study?

2. Were the persons with whom the children were left always callous and indifferent to the fate of their charges?

There is considerable evidence to suggest that the main reason why mothers left their homes and families and went out to work in the mills was because their families sorely needed the extra money to raise a standard of living which the low wages of the husband (or the occasional dissolute father) would otherwise have forced below the primary poverty line. The fact that most appear to have worked until the last minute before the birth of a child and to have returned almost immediately afterwards suggests a similar motivation. Only before they had their first child did many women work because they wanted to. Tables 2 and 3 support the hypothesis that necessity played an important part in encouraging wives to work, and also make clear the way in which the working wife was a major solution to family poverty.

The fourth column of Table 3 shows that over 60 percent of the families of the wives who worked in factories would have been in difficulties had they not done so. The fourth column of Table 2 shows that with the earnings of the wife, only one in six actually were. In a third of all families which would have been in difficulties without the wife's earnings, the wives did in fact work. Conversely, where the

TABLE 2
Relationship between Family Standard of Living and Working Wives: Married Couples for Whom Data Were Adequate, Preston Sample, 1951

Relationship of weekly family income to poverty standard	Of all families, families where wife worked:			Standard of living of families:	
	in factory %	else-where[a] %	All families (N)	of factory working wives %	of all working wives %
Below by 4s. or more	5	2	41	2	2
Below by under 4s. to above by less than 4s.	14	3	105	17	14
Above by 4s. to 11s. 11d.	23	9	151	41	38
Above by 12s. to 19s. 11d.	21	10	102	24	24
Above by 20s. and over	19	21	70	15	22
All	18	9	469	99	100
				(N = 86)	(N = 128)

[a] Includes "weavers."

TABLE 3
Relationship between Family Standard of Living and Working Wives, When Earnings of Wives (Standardized at 8s.) Are Excluded: Married Couples for Whom Data Were Adequate, Preston Sample, 1851

Relationship of weekly family income to poverty standard	Of all families, families where wife worked:			Standard of living of families:	
	in factory %	else- where[a] %	All families (N)	of factory working wives %	of all working wives %
Below by 4s. or more	29	7	59	20	16
Below by under 4s. to above by less than 4s.	26	10	135	41	38
Above by 4s. to 11s. 11d.	17	7	134	24	24
Above by 12s. to 19s. 11d.	8	11	89	9	14
Above by 20s. and over	10	10	52	6	8
All	18	9	469	100 (N = 86)	100 (N = 128)

[a] Includes "weavers."

family was well clear of the poverty line, most wives appear to have worked only if they had no children who would have suffered from lack of attention, and a larger proportion of those who did work did not work in factories. Nevertheless, even where the family was in poverty if the wife did not work, only one-third appear in fact to have been in employment[2] which suggests considerable affection towards children and perceived role conflict, rather than neglect. It is also important to stress that, at these levels of poverty, where mothers did work they may very well have been so much improving the standard of living of their families that the betterment of the family's satisfactions outweighed in the minds of the children the greater degree of neglect suffered by themselves and by their home.

About one-quarter of all children under 10, then, had working mothers, and at least half of these had mothers who worked away from home and whose ability to care for their children was consequently diminished. It was only a minority of these children, however, who were left all day with hired nurses indifferent to their fate.

[2] See line 1, Table 3.—Eds.

While the mother was probably the best and first choice as a guardian, in her absence kin and close friends and neighbors were usually available as substitutes. In 14 percent of all cases where the mother worked (17 percent of all cases where she worked in a factory) the house contained an otherwise unemployed grandmother. Most of these would have been available as guardians. In addition, in a further 7 percent of such cases (28 percent of those where mother was a factory worker) some other unemployed person in the house, usually a co-lodger but sometimes a sibling or other relative, was similarly available.

Nearly half of all the young children of women working in factories, then, were probably cared for at home by a close relative or by a friendly lodger. Many more, undoubtedly, were cared for by close relatives who lived next door or just up the street. Indeed, if it be assumed that only one-half of all infants (children under one year of age) with no potential guardian in the home were cared for by relatives or friends living nearby . . . then, at a point in time, less than 2 percent of all infant children in the industrial districts of Lancashire were being left with professional child-minders. As a source of neglect and a factor affecting children's attitudes to their parents, then, working mothers were probably in fact of comparatively minor importance.

Finally, to what extent is it true, as was frequently alleged, that parents exploited their children's laboring ability, by forcing them at an early age into the labor force instead of sending them to school and bringing them up "properly"? Thus, for example, J. P. Kay wrote: "Too frequently the father, enjoying perfect health and with ample opportunities for employment, is supported in idleness on the earnings of his oppressed children." One may cite also the allegations, almost equally frequent, of the instrumental attitude of parents "who will take their children away from a kind master, and place the child with another (less kind), for the purpose of getting higher wages."

It is of course true that some exploitation did occur and this was seen as exploitation even through the eyes of the working class at the time. Moreover, where this was so it does seem to have been important in encouraging children to terminate relationships with their parents. Often, however, when children were sent to work before the normal age it was for a reason, such as family poverty, which was seen as justifying behavior which might otherwise have been seen as improper, or it was because the alternatives, usually education or mischief, were seen as worse or at least were not highly valued.

There is no doubt that some children were sent to work long hours from a very young age, even as late as the 1850s and 1860s. Children as young as 7 were reported from some industries, while other industries regularly employed or had employed children under 10. In cotton, after 1833, children were not employed so young, most beginning at about the age of 12. Table 4 shows the proportion of children of different ages recorded as in employment by the census of 1851, though one may suspect that these figures are subject to considerable underreporting. Nevertheless, it seems legitimate to conclude that by the 1850s comparatively few parents were exploiting their children's labor by forcing them into work at a very early age, though numbers of parents still tried to evade the law by pretending their children were older than they were.

Moreover, in the large proportion of the cases where young children were employed, it is clear that they were sent to work because the family was so poor that their earnings were absolutely essential if the family was to continue to function at all as an effective unit. Thus a hand-loom weaver commented that "I could not support my children except they were to bring something in." Another said his child was only employed in a mill "because I could not make do unless he was employed: my family was increasing." Indeed, it was claimed that only the children of "the class a little above necessity" were usually still in education between the ages of 10 and 12. A spinner sent his first four children into the mill before they were 10, but the fifth he kept out of the factory until the age of 12 or 13, "because our

TABLE 4
Percentage of Children Aged 7–15 Recorded as in Employment at the Census of 1851, for Manchester and Salford, and for Preston

Percentage employed	Age of children								
	7	8	9	10	11	12	13	14	15
Manchester and Salford:									
boys	1	2	4	11	23	41	60	76	—
girls	1	2	3	8	14	27	44	61	—
Preston:									
boys	—	—	7	13	27	39	74	88	93

circumstances were better." Thus, again and again, parents who otherwise showed considerable affection for their children and concern to do the best possible for them were yet forced by large families and low wages to send their children to work as soon as possible.

It is moreover clear that the more extreme allegations to the effect that fathers lay in voluntary idleness while their wives and children were forced into work can seldom be substantiated, though, probably where excessive drinking prevented a man from holding down a job, cases almost certainly did occur. More often, however, fathers were idle while their children worked because age had meant that they had lost their factory jobs, or because they were not qualified for a regular job and were more or less unemployable except as casual light laborers.

In sum, therefore, I would argue that where children suffered from neglect or overwork, this was more usually the result of ignorance, lack of foresight, or necessity than the result of deliberate cruelty or exploitation, though both were by no means rare. Few children then, will have perceived themselves as exploited. This opinion is strengthened if attention is turned to evidence on the affectionate bonds to be found in many families between children and their parents (particularly their mother).

Thus Adshead, on a general level, notes a man returning in the slump of the 1840s to "his famishing wife and family, among whom love for their parents and love for each other seem in a remarkable manner to have survived the circumstances of comfort in which they were formerly placed." Similarly, the agent of the Liverpool District Provident Society argued that "It is really only the professed beggars among the Irish who will ill use their children; the respectable Irish poor are very tender to them, and will try to get them into schools, or to bring them on in the world, and do as much for them as the parents of any other country." Perhaps even more interesting is the comment of the informant cited at the end of the last chapter on the carelessness of feeling between parents and adult children. He observed that with regard to *young* children "Nothing can be more warm and keen than the affection of parents throughout the cotton districts for children, so long as they continue children. . . ." It was only in adolescence that the changes occurred, and that as much as anything at the children's volition.

Many of the arguments given by the operatives in favor of the reduction of working hours in the late 1840s seem also to show their concern for their children, particularly if one admits that most of them did realize that it would bring with it a reduction in their wages. Thus "thinks she has been long enough away from her children when she has been away 10 hours"; "much better for her children being with them in the evening"; "he now has the pleasure of being more with his children, and seeing to their general wants and comforts."

For when the children worked, parents seem typically to have treated them with as much concern as was possible, given the underlying need that they should work at all. Thus from the same source: "has several children employed in the factories, and is thankful to have their labor limited to 10 hours." There are several cases in the literature where parents who thought their children's health was being injured by factory work quickly moved them to other employment which they believed would be less arduous.

There is also considerable evidence to suggest that bonds of affection were particularly strong between *mothers* and their children, which seems to reflect both the greater role of the mother in the life of the child and also the fact that it was she above all who made sacrifices for her children and she who protected them from their father. She, in turn, therefore seems to have received from them affection and gratitude. The segregated conjugal roles which seem to have been typical of these families are probably also important here. Thus, while at weekends "the men and single women really make holiday . . . the married women, who seem the slaves of Lancashire society, are then, however, obliged to set to work harder than ever . . ." to do shopping and housework. This pattern seems to have been typical, and applied to child care too, though some husbands, particularly in times of crisis, did help out in these tasks. More usually, however, in critical times, the mother seems to have taken over complete control. "I have sometimes thought that a family undergoing such a trial [unemployment] is like a crew at sea, short of provisions, with a limited allowance meted out day by day. Here it is the wife that is captain, she is provider and distributor. The husband under such circumstances commonly leaves all to her, and right nobly does she discharge her part. . . ." Another contemporary comment is also worthy of note: "An observation constantly made by the medical men, that the parents have lost their health much more generally than the children, and particularly that the mothers, who most of all starve themselves, have got pale and emaciated. . . ."

I have already noted that drunk and cruel fathers caused considerable distress to many children. Where they occurred, wife beatings, desertions of the family, adulterous relationships, and other misdeeds on the part of the father must often have further influenced the attitude of children to him, particularly if the children had to some extent identified and developed a strong bond with the mother. Cases or general descriptions of such activities abound in the literature, though it is impossible to know how widespread they were. A London case is perhaps particularly interesting since it shows the operation of the mother-child bond under such circumstances: "Sometimes he illtreats me. If he don't with his hand, I know he does with his tongue. He has the most dreadfullest tongue ever heard of. He drinks very hard. He's drunk whenever he's the money to be so. . . . I can assure you I have been obliged to live upon my two shillings. . . . I have, indeed, sir, a very hard time of it. I'm ready to run away, and leave it very often. If it wasn't for my children, I should do it." It is not surprising that for many it was the case that "should the mother die . . . her little ones weep indeed, as their only friend is gone."

In sum, then, the balance of the evidence on my interpretation suggests that to the best of their ability most working-class mothers do seem to have been affectionate and to have done what they saw as the best for their children while they were young and that young children will have perceived this as being the case. Many fathers, too, were similarly much loved and appreciated, though some were feared as intolerant or as heavy drinkers. I shall suggest later that it may have been above all the children of these parents who sought to terminate relationships with their families, but it seems unlikely that in general the attitudes and behavior of adolescent and adult children towards their parents can simply be attributed to excessive ill treatment while the children were young.

Sidney Pollard

THE IMPROVEMENT
OF LIVING STANDARDS
IN SHEFFIELD AFTER 1850

Sheffield, a center of metallurgical production and light manufacturing in England, grew from 135,000 inhabitants in 1851 to 324,000 by 1891. In this selection, written by Sidney Pollard, an economic historian who teaches at the University of Sheffield, we see the town government attempting slowly to come to terms with the results of intensive migration. Pollard analyzes changes in workers' life-styles as their incomes rose and as physical conditions improved during the second half of the nineteenth century.

The Beginnings of Sanitary Reform

. . . Sanitary provisions failed to keep pace with the growing population, and the nadir in the sanitary condition of Sheffield was reached in the 1860s. Only after the turning-point of the early 1870s were more vigorous steps taken to improve the state of health in urban areas, furthered by a growing specialist medical and sanitary staff.

The staff was not yet a large one, even in 1893, for a town of a third of a million inhabitants, but while in 1864–65 the expenditure on the Health Department's activities was under £450, it reached £50,000 in 1893–94. . . . The Public Health Act of 1872, passed when the fear of the cholera still stalked the country, was the signal for major reforms. In 1872–73, the Nuisance Department was reorganized and the staff enlarged, a Medical Officer of Health [M.O.H.] and a Public Analyst were appointed and other reforms followed in rapid succession.

Up to the 1870s, middle-class opinion was hostile to expenditure on sanitary improvements. In 1860 the Town Council resolved "that it is not expedient at the present time to consider the most efficient means of improving the sanitary condition of the Borough," and the Sheffield Vestry refused to spend £15,000 on sewers. In 1864 the Town Council refused a request of the Sheffield Burial Board for a

From Sidney Pollard, *A History of Labour in Sheffield* (Liverpool: Liverpool University Press, 1959), pp. 93–95, 96–101, 102–104, 105–110, 111–117, 119, 122–124, 339–340. Reprinted by permission of the publisher.

sum of £15,000 for the site of a new cemetery, and in 1865 it was induced only by strong pressure from the Local Government Board to adopt the Nuisances Removal Act of 1855 with its Amendments of 1860 and 1863, and to sanction a main drainage scheme, though it rejected a more ambitious, and more costly, rival scheme which promised more permanent benefits. Further by-laws to prevent nuisances from accumulations of refuse were also passed, though the Report of the Medical Officer of Health of the Privy Council of that year still noted large gaps in the local by-laws.

The depths to which Sheffield had sunk is evidenced by the comprehensive surveys made by the *Sheffield Independent* in 1872. . . .

In the Park, according to the survey of 1872, things had become worse in the past two decades; the newly erected terraces in the Eyre Street area had added yet another vile slum quarter to the town; St. Peter's Ward, the shopping center, was "but a scattered midden" behind imposing frontages; worst, perhaps, were the quarters around West Bar and St. Philip's Road, where respectable artisans tried to preserve the decencies of life in intolerable conditions. On and on went the reporter, from the filthy dens of expanding Brightside to the "crofts" near the parish church, with their "swarming courts, so full of life as sewers are of rats, nay more so, and quite as foul." Virtually everywhere the picture was essentially the same: working-class families struggling to lead decent lives in conditions of unimaginable dirt and neglect.

The first report of the Medical Officer of Health for 1873 claimed that the ending of the small-pox epidemic of 1871–72 was due largely to better cleansing and greater vigilance on the part of the health committee and to vaccination, but warned that "many of the dwellings of the poor are unfit for them . . . whole families, without regard to sex or age, the single and the married are promiscuously mingled. . . . Personal midnight and other inspections lead to the conclusion, that so long as such dangerous conditions continue to exist, there is danger to the community." . . .

A really effective combined sewage system was decided on only in January 1884. The drainage of the town was brought up to a uniform standard, and the new sewage works at Blackburn Meadows filtered the sewage before discharging it into the rivers, using the principles of lime precipitation. The works, which ultimately cost £195,000, were completed in 1886. . . .

The survey of December 1883 showed considerable improvement

on previous inquiries. There were still insanitary areas, filthy and neglected, but the significant fact was that they no longer extended over the whole of the working-class residential quarters, but had been driven back to a few districts only: the Crofts, Smithfield, Cotton Mill Walk, Pond Hill, the Park, Westbar and Green Lane. This remained the main achievement of the period 1850–93; it was substantiated by the systematic survey contained in the Report on the Sheffield Small-pox Epidemic of 1887–88. . . .

There was much progress in other matters affecting health. The paving of streets was taken seriously in hand and from 1877 onward the Town Council undertook the extension of paving to all main roads. Even the undedicated streets, numbering 510 out of the 1,343 in the borough in that year, began to receive attention. Under clause 150 of the Public Health Act of 1875 the corporation could deal with the worst of them as nuisances, and the control of the corporation over them was steadily extended; between 1882 and 1893 about 12¾ miles of private streets were dedicated, and a further 6 miles were in process of dedication in 1893.

In the campaign for pure food, several successful prosecutions of vendors of unwholesome meat were instituted in the 1860s, but in 1865 the Chief Sanitary Inspector considered the inspection of cattle unnecessary. Ironically enough, the cattle plague reached Sheffield three months later, and the Mayor had to close the market for beasts for six weeks. In the same year, the Town Council refused to prosecute in cases of openly admitted adulteration of flour with alum. From 1872 on, however, the sanitary staff undertook these prosecutions and the inspection of meat. A list of foodstuffs condemned as unfit in 1875 included 96 carcasses, 493 other pieces of meat, 106 tubs and baskets of fish and 318 lots of fruit and vegetables. In 1886 the M.O.H. obtained powers to close the worst slaughter-houses and to force drastic improvements on others by a system of licensing, registration and inspection.

Epidemic diseases, which furnished perhaps the main impetus to sanitary reform, were themselves still largely beyond the powers of medical science. Although endangering all social classes, they caused more deaths in the poorer and more overcrowded quarters, because of lack of sanitation and undernourishment. Throughout the period, the death rates in Sheffield from all zymotic diseases were among the highest in the country.

The water supply continued to be the subject of much complaint.

The West End received Company water only in 1864–65, Walkley and neighborhood in 1867–68 and Crookes in 1870–71. In 1864, the reluctant Water Company was forced to supply water for twelve hours per day, and in 1869 it preserved its independence only by undertaking to maintain a day and night supply. It was finally bought out in 1888, and by 1893 the total capacity was 20 million gallons per day, and two further reservoirs were then under construction, planned to increase the daily supply to 30 million gallons. The exceptional purity of the Sheffield water became a problem when it was discovered that the absence of lime was partly responsible for rickets and poor teeth in the town, while the water, if left to stand, tended to absorb lead from the pipes. Cases of lead poisoning, apparently from this cause, increased after 1887, and induced the Water Sub-Committee to add lime to the water in 1890.

The Gas Company, like the Water Company, was also often under fire from the consumers. The Corporation's attempts to purchase the works of the existing company in 1869–70 failed, but the price of gas was gradually reduced, while its use spread among the working classes. The 49,000 consumers of 1893 represented about three-quarters of all householders. The number of public gas lamps rose from 1,165 in 1853 to 6,301 in 1892, a sign that the poorer quarters had also begun to be illuminated.

The provision of public open spaces began with the Duke of Norfolk's gift of the "Park." Weston Park, of 12½ acres, bought in 1873, was the first municipal purchase. Two years later Firth Park, of 36 acres, was presented to the town, and between 1886 and 1890 Meersbrook Park, Endcliffe Woods and Hillsborough Park were purchased, with a combined area of 112 acres. By 1893 the Council also administered 7 recreation grounds, most of which were in closely built-up areas, and it resolved in 1891 to turn part of the land acquired under the Housing of the Working Classes Act, 1890, into open spaces in the poor and congested areas of the town.

The combined effects of all these improvements were seen in the slow, long-term fall of the death rate in Sheffield. Statistics of the crude death rate and of infant mortality are given in Table 1. Infantile mortality remained high, well above the level of other large cities, and was not lowered until the turn of the century. Throughout the period almost one child in five died before reaching the age of twelve months, and about one in two died before reaching the age of five. Mortality was particularly high in the central districts, and among illegitimate children, whose mothers generally had to go out to work.

TABLE 1
Mortality Rates in Sheffield, 1861–95

Annual Average	Crude Death Rate (per 1,000 population)	Annual Average	Infantile Mortality Rate (deaths of children under one year per 1,000 births)
1861–65	27.4	1861–69	184
1866–70	27.4	1870–78	182
1871–75	26.8	1879–87	164
1876–80	24.2	1888–93	180
1881–85	21.6	—	—
1886–90	22.1	—	—
1891–95	20.9	—	—

General mortality rates showed a considerable improvement, but were still high compared with other areas. Taking the "corrected death rate" for England and Wales as 100, the Sheffield rate was 124 in 1874, 117 in 1885, 110 in 1886 and 129 in 1893. Yet the Sheffield rates for the age-groups 10–45 years was more favorable than those for England, perhaps owing to the large number of immigrants.

In 1865, the average expectation of life in Sheffield was given as 17 years for the "working classes," 25 for the "middle classes" and 33 for the "wealthy classes." In part, the high rates of mortality were accounted for by the unhealthy nature of some of the local trades; but in large measure they were caused by insanitary living conditions. The differences, shown in Table 2, between the central town-

TABLE 2
Mortality in Sheffield, by Districts, 1858–90

	Deaths per 1,000			Infant Mortality Rate	
	1858	Av. 1861–87	Av. 1888–90	Av. 1861–87	Av. 1888–90
Sheffield West		25.6	30.4	204	217
Sheffield North	30.4	25.4	29.2	199	218
Sheffield South		24.8	25.0	188	218
Sheffield Park		25.4	25.1	185	192
Brightside	25.7	23.1	21.6	172	183
Attercliffe	26.4	22.0	21.1	173	203
Heeley	22.3	20.5	18.8	161	160
Nether Hallam	20.8				
Ecclesall	24.1	20.1	19.8	155	150
Upper Hallam	21.4	16.4	12.0	113	67

ship and the newer working-class quarters, Brightside, Attercliffe and Heeley, were remarkable enough; still more striking was the correlation between mortality and sanitary conditions found in investigations of smaller districts. In the special areas reported on under the Artizans' Dwelling scheme, for example, the death rate was 35.3 per thousand in 1876, compared with 24.2 for the Borough as a whole.

Working-Class Housing

When the building of "back-to-backs" was prohibited by by-law in 1864, 38,000 houses of that type were in existence, forming the typical working-class dwelling. They did allow most families to live in separate houses, but were bound to be overcrowded in the case of large families or where lodgers were taken in. In 1891, the bulk of the working classes lived in tenements of three or four rooms, which accounted for 32,864 out of the total of 67,501 enumerated in the town in 1891; there were 6 persons or more in 4,941 of the three-roomed tenements, and in 5,221 of the four-roomed tenements. In smaller tenements overcrowding was worse: there were, for example, 4 persons or more in 64 one-roomed tenements and in 1,794 two-roomed tenements. The average number of persons per house had remained unchanged at 4.8, and was lower than in most other industrial towns.

Gas lighting was found in many working-class homes by 1893, but water was still obtained chiefly from standpipes in the yards, and few sitting-room floors had wooden boards as yet in place of stone paving. Only in 1888 were by-laws submitted which specified in some detail the materials to be used and laid down some elementary rules on the style and quality of building.

There were several wealthy landowners who developed their property themselves, generally in the form of "estates" for which certain minimum building standards were laid down, but these were accessible to middle-class lessees only. About 1870 the bulk of the working-class dwellings was owned in blocks of from 10 to 50 houses, representing investments of between £1,000 and £10,000, made by tradesmen, publicans and men of like status. These were the landlords who could least afford repairs and improvements. The owners of the large new firms in the "East End," in contrast with those in nearby villages and towns, did not apparently engage in building for their immigrant workers. House ownership by building societies was negligible. . . .

In years of high earnings, some families moved into better-class houses, and returned to the slums in depressions. Rents showed little short-term fluctuations, but rose substantially over the period 1850–93, most of the rise occurring in the exceptional boom conditions of the early 1870s, when many rents went up by as much as 50 percent. They did not fall again very far in the following depression, and a slow increase continued until 1893. The typical rents of 2s. 6d. to 3s. per week for a "back-to-back" in a poor district and 3s. 6d. per week for a better working-class house, had risen to 3s.–3s. 6d. for the former and 5s. for the latter in the period between 1873 and 1893.

The first important housing act, the Cross Act of 1875, permitting re-housing by local authorities, found a quick public response in Sheffield. As a result of a memorial presented to the M.O.H. in November 1875, a subcommittee of the Town Council instituted an inquiry into a large area stretching from the parish church to St. Philip's Road and St. George's Square, and containing much of the poorest property in Sheffield. The inquiry was opposed on account of its cost by prominent citizens like Ald. Clegg and Ald. Carr, while the M.O.H. insinuated that the scheme had been proposed by slum property owners in order to obtain high compensation premiums; but it could not be stopped, and the report was published in the summer of 1877. Although the area was not the worst in the town (sectors of the Park and Sheffield South showed higher death rates), and within it some areas were much better than others, its statistics made grim reading. The population density was 182 per acre, rising in one subdistrict to 261. There was one privy to 11.8 persons and 2.8 houses, and one privy in four was in an offensive condition. Well over two-thirds of the houses had no back doors and almost two-thirds no back windows. Most of the cellars were damp, and although these were not inhabited, they were used for keeping foodstuffs and live-stock. In addition to its 23,261 persons, the area contained 112 horses, 60 cows, 12 asses, 211 pigs, 336 dogs and 844 heads of poultry. Despite the pressure by the public and the Local Government Board, the report was not followed up by any action.

In the following years the attitude of the public towards housing reform was greatly changed, and the response of local authorities to the Act of 1890, was far more positive than that to the Act of 1875. A conference on the "Housing of the Poor in Sheffield," held on 28th May 1889 and attended mainly by workingmen and ministers of religion, led to the formation of a permanent committee and ultimately to the establishment of the "Sheffield Association for the Better Housing of the Poor," which received wide public support. At a public meeting of the Association on 8th October 1889, W. C. Leng, the influential editor of the Conservative *Sheffield Telegraph* proposed from the chair to curb the jerry-builder and facilitate the buying of houses by working men, and declared that "rotten houses and houses falling into decay should be taken by the local authority and demolished without compensation."

A special subcommittee of the Town Council, set up to deal with the housing of the poor, attempted to delay action, but the hands of the M.O.H. had been greatly strengthened by the Act of 1890 and by its public support. He began almost at once to condemn the worst houses as unfit for human habitation, and in September 1892, as a result of a rate-payers' petition, he started an inquiry into the condition of the "Crofts" which had formed part of the area investigated in 1876–77. This was to lead to the Corporation's first slum-clearance and housing scheme, sanctioned in 1894. . . .

The Rise in the Standards of Comfort

Improvements in general housing were slow and marginal only, because of the deadweight of existing buildings. By contrast, standards of consumption of less durable goods could be raised fairly rapidly. There is little doubt that the real earnings of the working classes showed a substantial improvement in the half-century ending in the mid-nineties, despite rising rents, wider fluctuations of trade, and the apparent growth in the number of the very poor in the large cities.

The skilled man, in particular, had been the gainer:

> *The home of a steady, skilled and fortunate artizan would bear comparison with that of the lamented yeoman of old times.* Mutatis mutandis, *the conscious wants are about as well met, and there is therefore progress, as the mechanic of one hundred years ago was worse off than a yeoman. Unstinted food, clothes of the same pattern as the middle class, when house rents permit, a tidy parlor, with stiff, cheap furniture which, if not itself luxurious or beautiful, is a symptom of the luxury of self-respect, and an earnest of better taste to come, a newspaper, a club, an occasional holiday, perhaps a musical instrument—these represent the nineteenth-century equivalent to the yeoman's pony, shining pewter, bits of ancestral oak, and homespun napery. . . . The prosperous operative is better off in comparison with the unprosperous middle-class man than ever before.*

The extent of the gains of the Sheffield trades, made up of skilled men or men in rapidly expanding industries, may be judged from the year-by-year statistics collected in Table 3, Appendix B.[1] Improvement was slow until the middle 1870s, when rising prices absorbed most of the increases in wages. The rise in real incomes was largely concentrated in the following twenty years, the period of the so-called "Great Depression," when prices had a downward tendency. Local price statistics show that the fall in prices was particularly marked in the case of imported foodstuffs, like grain and colonial products, while mainly home-produced food, like meat, milk, butter and eggs showed no price fall and in some cases continued to increase in price.

Working-class spending power may also be measured in a slightly different way. Several local working-class budgets in this period show an expenditure of 60 percent of income on the main irreducible necessities, distributed in the following proportions:

	%
Bread	10
Flour	2
Milk	3
Meat	15
Clothing	12
Coal	5
Rent (incl. rates)	13
	60

These items represent bare necessities; the remaining 40 percent of incomes were spent largely on goods and services with strong seasonal fluctuations (vegetables, fruit) or varying with the composition of the family (education), or else most easily reduced in hard times. Changes in the residual 40 percent may thus measure more clearly the worker's freedom of action than changes in "net earnings," much of which is mortgaged on irreducible regular expenditure. The index of this residuum showed a rise of 40–50 percent from the early fifties to the early seventies (taking the good years with the bad), which was larger than the rise in prices and represented a genuine increase in standards; it remained constant in the face of

---

[1] Reprinted at the end of this selection.—Eds.

falling prices after 1873, continuing, in effect, the upward trend. This index thus tends to confirm the rise in living standards in 1850–93.

Though the typical Sheffield artisan fed well, the proportion of his income spent on food remained between 52 percent and 60 percent throughout the period; this may be compared, for example, with Miss Mackenzie's reconstructed representative budgets which show the proportion spent on food by the median family as 67 percent in 1860 and 61 percent in 1880. The comparison shows the relatively high standards of living of Sheffield workmen, since a high proportion of expenditure on food is generally taken to be a sign of poverty.

Within the food budgets, the high level of expenditure on meat stands out as another sign of relative comfort, though men doing heavy work are likely to forgo other necessities to have a minimum of meat. In 1878 the American Consul complained that it was chiefly the "ignorant poor" who were prejudiced against American fresh and tinned meats and insisted on good English meat, while the "better and more intelligent classes" were glad to avail themselves of the cheaper alternative. Sheffield workmen, he reported in 1876, "spend their money freely on meats of the best quality, and the general appearance of the working-men is that of a well-nourished and vigorous people." The author of the S.P.C.K.'s[2] volume on Sheffield, published in 1864, believed that workmen did not stint themselves on food: "It is he (the brawny broad-shouldered man of the forge) who buys the early peas, the winter salads, the first asparagus . . . and it is the aristocrat of labor—the workman who earns his three or four guineas a week, and *spends it all*—that carries off the fattest capon, the plumpest goose and the biggest turkey the market affords."

These descriptions, if based on fact, could have applied to the highly paid head melters, rollers or forgemen only. The working-class housewife normally bought cheap, made-up dishes, like sausages and "ducks," but in this respect the period 1850–93 also saw a number of improvements. Imported food began to offer wholesome alternatives to expensive home-grown products; Free Trade reduced prices of sugar, tea and other foreign products; adulteration of foods and medicines began to be suppressed by the local authority; and high retail margins and incompetent shopkeeping were, to some extent, circumvented by the formation of cooperative retail societies.
. . .

[2] Society for Promoting Christian Knowledge.—Eds.

The rising standards of comfort were also seen in furniture and furnishings. By the middle 1860s, the top ranks of the skilled local artisans had become used to carpets and wallpaper; a few men even boasted a piano, pictures or statuettes, while "a well-stuffed haircloth sofa, and chairs to correspond, are considered indispensable." By 1893 most of these comforts and luxuries had become diffused among all but the poorest in the unskilled and sweated trades. Perhaps the most notable additions were floor coverings and curtains. In the middle 1890s, linoleum was about 2s. per yard, carpets were 1s. to 4s. per yard and rooms could be covered with reasonable "Brussels squares" for £2 to £3. The flock or feather bed had ousted the palliasse; cheap sofas or couches were found in every home and chairs covered in leather were becoming popular. Sewing-machines (at about £4) and pianos (at £11 to £30) could be bought by instalment payments (as could, indeed, other furniture) and pictures and ornaments, clocks and china, testified to a substantial rise in the freely available margin of expenditure.

There was also a larger margin for savings and provision for sickness and old age. Deposits in the Sheffield Savings Bank increased from £356,000 in 1860 to £1,161,000 in 1890, and the proportion of artisans among the depositors remained high: in 1890, a brief count of the first 100 depositors revealed 36 artisans and 7 artisans' wives.

In 1855, there were 66 lodges of friendly societies with a total of over 9,000 members returned for Sheffield, the majority in national societies like the Manchester Unity of Oddfellows (15 lodges, 1,287 members) and the Ancient Order of Foresters (17 lodges, over 1,187 members). The largest local societies were the Park Free Gift (225 members) and the Royal Jubilee (189 members). By 1891 membership had greatly increased, and local societies alone had grown from 2,100 members in 1855 to well over 7,000, while the Sheffield Independent Druids, who broke away from the Ancient Order in 1892, had nearly 14,000 members in the area in 1893. The local membership of national societies cannot be established with any accuracy. Workmen were also able to increase their contributions to local hospitals. The average annual sums contributed by trade unions and shop collectors in the years 1890–93 were £1,787 in the case of the Royal Infirmary, £258 in the case of the Jessop Hospital and £767 (in 1889–90) in the case of the Royal Hospital. With insignificant exceptions, these sums were found by men in the staple trades.

The secular improvement did not detract from the urgency of the distress during the prolonged depressions. To some extent, the wide fluctuations of earnings were neutralized by parallel changes in the cost of living: thus, it was stated in 1879, "the chief necessities of life are cheap and abundant, or the sufferings of the working classes would be intense"; and in 1885, "the unusual cheapness of living has had much to do with the extent of pleasuring (at Whitsun), going far in a vast number of cases to counterbalance the diminution in wages, and so leave a surplus for out-door recreation." Similarly, high prices often absorbed the high earnings of boom years, and while the wage increase often remained in the hands of the men, the housewife had to manage an unchanged budget on higher prices. But, on the whole working-class real incomes tended to be severely reduced in depressions and, conversely, rose in prosperous years, with the possible exception of the period near the turning point of the trade cycle, when the rise in prices may have temporarily overtaken the rise in earnings.

Unemployment had lost little of its terror by the end of the century. The skilled craftsman, who had lived near the limits of subsistence in 1850, had a margin out of which he could build up savings to withstand short periods of unemployment in the 1890s, but by that time a whole new army of laborers and others with little specialized skill had been created in the heavy industries. These men had no margin of expenditure, no trade-union funds, and no hope of partial employment such as was common in the light trades in 1850. . . .

From 1874 onward depressions became more prolonged. In January 1877, after three years of decline, soup kitchens were started again, and by January 1878 a distress fund had distributed £4,700, while the Duke of Norfolk spent £3,500 on relief works on his estate. The distress of the following winter exceeded all previous experience: a new relief fund spent £12,000, and it was stated that some departments in the East End had averaged little more than one day's work per week for some years. Soup and bread issues to poor children were continued even in the winter of 1880–81.

In 1884–85 pauperism was once more on the increase, and in the winter of 1885-86 all the tragic scenes of the winter six or seven years before were reenacted. A new relief fund was started in February 1886. From details published at the time, it appears that of those relieved on the second day of the fund's operation, 26 of the breadwinners were in the heavy staple trades, 60 in the light staple trade, 76 in the building trades, 9 in other skilled occupations and 437 were "laborers and unspecified."

Even without the Goschen Poor Law Minute of 1869, which urged the Guardians to relieve "general cases" and leave special cases to private charity, the Poor Law would have been utterly unsuited to cope with the new type of mass unemployment which appeared from 1874 onward. The Chamberlain Circular of 1886, which encouraged Guardians to apply a labor test by setting able-bodied paupers to work on roads or other municipal contracts in times of depression, caused rates to rise at the most difficult times. In practice, the unemployed came to depend increasingly on distress funds, raised and administered by voluntary effort, and on relief works, undertaken by the authorities which were under strong pressure from organized labor, represented by the Trades Council, and from *ad hoc* bodies delegated by public meetings of the unemployed. There were also the permanent private charities, which disposed of about £15,400 p.a. in 1873–75 and £34,500 p.a. in 1895, of which about £10,600 and £23,500 respectively were available for "public uses and the poor." These local methods, gradually evolved by experience, were applied with little change in the winters of 1887–88, 1890–91 and 1892–93.

Educational Reform and Working-Class Culture

Education for the children of the poor changed little between 1850 and 1870; the Education Act of 1870, establishing the principle of general and compulsory elementary education, formed the watershed. It raised at once the age at which children could be put to work, and, as a long-term effect, it abolished illiteracy, which had by no means disappeared in the second half of the century.

The searching inquiries into the school provisions within the borough which preceded and followed the Act of 1870 showed that school accommodation was grossly inadequate, and that a considerable proportion of schools was inefficient, both in respect of the teaching and the buildings and equipment.

According to the report on the elementary schools in the town compiled by J. F. Moss, the Clerk to the Sheffield School Board, in March 1871, the majority of the grant-aided schools and those maintained by the denominations consisted of schools of reasonable standard; of the 50 "private adventure" schools charging fees, like the "dame schools," 33 were condemned as inefficient. Joseph

Beeley, Master at the Collegiate School, who had inspected 24 dame schools, reached similar conclusions in his report to the School Board in the same month. Accommodation was almost invariably unsuitable and cramped, and "the teachers are mostly persons who have had no training in the art of teaching, but who have taken upon themselves the responsibility of communicating to others what they themselves never knew." Some of the teachers, added the *Sheffield Independent*, were found incapable of spelling two-syllable words.

The total number of school places available was 31,000, of which about 25,000 were filled. But of those 25,000 scholars, nearly 8,000 were outside the normal school age of 5–13 years, and only about 20,000 attended regularly. The total population of school age was 40,000–41,000 so that less than half the number of children of school age actually attended any sort of day school. Even if all the existing accommodation could be used for scholars of school age, there would still remain an estimated deficiency of between 8,000 and 11,000 places, spread unevenly between the parishes. Other inquiries showed broadly similar results. The Rev. F. Watkins, for example, estimated in 1872 that only 43 percent of the working-class children attended efficient schools.

After the election of the first Sheffield School Board, fought on religious and sectarian lines, the expansion of school facilities was remarkably rapid. By adaptation of existing buildings, by the temporary requisitioning of chapels and by much building on its own account, the School Board realized its ambitions of providing education for all children of school age within a few years. By 1874, 9,000 school children had been accommodated in new schools, and between 1873 and 1892 the total numbers on the registers increased from 35,000 to 61,000, of whom nearly 35,000 were in Board schools, and the proportion of school attenders in Sheffield was higher than in most other industrial towns.

Almost from the first working-men took a considerable interest in the School Board. At the School Board election of 1879, the hours of voting were extended from 12 noon to 7 p.m., to permit working-class electors to record their vote, and in 1885 the "Sheffield Labour Association" succeeded in getting its candidate, W. H. Smith, elected to the Board. It was also agreed to hold meetings in the evenings and elections on Saturdays, to facilitate participation by working-men.

The importance of the activities of the School Board for the future welfare of the working classes lay not exclusively in the field of education. Out of the experience of men connected with the education of the children of the poor arose the first beginnings of several present-day social services.

Thus, in March and again in September 1873, the Clerk to the Board had to draw attention to the influence of poverty and the lack of sufficient clothing on school attendance, and the School Board began to act as a voluntary agency for collecting clothing for poor children. It established regular medical inspection from 1873 onwards, it encouraged Penny Banks in the schools, and in 1884 the first school was permitted to supply "penny" dinners for poor children for one or two days per week. These dinners were, apparently, suspended during the following years, but in 1890 half-penny dinners were again started at the Crofts School. In the winter of 1893–94, about 800 children were provided with bread and soup by the N.S.P.C.C.,[3] and some schools also provided breakfasts and dinners.

The Sheffield Board was one of the first to establish a Central High School in 1880, to which the most promising children of elementary schools could be sent, with Board scholarships, if required, to be taught ordinary subjects at higher levels or technical subjects connected with local industries, or to be trained as teachers. On the other hand, it compromised on the question of releasing children under the age of 13 for work, and the working-men on the Board were among those who favored early release to increase the family income, at the expense of the children's education.

Adult education remained the concern of voluntary bodies, but much of the original enthusiasm, which had brought into being the People's College and the Mechanics' Institute, was lost. The People's College closed in 1879 and the Mechanics' Institute was wound up in 1897, handing over its stock and balance to provide scholarships at the University College for "persons of the artisan or laboring classes."

The fate of these two institutions illustrates the tendency away from the ideal of a liberal education which had inspired much of the earlier adult working-class education movement, and towards purely technical education, making individuals more efficient at their trade, while accepting the broad framework of their society. The former had rested largely on the workmen's unaided efforts; technical education, on the other hand, attracted considerable support from employers,

[3] National Society for the Prevention of Cruelty to Children.—Eds.

especially those who had reason to fear foreign competitors and who required increasing skill and artistic or technical training from their workmen. Liberal adult education for the general public was limited to the Adult School, founded by James Barber and to the University Extension lectures, started early in 1876, which had few working-class students.

By contrast, technical instruction, in its wider sense, made great strides. An inquiry by the School Board in 1871 showed that in addition to the colleges noted above and the School of Art (the College of Arts and Crafts) several denominational schools prepared students for examination by the Science and Art Department. In 1874 the Board itself inaugurated evening science classes. Those held at the Central School attracted a growing number of artisans and apprentices, and in 1886 these were transferred to a new technical school which became, in 1897, part of the new University College. Following the Technical Instruction Act of 1889, a substantial grant from the Town Council permitted the number of evening classes in technical subjects, particularly at higher levels, to be increased while the fees were reduced. By the end of the century, therefore, the means of working-men for obtaining technical or vocational instruction had been considerably improved, though most of the advances had been made in the last decade only.

The Free Library, steadily expanding in scope, found in 1861 that 89 percent of its membership worked in the staple light and heavy industries. Branch libraries were opened in the growing working-class suburbs (Upperthorpe, 1869; Brightside, 1872; Highfields, 1876; Attercliffe, 1894) in the following years. Other institutes and schools as well as private foundations, such as the Working-men's Reading Room in Snig Hill, opened in 1866, also offered facilities for cheap reading.

The foundation of the Walkley Museum by Ruskin's Guild of St. George deserves special mention. John Ruskin, on his brief visit to the town in 1875, had been much impressed by the wide opportunities for artistic craftsmanship still preserved in the local trades, and affirmed that "it is fitting that of the schools [of St. George] for the workmen and laborers of England, the first should be placed at Sheffield." The Guild's communal farm established near Sheffield was a failure, but the Museum, erected at Walkley "in order to entice workmen out of the smoke to study in a country retreat," and housing works of art as well as objects illustrating natural history, gained much support and helped to discover at least one local artist in the person of Benjamin Creswick, a grinder. It was transferred to the Corporation's Meersbrook Park in 1890.

The payment of wages in public-houses declined after the 1860s, but the growing number of men in the heavy trades, who lost much moisture during working hours by heavy perspiration, maintained the local tradition of drinking ale at work, since it was held that any other beverage, drunk in the necessary quantities, would be physically harmful. The public-house itself, Ald. Wm. Fisher told the Select Committee on the Sale of Liquors in 1867, became on weekday evenings a study and newsroom to the working-man, where he could talk politics and discuss other matters not of interest to his wife and children; and during Sundays and holidays the inns of the vicinity formed the necessary resting-places for the Sheffielders who undertook, generation after generation, long walks into the beautiful countryside surrounding their town. The number of public-houses per head of population showed a slight increase in this period, but excessive drunkenness was on the wane. This was attested both by the number of apprehensions for drunkenness and, more significantly, by the evidence of independent observers. The Public House Licensing Act of 1864 was adopted in 1865, but there was a large popular majority against restriction of what was considered a legitimate form of recreation for working-men.

There are many indications to show that the influence of religion on working-class lives was increasing in this period. Sunday-schools, catering for about half of the children of school age, recruited new members for their faiths from the working classes; the efforts of the Christian Socialists, the failure of secular Utopian hopes of salvation, the deliberate wooing of the working-man by the churches, and the acceptance of "respectable" workmen as equals within their congregations, all favored this development. Increasingly, workmen were to be found acting as class leaders, lay preachers or other officers. . . .

Attendance at places of worship changed little between 1851 and 1881. According to the "religious census" organized in November by the *Sheffield Independent*, 31 percent of the population attended divine services, exactly the same proportion as in 1851. The distribution among the denominations also showed no major changes, except for a significant loss of the Wesleyans to other Methodists, and the rise of the Salvation Army. . . .

Among the energetic outdoor recreations of the Sheffield workman were cross-country running, cricket and football. At Whitsun and on many Sundays, local workmen took their families to Grimsby, to the Dukeries, to Wharncliffe Crags or into Derbyshire by special train. "A great many of the population of Sheffield have been born in the villages around. The town is ugly and smoky, and the country is exceedingly beautiful about, and they pour out on foot, and by railway, and in vehicles in very great numbers."

Gardening became more restricted as the town spread outwards, though strangers from other industrial areas, like Edward Baines, were still impressed in the 1860s by its extent. "Everywhere in my youth," confessed a blade forger and noted amateur gardener, born in 1844, "you found workmen's gardens, but the builder has swept them away, and the increasing smoke and dirt have discouraged many flower-growers from continuing the hard fight in the gardens." In 1890 the Town Council decided to give support to the Duke of Norfolk who had turned 89 acres into 852 garden allotments and was preparing 50 acres for 300 more.

For indoor recreation there were the Music-hall in Surrey Street, the Theatre Royal and Alexandra Theatre with 2,000 and 4,000 seats respectively, all in existence before 1850, and the more recent Variety Theatre in West Bar and Sangers and Stacey's Circuses. There were also the Working-men's Clubs, of which the first was formed in 1866. . . .

The Growth of "Respectability"

A cursory examination of some aspects of social changes in Sheffield between 1850 and 1893 may slur over one important development which colored them all; the growth of what, for want of a better term, may be called "respectability" among the working classes. This phenomenon has often been noted, not least by the economists who discussed the rise in material standards of living, and it was clearly evident in Sheffield, even though in Sheffield the lack of "respectability," or the social gulf which divided Disraeli's two nations, was far less marked before 1850 than in most other industrial areas of Britain.

"Respectability" meant, essentially, the approximation of working-class codes of behavior to those of the middle classes. "The most repulsive thing here," lamented Friedrich Engels in 1889, "is the bourgeois 'respectability' which has grown deep into the bones of the workers." In the first half of the century, trade unions, co-operatives and other organizations expressed the working-man's hostility to his environment and its ideal of individualistic competition; within the following generation he had come to accept the dominant ideals of individual self-help. At the basis of this change lay undoubtedly the material opportunity of doing so, now that working-men were, for the first time, escaping from the "iron law of wages," which had kept wages down to subsistence levels.

After 1850, the wages of most men in the staple trades were above those levels for long periods. The opportunities of saving, of moving into better houses, of appearing in public in decent clothing, even of buying books or newspapers, became open to many. At the same time education and political rights opened up further opportunities of individual advancement. Working-class thinkers could cease to attack the "system" and advise instead how to make the best of it; the great mass of their fellows adapted themselves, perhaps less consciously, but with equal ease.

The change was seen even in outward appearances. The dress and bearing of working-men and their wives were less distinct from those of the middle classes in 1893 than in 1850. The gap in health and expectation of life had narrowed, and the same might be said of housing and sanitation.

In the field of attitudes towards social status, the change was greater still. In 1824 enrollment in the Mechanics' Library was a failure at first, because application forms could be had only at banks, newspaper offices and "other respectable institutions." "Do you suppose," wrote one workman indignantly to a local paper, "that we should have the presumption, or impudence or hardihood, or any other term equally harsh, to enter such places?" When the forms were sent to local employers instead, 140 members enrolled. By the end of the century, working-men had not only become used to visiting Savings Banks and Post Offices as investors, but also Building Societies, and, if they were trade secretaries, perhaps even commercial banks. Before 1850, they entered politics as a class apart, feared and despised by the middle classes; by 1893, working men sat on the Town Council and on the School Board as respected members of the existing parties, and they were demanding places on the bench of magistrates. The religious congregations and educational institutions accepted them into leading positions, and official government inquiries listened to their evidence with courtesy and respect.

Contemporaries noted evidence of greater sobriety and responsibility, "better" behavior in public and more moderate views on political questions. Women in local industries devoted more care to their children and their homes than formerly. Ideas on family limitation began to spread for the first time, and medical assistance came within easier reach of working-men. The distribution of the family budget became less capricious, while the support for friendly societies and hospitals grew out of recognition. Although Sheffield workmen had started from a much better position in 1850 than most others, the progress made even in their town within little more than a generation was substantial.

APPENDIX B

TABLE 3
Wages and Earnings in the Sheffield Trades, 1851–1914[a]
(Index, 1900 = 100)

		Light Trades		Heavy Trades		Sheffield Trades	
	Cost of Living	Money Earnings	Real Earnings	Money Earnings	Real Earnings	Money Earnings	Real Earnings
1851	100.5	78	78	71	71	77	77
1852	100.5	79	79	73	73	78	78
1853	107.6	82	76	77	72	81	75
1854	121.5	82	67	72	59	79	65
1855	125.1	80	64	72	58	79	63
1856	124.6	89	71	68	55	84	66
1857	119.0	88	74	75	63	86	72
1858	110.8	82	74	65	59	79	70
1859	109.7	82	75	65	59	78	71
1860	113.3	83	73	68	60	80	71
1861	115.9	75	65	73	63	74	64
1862	113.3	74	65	75	66	74	65
1863	110.3	75	68	79	72	76	69
1864	109.2	81	74	77	71	80	73
1865	110.3	89	81	84	76	87	79
1866	116.4	97	83	82	70	93	80
1867	122.6	91	74	75	61	87	71
1868	120.5	82	68	70	58	79	66
1869	115.9	83	72	78	67	81	70
1870	115.9	86	74	83	72	86	74
1871	116.4	100	86	89	76	97	83
1872	122.6	104	85	97	79	102	84
1873	123.6	100	81	104	84	101	82
1874	120.0	93	78	91	76	93	74
1875	116.4	87	75	86	74	86	74

TABLE 3 (*continued*)

	Cost of Living	Light Trades		Heavy Trades		Sheffield Trades	
		Money Earnings	Real Earnings	Money Earnings	Real Earnings	Money Earnings	Real Earnings
1876	114.4	83	73	82	72	82	74
1877	116.4	83	71	83	71	83	71
1878	114.4	83	73	72	63	80	70
1879	109.2	82	75	68	62	78	71
1880	112.3	83	74	79	70	82	73
1881	110.8	86	78	87	79	86	78
1882	111.3	92	83	93	84	93	84
1883	109.2	92	84	92	84	92	84
1884	107.2	81	76	85	79	82	76
1885	103.6	77	74	76	73	77	74
1886	100.5	76	76	68	68	73	73
1887	98.5	79	80	74	75	77	78
1888	98.5	83	84	77	78	80	81
1889	100.5	91	91	86	86	90	89
1890	100.5	93	93	90	90	92	91
1891	101.5	96	95	83	82	91	90
1892	101.5	88	88	72	71	82	81
1893	99.0	84	85	68	69	78	79
1984	97.4	86	88	73	75	81	83
1895	95.4	89	93	79	83	85	89
1896	94.9	98	103	86	91	93	98
1897	96.9	103	106	90	93	98	101
1898	98.5	98	99	94	95	97	98
1899	97.4	101	104	101	104	101	104
1900	100	100	100	100	100	100	100
1901	101.0	95	94	94	95	95	94
1902	102.0	93	91	86	84	90	88
1903	101.2	88	87	92	91	90	89
1904	101.2	85	84	87	86	86	85
1905	101.4	83	82	90	89	86	85
1906	101.2	90	89	97	96	93	92
1907	103.4	88	85	104	101	95	92
1908	104.6	84	80	90	86	87	83
1909	104.9	86	82	90	86	88	84
1910	105.7	93	88	101	96	97	92
1911	105.9	98	93	109	103	103	97
1912	109.8	104	95	114	104	109	99
1913	109.8	105	96	117	107	111	101
1914	111.5	102	91	111	100	107	96

[a] Based on S. Pollard, *Wages and Earnings in the Sheffield Trades, 1851–1914,* and *Real Earnings in Sheffield, 1851–1914.*

Hsi-Huey Liang

LOWER-CLASS IMMIGRANTS IN WILHELMINE BERLIN

Hsi-Huey Liang, Professor of History at Vassar College, here uses oral as well as written sources in order to describe the living conditions of the hordes of lower-class migrants who streamed into Berlin during the quarter century before World War I. His theme is their gradual adaptation to an environment which they found both threatening and attractive.

I

During the Second Empire, tens of thousands of poor people from East and West Prussia, Silesia, Pomerania, and Posen moved to Berlin every year.[1] They came primarily to improve their economic position. A large number of them were transient agricultural laborers who had been accosted by private employment agents in Berlin railway stations. Others were provincial craftsmen in declining trades who sought to start a new life in the city: for example the cigar-maker hoping to make enough money to buy a tobacco shop. Coming on the mere chance of a job, such men were likely to end up as anything from a coal carrier or hackdriver to kitchen help in the Charité hospital. Most of them became factory hands. Journeymen on the tramp who arrived on foot from as far as the Bohemian border were better off as far as job opportunities went. They had not as yet burned their bridges and could still move on with a small travel allowance from their guilds if nothing lucrative turned up in Berlin. But Berlin needed young locksmiths, turners, carpenters, molders, tinsmiths, and harnessmakers. (In 1905, 72 percent of the workers in Ludwig Loewe's machine-tool factory were immigrants from outside Berlin.) There were also those who became Berliners in the course of their military service: after two or three years of garrison duty in or near Berlin, a country boy often had no wish

From *Central European History* 3 (1970): 94-111. Copyright 1970 by Emory University. Reprinted by permission.

[1] The following article is an excerpt from a forthcoming study on "The Working People in Wilhelmine Berlin, 1890–1914." Much of the information was gathered in personal interviews with about one hundred twenty elderly Berlin workmen and workwomen, doctors, clergymen, teachers, trade union officials, welfare officers, and Social Democratic Party functionaries in 1953–54.

to renounce the "big-city life" and would go to great lengths to find a living there.

To enter the competitive labor market of modern industrial Berlin was a challenge. To be employed in one of its world-renowned firms was an honor.

> *Wer nie bei Mix und Genest war,*
> *bei Schwartzkopff, A. E. G. und Borsig,*
> *der kennt des Lebens Tücke nicht,*
> *der hat sie erst noch vor sich!*[2]

ran a proud ditty among the metal workers. The same went for people in the catering industry. There was no better way of perfecting one's education as a waiter or cook than working in one of Berlin's large eating places like Terrassen am Halensee, or even better, in an exclusive establishment like Weinhaus Kempinski. As for country girls in search of suitable employment, the move to the city was almost mandatory—house servants were in little demand in the provinces. Women were also willing to enter the garment industry, provided the recruiters from Berlin, as usual, had managed to pass over in silence its sweated condition.

Not that Berlin's attractions needed much recommending to the country poor. The capital was widely believed to pay the best wages in Germany and yet to be cheap to live in: a bridegroom's outfit for twenty-six marks, a tailor-made suit for fifty! True, the demands made by the city were correspondingly higher than in the village. People here dressed better, they spent more on entertainment and transportation, and for the newcomer there were the added initial outlays for the workers' hostel (*Penne*), the employment agency, and the trade-union membership card. But the amenities of city life were surely worth all this extra cost. Once you had a job and some pocket money to spare, you could enjoy the freedom of anonymity found only in the metropolis. There were theaters and museums, public libraries and evening lectures, the bioscopes and the panoramas, the zoo, and the glittering shops in Leipziger Strasse whose windows were a constant source of stimulation for new tastes and new wants. Even *Vorwärts,* one of the official organs of the Social Democratic Party (though admittedly not the most widely read paper among the workers), carried advertisements for dance halls and variety shows: Ostbahnpark,

[2] He who has never worked for Mix and Genest,/For Schwartzkopff, A. E. G., and Borsig/ Doesn't know the trick of life/ And still has much to learn!—Eds.

Prater, Wintergarten. Department stores bought up whole pages to advertise the sale of box cameras for only one mark, and children's clothes for the summer holidays. A popular saying of the time put Berlin's chief appeal in a nutshell:

> *Berlin ist schön, Berlin ist gross,*
> *Nur in Berlin allein da ist der echte Rummel los!*[3]

Another attraction was its freedom from particularism. French Huguenots in the seventeenth century as much as emancipated peasants after the Napoleonic wars had made their fortune in this city without meeting any hostility. "The Berliner despises parochialism, and treats his own kind with a harshness bordering on injustice. It is easier for the man from the provinces to succeed in Berlin than for the Berliner."

Finally, there were workers from other parts of the empire who came to Berlin for political reasons. They wanted to escape the restrictions of the authorities in their home towns and yearned to join more aggressive and powerful organizations. Berlin by the beginning of the twentieth century was about to replace Hamburg and Leipzig as the capital of the labor movement. The city harbored 13.4 percent of all socialist trade-union members in Germany, and 22.4 percent of all organized metal workers. We may cite the case of Hugo Hoffmann, an independent stove-fitter in a rural community near Magdeburg. Because he gave his journeymen a holiday on May Day, 1903, he was ostracized by the townspeople as a "Red" and practically run out of business. In disgust he sold his shop and moved to Berlin to become a worker and join the Movement himself.

It was another question, of course, whether the masses in the teeming working-class quarters of Greater Berlin were equal to the expectations of a dedicated socialist like Hoffmann. Every worker was anxious to make a success of his life, most workers were conscious that their status as proletarians deprived them of avenues for advancement, but how many of them would stake their hopes on a political movement and Marxist ideas?

II

For many newcomers the trip from the railway station to their first domicile was like the beginning of a great adventure.

---

[3] Berlin is beautiful, Berlin is big,/ Only in Berlin is there a real hubbub!—Eds.

The carriage rattled through well-lighted and somber streets, the children glued to the windows, only the little girl cried on her mother's lap. They stopped in a wide street in front of a house with a red lamp. The man opened, they climbed four narrow flights of stairs, the children had never walked such high steps, the passageway had many narrow doors with mail boxes, he opened one, it was a small, dark, and vile place, the kitchen right at the entrance, one other room.

The family lay down to sleep on mattresses on the floor, undressing in the dark. The boys, all excited, pressed their noses to the window.

The black mass of houses with their silent windows and closed blinds stretched like a single wall. It was a gigantic fortress. Few street lamps were burning, none of the houses was lighted, though they surely were crammed full of people. This was the street, oh, what a vast and mysterious city.

The tenement houses (*Mietskasernen*) were the hallmark of proletarian Berlin. Some of the worst examples could be found in the old streets of the inner city not far from the Alexanderplatz. In the Stralauer Viertel to the south of this square, a busy district of woolen and silk weavers, they lined the banks of the Spree. Sooty wooden fences hid river boats, barges, mountains of coal, and the city dump, picked over by professional scavengers. More to the north, the houses in and around Linienstrasse and Füsilierstrasse gave the "*Scheunenviertel*" its name for squalor and degradation. The quarter was haunted by underworld characters, by Jewish pedlars from Galicia, furrier's shops below street level. "Listen to the cracking, and to the plaster falling behind the wallpaper!" roars the foreman-mason John in Gerhart Hauptmann's *Die Ratten* (1911) as he treads on a loose plank in the floor. "Everything is rotten. Everything rotten timber! Everything undermined by vermin, eaten by rats and mice! Everything totters! Everything is about to crash right down into the cellar!" Shortly before the First World War, some of the streets of the *Scheunenviertel* were finally condemned and torn down to make room for the Bülowplatz and a new People's Theater. But by then the principal working-class districts had long moved to the periphery of Greater Berlin, where real estate was cheaper and where most industries had been located since the 1890s.

The principal working-class districts, known by their low taxation yields, high social welfare budgets, and overcrowding, were in Wedding, Reinickendorf, Gesundbrunnen, Moabit, Friedrichshain, Prenzlauer Berg, Spandau, Treptow, Neukölln, and Kreuzberg. There were also smaller enclaves of working-class housing in wealthier townships like Charlottenburg and Schöneberg; shortly before the war of 1914, a handful of factories built modern apartments for their employees; and not a few workers lived outside Greater Berlin altogether, commuting twenty-five to thirty kilometers daily from Nauen, Velten, Beelitz, or Trebbin, where they owned a small cottage and garden. For the vast majority of the working class, however, home meant a cubicle in one of the tenement houses in the northern, eastern, or southeastern parts of Berlin.

Contemporary observers who did not trouble to take a good look sometimes came away with high praise for the order and cleanliness of the workers' quarters. John A. Catterall was one of a succession of self-appointed inspectors from England in the opening years of this century, who came to Berlin intent on proving the German workman better off than his English confrere. In 1910, he wrote:

> We were driven through, according to a Berlin interpreter, "the very poorest quarters of Berlin." Here, indeed, was an object lesson; imposing well-appointed dwellings, with apparently contented inhabitants, no shoeless children romping on the pavements, no down-at-heel adults standing at street corners, waiting Micawber-like for "something to turn up." What we did see in these poorest parts of the city, were cabs and conveyances, whose owners evidently find a profitable clientele in the poor people. Would that our poorest were those who could afford to seek rest, recreation, or enjoyment in the harmless luxury of a drive.

No local housing surveyor or welfare doctor would have borne him out. And yet Catterall's testimony was not without value. It confirmed what Werner Hegemann and others were saying about the tenement houses at that time, namely that Berlin slums, though probably worse than many in America and England, were less conspicuous because they were distributed over many districts and hidden in closed courtyards behind prim facades. It also pointed to the absence in these parts of beggars and vagrants, or of radical political slogans on house walls. Proletarian Berlin contained no Faubourg Saint-Antoine. Barricades were virtually unknown between 1848 and 1918. Instead, many beer houses displayed busts of Kaiser Wilhelm II.

Indeed, everything pointed to social peace. "One could see at a glance that the entire population led orderly lives," wrote an anonymous chronicler about Spandau at the turn of the century. The old workers who were asked in interviews how their neighborhood looked fifty years ago talked of disciplined crowds on their way to work at the crack of dawn (the workers' steetcar tickets were only valid before 7 a.m. or after 5 p.m.) and of their return after sundown, all the men anxious to wash up, eat, and rest. "The scene never changes," wrote Paul Piechowsky in 1927, describing a street at the end of a workday in Berlin-Neukölln. "The thin faces show exhaustion and wear. Some men smoke. Their shoulders are bent, their calloused hands clutch a satchel or an enameled coffee flask. The smell of sweat and poverty exudes from their clothes. When they reach the top of the stairs they lift their eyes." Women, in response to the same question, mentioned the pedlars who called in the daytime (the working-class districts being poorly provided with retail shops): old men with handcarts trading kindling for potato peels, the vegetable man bringing fresh produce from the nearest district market hall to sell at the curb, the scissor grinder and the street musician, not to forget the *Sandmann* who hauled the white sand that still kept Berlin's kitchen floors clean in the 1890s. Anna Lier, a socialist pub-owner in those years, referred to Naunynstrasse in Kreuzberg as *"Naunynritze"* on account of the multitude of children in the courtyards and on the street. In the evenings, her place was always well-filled, she related, with people gossiping, singing, and playing cards.

All these reminiscences contained an element of sentimental attachment to the sound and colors of the narrator's own city block. Franz Lederer, the Berlin historian, was not wrong in speaking of a petit bourgeois idyll (*Wilhelm Raabescher Kleinbürgerzauber*) in some of the proletarian districts. The superlatives of passing English trade unionists would have made the old workers smile. But they would equally have rebuffed the middle-class reformers who spoke of their streets with pathos as "the districts where the rare laughter one can hear is brutal and bitter, where sorrow dwells heavily, and the joys are limited to . . . the organ-grinder and the furtive ray of sunshine." This is not to say that the Berlin workers lived well, only that they thought how they lived was their own affair.

To drive home the point that Wilhelmine Berlin had no districts solidly held by the fourth estate, and certainly none that was a refuge of pauperism or a stronghold of social revolt, we should mention that the percentage of working-class dwellings in any one district did not exceed 80 percent of all housing. Wedding, for example, was not only the seat of large breweries, tanneries, metal workshops, and the residence of many workers, it also harbored scientific research institutes, the Rudolf Virchow hospital (since 1906), a Jewish hospital, the Paul-Gerhart Foundation for the aged, and many churches. A census in 1925 revealed that only 57 percent of the residents in Wedding actually belonged to the working class. In the 1880s, a number of good residential streets had been laid out west of the Müllerstrasse in the hope of attracting more people of middle-class standing and thus improving the reputation of the district. The same consideration prompted the city fathers of Rixdorf to rename their town Neukölln in 1912. Too many prejudices were attached to the old name, they found, and as things stood, not enough self-respecting burghers wanted to move there. Finally, the design of the tenement houses itself worked against exclusive proletarian inhabitation of any one part of Greater Berlin.

III

Ironical though it sounds, the tenement houses which symbolized capitalist exploitation in modern Berlin, were originally conceived as means to overcome the class conflict. Just as the city fathers of Wedding and Rixdorf believed in the virtue of social diversity, so the chief promoter of the Berlin Building project of 1858, *Baurat* James Hobrecht, had stood up for apartment buildings with mixed quarters for middle-class and working-class tenants. Proximity, he explained in an article in 1868, breeds mutual understanding between rich and poor. For the worker on the fourth floor, neighborliness across class lines would mean a plate of soup when his wife was ill, and for the grocer's wife in the large apartment up front who had cooked it, a lesson in human compassion. In 1904, the *Vaterländischer Bauverein* in Berlin-Wedding went so far as to call a lane connecting the wings of a new apartment complex *Versöhnungs-Privatstrasse* [Reconciliation Street]. A nearby church in Bernauer Strasse was named *Versöhnungskirche.* Yet surely the inadequacy of such naive schemes as remedies to the social question should have become evident in the half century since Hobrecht's project of 1858. Already in the 1890s, Leixner was complaining that in the *Mietskasernen,* the workers were not being reconciled to capitalism, but instead infected the lower middle classes with socialist thought. Always blunt, Werner Hegemann dismissed Hobrecht's idea of social reconciliation as "quackery."

The tenement houses had one great virtue. They accommodated a large number of people. This was important since throughout the last third of the nineteenth century Berlin suffered from a serious shortage of cheap housing. Eighteen sixty-three had seen the first major street disturbances on account of high rents and evictions; in some parts of town there had been pitched battles between tenants and police. During the early founding years, whole shantytowns had sprung up on the edge of the city. Some 600 families were relegated to the public shelters in 1872, and 163 families lived in tents outside Kottbuser Tor. The summer of that year brought more fighting between police and squatters, in the course of which a red flag was hoisted by the rioters—the first red flag seen in Berlin since the revolution of 1848. At Kottbuser Tor, 159 civilians and 100 policemen were wounded. The housing crisis in Berlin remained highly acute until 1875.

Most of the tenement houses inhabited by the working people in the period of this study were built in the 1870s and 1880s by private speculators on the lookout for handsome profits. Using cheap materials and indifferent craftsmanship these men erected five-story structures with many wings, separated by narrow inner courtyards to allow for some light and fresh air—not very much light and fresh air as it turned out. Walking from the street through the archway of one of these living machines, one came to a succession of such courtyards, each like the bottom of a mine shaft reaching toward a shred of sky past dozens of small, stuffy dwellings. The notorious Meyerhof in the Ackerstrasse (Wedding) had no less than nine such courtyards and housed five thousand people. Children were usually not allowed to play in the courtyards because all sounds rebounded loudly from the house walls. There was enough noise as it was from the slamming of trashcan lids, carpetbeating, quarrels among the grownups, the squeaking of the communal water pump, and in older houses the traffic to the outhouse—one outhouse for ten apartments.

Children's games were forbidden and so were wooden shoes, flower pots on window sills, standing around in corridors and stairways, singing after 10 p.m., and much more. The house rules in the *Mietskasernen* reflected the "feudal" relations between tenants and landlords, to use an expression of the socialist *Arbeiter-Sanitätskommission* [Workers' Sanitary Commission] in 1893. The rule of the "house pashas," the commission reported, was oppressive and sometimes outright degrading. Tenants who were evicted for arrears in rent were still charged for their rooms until a new lodger was found to take over their lease. They were liable for all damages in their dwellings but given no credit for improvements. Damp apartments had to be kept well heated to avoid penalties for neglect. According to Georg Rinkowski, a worker and his wife and nine children were locked in by their landlord for two weeks in 1904 because they could not pay their rent. In 1903, Rinkowski's own family had been evicted from their one room and kitchen apartment in the *Scheunenviertel* for the same reason. The landlord kept one of his father's three sewing machines as a pawn, which was a heavy blow to the family since it depended on home-sewn articles for a living.

In fact, working-class families were forced to move their domicile frequently—as often as twice a year, according to Dr. Albert Südekum—especially if they had many children. Some homeowners allowed people to live rent-free in newly constructed housing, for the tenants had to heat their apartments well to keep out the damp chill, and thereby speeded the process of drying the house. After six months, when the police released the house for general occupancy, these "moisture tenants" (*Mieter per nass*) were asked to move out. The police vainly issued warnings against this practice, which made the tenants pay for their lodgings by contracting tuberculosis. Heinrich Zille, the poor's man's artist, quite aptly once called tenement houses "deadlier than an ax."

Berlin's lower-class housing constituted a health problem to the city. The files of the former imperial ministry of health still contain a large collection of housing reports from the turn of the century, all of them testifying to the seriousness of the situation. The most thorough studies were the survey of the *Berliner Arbeiter-Sanitätskommission* in 1893, and the yearly reports of the *Berliner Ortskrankenkasse für den Gewerbebetrieb der Kaufleute, Handelsleute und Apotheker*,[4] especially those of 1902 and 1910.

The fundamental evil of working-class housing was overcrowding. A contemporary architect, Friedrich Wagner, stipulated at the beginning of the twentieth century that a worker's family of four to five persons needed a minimum of one corridor, one kitchen, one pantry, one toilet, one bedroom for the parents and infants, and one or two bedrooms for the grown-up children separated by sexes. Yet a survey

[4] Local Berlin Health Insurance Fund for the Business of Merchants, Tradesmen, and Pharmacists.—Eds.

of almost 400,000 low-income apartments in Berlin in December 1900 showed that

- —4,086 of these apartments were "kitchen flats" (*Wohnküchen*), i.e., kitchens serving also as living room and bedroom.
- —1,761 consisted of one heatable room only. Of these, 658 had no separate kitchen and were called *Kochstuben.*
- —197,394 had one heatable room and one kitchen.
- —132,144 had two heatable rooms and one kitchen.
- —55,628 had three heatable rooms and one kitchen.

In other words, 70 percent of all Berlin dwellings in 1900 consisted of no more than two rooms with a kitchen, and 50 percent consisted of only one room and a kitchen. The latter were the homes of 43.64 percent of the Berlin population.

Two years later, the *Ortskrankenkasse* reported that approximately 40 percent of the sick patients on its visiting list lived in apartments with one room and kitchen; 39 percent lived in two rooms and a kitchen; 14.44 percent lived in *Kochstuben;* and 1.83 percent in *Wohnküchen.*

The individual rooms in the *Mietskasernen* were small and un-hygienic. Friedrich Wagner had demanded a minimum area of 20 to 25 square meters for any room serving as bedroom and living room simultaneously. The *Ortskrankenkasse* found that 65 percent of the dwellings it inspected in 1902 failed to meet this standard. Nearly 10 percent were smaller than even the 12.18 square meters set as a minimum by most building societies and by the Berlin police. The police also stipulated 2.80 meters as the minimum height for ceilings, a condition not met by 33 percent of the dwellings covered in this survey. Dampness was another problem. The *Ortskrankenkasse* in 1902 called 5.40 percent of the dwellings which it inspected "ex-tremely damp." Ten percent were in perpetual darkness; some had no windows at all. None had private toilets. All of them lodged too many people.

Taking four or more persons per heatable room as our standard of overcrowding, we find that in 1875 there were 28,238 such congested lodgings in Berlin, affecting a total of 148,230 people. By 1912, the figure had risen to 100,000 overcrowded dwellings inhabited by 600,000 persons. This situation was especially alarming when a lodger in an overcrowded apartment was afflicted with a contagious disease. The *Ortskrankenkasse* reported in 1902 that 12.67 percent of the male and 14.24 percent of the female tubercular patients it had visited lived in rooms which they shared with more than four other people.

The evil of overcrowding was compounded by the pernicious night-lodging system, or *Schlafgängertum*. The poorest families were forced to sublet one or two beds to strangers at night in order to pay their rent. At times several night lodgers shared the same room—in some cases even the same bed—with the family. Statistics for December 1900 show that in the borough of old Berlin alone, 61,765 households accommodated strangers at night. In 1,958 cases, the night lodgers slept in the same room as the family. In 48 cases, night lodgers of both sexes shared the same room. There were instances when the same bed was used alternately by a worker on day shift and a worker on night shift. Admittedly, the practice of night lodging did not prevail throughout lower-class Berlin. It affected 21 percent of all Berlin households in 1875, and 10 percent in 1912. But its concentration in precisely the smallest and poorest lodgings added to the overall housing problem among the poor. The following are three samples taken from the worst housing encountered by the inspectors of the *Ortskrankenkasse* in 1910:

> *Kottbuser Strasse, inner wing, first floor. The dwelling has not been repaired in six years. The walls and the ceiling are blackened by smoke. The walls have large moist patches. The rooms are cold and have little light or sun. The woman is ill and cannot work. Eight people sleep in one room, three to one bed. The air is stuffy although the windows are open.*
>
> *Kösliner Strasse, side wing, third floor. The patient sleeps in the kitchen. The latter is damp, the wallpaper is peeling off. The landlord refuses to repair the rooms. The man, whose tuberculosis is incurable, draws invalid pension since 1908. He shares a very unclean bed with his wife. There is, therefore, the danger of infection. The family depends on the income of the wife.*
>
> *Reichenberger Strasse, side wing, cellar. The rooms are two meters below the ground. When it rains, water floods the apartment. The windows are seldom opened, since they have no iron bars and children have fallen into the cellar from the courtyard. The rooms are very damp, the plaster is falling off the walls. The floor boards are rotten with moisture. The neighboring cellar dwelling is even worse. The windows are boarded up with cardboard because the landlord will not have them repaired. An old baking oven serves as stove. The rooms are repellent due to filth and polluted air. The toilet in the courtyard is used by 25–30 persons.*

It would seem that wretched dwellings such as these should at least have been inexpensive to rent. Yet the average rent per head in

1901 was still 195 marks per year. For an apartment consisting of one room and a kitchen the average rent was 230 to 270 marks per year in 1903; and for an apartment with two rooms and a kitchen 315 to 350 marks. Prices were high precisely because there was so much demand for small working-class flats. Not even the poorest were spared this expenditure. An inquiry among the destitute in Rixdorf who received city alms in 1910 showed that only 7.1 percent paid less than 100 marks per year for their rooms. Nearly a third, or 32.8 percent, paid from 100 to 200 marks a year; 40.3 percent from 200 to 300 marks; and 16.8 percent more than 300 marks a year. These figures do not include the cost of frequent moving.

There were some improvements in housing conditions after the turn of the century. Dr. R. Kuczynski informs us that while in 1875 10 percent of the Berlin population lived in cellar apartments, the corresponding figure for 1912 was 3 percent. Attic apartments, still numerous in 1875, had almost disappeared by 1912. Half of the apartments in houses built since 1905 had private baths; many courtyards in newer buildings were planted with trees and flowers. And yet, while these indices speak for a genuine concern over the housing problem in Berlin—as indeed the many surveys in this period do too—the life of the common people before 1914 could hardly have been affected by these incipient reforms.

IV

The *Berliner Arbeiter-Sanitätskommission* was sponsored by the Social Democratic Party and the *Zentralstelle für Wohlfahrtseinrichtungen,* a central clearing house for private welfare bodies in the city. Not only *Vorwärts* published the commission's final report, but also conservative and liberal papers like the *Kreuzzeitung, National-Zeitung,* and *Vossische Zeitung.* If we remember that besides the aforementioned commission there were at least a dozen other institutions engaged in housing surveys in the opening years of this century—among them private insurance funds and the Berlin statistical office, the factory inspectorate and the Society for Social Reform—then one may well conclude that housing conditions among the city poor belonged to the most widely debated topics of social reformers before the First World War.

Nevertheless, concrete improvements were unlikely in the foreseeable future. The reform efforts before the war were both belated and insufficient in scope. The two housing bureaus of Charlottenburg and Berlin, in 1914, were still limited to giving technical advice and mediating minor disputes between tenants and landlords. The *Berliner Mietverein* [Berlin Renters' Association] in the same year could not go beyond petitioning the city assembly to restrict mortgages to slum landlords. There were a few cooperative building societies (*Baugenossenschaften*) from the 1890s on, but their inexpensive flats were restricted to members. Only the Social Democratic regime in Prussia during the Weimar Republic managed to arrest the further spread of the tenement house system in Berlin. Yet to cure it was even beyond its power. The trouble with modern massive construction, complained Hegemann in 1930, is that it deprives our towns of periodic purgatives by fire. To rectify the mistakes of Berlin's bureaucratic town planners in the nineteenth century, he predicted, would take a colossal earthquake. (Hegemann's earthquake came fifteen years later in the form of Allied bombers blasting the cheap plaster of Berlin's founding years all over its working-class pavements.)

The reform efforts before the First World War were furthermore hampered by the existence of rather austere notions in certain quarters concerning the dangers of pampering Germany's proletariat. There was something spartan in the Berlin police order of January 19, 1893, stipulating one straw bag, one straw pillow, and one woolen blanket as the minimal rights of a night lodger, and a separate bed only if he was over fourteen. There was something harsh in the eviction of the impecunious residents of the *Scheunenviertel* a decade later, while alternative housing was not available. But then public housing projects for the poor were not necessarily considered in the best national interest. "Obtaining good and cheap lodgings," wrote the *Deutsche Volkswirtschaftliche Correspondenz* on April 22, 1913, "is up to the worker and the little man. It depends primarily on [each man's] strength, his skill, endurance, and initiative. . . . You cannot make a nation strong with acts of charity and material benefactions—this only produces an ugly national obesity. . . . For this reason it would be wrong to pass an imperial housing bill that provides for comfortable housing in the large cities through welfare grants and privileges at the expense of other *Stände* [social estates]. This would lower the people's initiative, energy, and birth rate. . . ." In conservative circles it was also not uncommon to associate run-down housing with Social Democratic tenants, while the apartment of an honest worker was pictured as clean and tidy, and adorned with portraits of the imperial couple or scenes from the

Franco-Prussian War. Socialists, according to this reasoning, were people whose slovenliness made their homes unattractive, and unattractive homes, in turn, explained their envy of others and their rebelliousness.

Bizarre though the conservatives' association of politics and housekeeping sounded, this train of thought was not wholly unique to them. Left-radical intellectuals in the leadership of the *Neue Freie Volksbühne* hoped that the people's theater movement might teach the common workers a higher standard of *Wohnkultur,* also for political reasons. Not so the Social Democratic Party and trade unions, which, except for a few individuals, worried about overcrowding and sanitation—the pioneering work of the *Arbeiter-Sanitätskommission* in 1893 is proof for that—but not about the workers' style of living. To them the political issue in the housing problem was whether the labor movement should or should not support Pastor Bodelschwingh's land-reform movement in northern Germany, the aim of which was to make every workman a houseowner, or the company housing projects of major industrial firms.

What about the workers themselves? If one can distinguish between housing statistics and private living arrangements as two ways of tackling the workers' housing problem, the workers, no doubt, were chiefly concerned with the latter. The residents in Berlin's *Mietskasernen* by and large accepted their harsh surroundings. They drew what satisfaction they could from their small victories in the perennial struggle for a decent living: a new sofa, a handsome tile stove, moving to a flat with a balcony, or living near the meadows of Jungfernheide. For those without such amenities, the tenement house was complemented by the local beer joint and the popular dance hall.

The workers' submissiveness is not difficult to understand in light of the fact that so many of them had recently lived in villages and were quite unspoiled. The psychology of the provincial have-not seeking his fortune in metropolitan Berlin favored individual ambition over collective action. By all accounts, tenants in the same *Mietskaserne* rarely helped one another against heartless landlords. "A neighbor could expect a helping hand in appropriate cases [*wo es angebracht ist*]," was the way Frau Schönobrod of Hussitenstrasse 40 put it, primly stressing the word "appropriate." Always anxious to protect their privacy outside working hours—and therefore disinclined to move into company housing—the workers generally held aloof from their fellow tenants. An element of slyness was probably involved too. It was easier to indulge in a little make-believe if the family's circumstances were not laid bare to the whole neighborhood. Then one could pretend that the grown daughter worked in an office and not in a factory, or that the family could afford meat when the people next door were having fish. There is no evidence that relations were any more cordial among socialists sharing the same staircase. In the recollections of the old workers who were interviewed for this study, there was more talk of quarrels among the lodgers than of communal coffee parties in the courtyard, of people moving out than of their protesting abuses.

Sociologists and historians of Berlin have often asked themselves whether the masses in the tenement houses were actually content, whether they were capable of striking roots in Wedding and Lichtenberg, whether modern Berlin could ever mean home to them. They wondered about the psychological effect of overcrowding and noisy streets on the urban worker at the end of a working day, and speculated about the loneliness of the immigrant in this city of over three million inhabitants. The answer can be found in the population statistics of the prewar years. Even with growing unemployment in the first decade of the new century, there was no "return migration" to the countryside. The efforts of the Rixdorf authorities to provide agricultural work for its 730 unemployed in 1901 failed because all of them, save one, refused to move out of Greater Berlin.

It would go too far to suggest that the unemployed in Rixdorf stayed because of local patriotism, because of *Heimatgefühl*. But then *Heimatgefühl* is too poetic a name to describe the relation of a Berliner to his city. The city meant economic competition and untold opportunities, it demanded independence of mind and resourcefulness. Many people did not like Berlin at first, but this changed with the years as they acquired relatives among its residents and made friends. The dream of returning to one's native village one day, to buy a plot of land there and a cottage, was precisely that and no more. It was a dream, just as childhood memories of picking berries for supper in Pomerania and tending the geese were dreams, or youthful recollections of tramping through half of Europe. Such thoughts do not represent actual goals. They are the little man's private refuge when the gigantic metropolis wants to engulf him.

Suggestions for Additional Reading

Bibliographies

Lewis Mumford, *The City in History: Its Origins, Its Transformations, and its Prospects* (New York, 1961), and F. Roy Willis, *Western Civilization: An Urban Perspective* (2 vols., Lexington, Mass., 1973), are surveys of urban history that provide useful guides to further reading. In Charles Tilly, *An Urban World* (Boston and Toronto, 1974), the student can find a wide sample of recent social science literature on the city. The latest publications on British cities are reviewed in the *Urban History Yearbook,* which began to appear in 1974 as an offshoot of H. J. Dyos's *Urban History Newsletter.* Philippe Dollinger has edited the *Bibliographie d'histoire des villes de France* (Paris, 1967), and Erich Keyser has edited the *Bibliographie zur Städtegeschichte Deutschlands* (Cologne and Vienna, 1969).

Early Modern Cities

Gideon Sjoberg develops a theoretical model of preindustrial cities which has both historical and contemporary relevance in *The Preindustrial City: Past and Present* (Glencoe, 1960). Much of the most interesting literature on early modern urban history focuses on German cities, many of which were already well developed long before the nineteenth century. Hans Mauersberg, *Wirtschafts- und Sozialgeschichte zentraleuropäischer Städte in neuerer Zeit: Dargestellt an den Beispielen von Basel, Frankfurt a. M., Hamburg, Hannover und München* (Göttingen, 1960) is an important comparative study. Gerald Strauss provides a sympathetic and fascinating account of life in a highly traditional city in his *Nuremberg in the Sixteenth Century* (New York, 1966). Another local study, focusing on the relations between social and political conflict, is Gerald Lyman Soliday, *A Community in Conflict: Frankfurt Society in the Seventeenth and Early Eighteenth Centuries* (Hanover, N.H., 1974). Mack Walker, *German Home Towns: Community, State, and General Estate, 1648–1871* (Ithaca, 1971), explores the changing nature of the pre-urban communities for which many Germans were to feel increasingly nostalgic in the course of the nineteenth century. For England, see M. Dorothy George, *London Life in the Eighteenth Century* (London, 1925), Dorothy Marshall, *Dr. Johnson's London* (New York, 1968), and E. A. Wrigley, "A Simple Model of London's Importance in Changing English Society and Economy, 1650–1750," *Past and Present,* no. 37 (July 1967), pp. 44–70. French cities are treated in Orest A. Ranum, *Paris in the Age of Absolutism: An Essay* (New York, 1968), and Maurice Garden, *Lyon et les lyonnais au xviiie siècle* (Paris, n.d.), which provides a detailed analysis of social structure in an early industrial center.

The Process of Urban Growth

Two useful overviews are Kingsley Davis, "The Urbanization of the Human Population," *Scientific American* (1965), and Eric E. Lampard's wide-ranging synthesis, "The Urbanizing World," in Volume I of H. J. Dyos and Michael Wolff, eds., *The Victorian City: Images and Realities* (2 vols., London and Boston, 1973). For Britain, see Arthur Redford, *Labour Migration in England, 1800–1850* (2nd ed., rev. and ed. by W. H. Chaloner, Manchester, 1964), and Dov Friedlander, "The Spread of Urbanization in England and Wales, 1851–1951," *Population Studies* 24 (1970): 423–443. Louis Chevalier has treated the growth of the Parisian population throughout the nineteenth century in *La formation de la population parisienne au xixe siècle* (Paris, 1950). David H. Pinkney uses both statistical and qualitative sources in an interesting article, "Migrations to Paris during the Second Empire," *Journal of Modern History* 25 (1953): 1–12. Wolfgang Köllmann has written a number of important articles on German demographic history. In addition to the article reprinted above, one of the most useful is "Industrialisierung, Binnenwanderung und 'Soziale Frage': Zur Entstehungsgeschichte der deutschen Industriegrossstadt im 19. Jahrhundert," *Vierteljahrschrift für Sozial- und Wirtschaftsgeschichte* 46 (1959): 45–70.

Urban Society in the Nineteenth Century

There are practically no internationally comparative works on urban social history during the nineteenth century. One of the few exceptions is Lynn Lees, "Metropolitan Types: London and Paris Compared," in Volume I of Dyos and Wolff, *The Victorian City* (cited above). Most of the items worth mentioning fall clearly into a particular national category.

For Britain, *The Victorian City* provides a rich panorama; in addition to the two articles mentioned above, and the one from which we have reprinted a selection, it contains thirty-five essays on all aspects of English urban life, from prostitution and crime to literature and religion, and several hundred illustrations. Asa Briggs, *Victorian Cities* (New York and Evanston, 1963), is another important and readable synthesis. There are several recent works that treat particular aspects of urban development in a number of cities: John R. Kellett, *The Impact of Railways on Victorian Cities* (London and Toronto, 1969); Enid Gauldie, *Cruel Habitations: A History of Working-Class Housing, 1780–1918* (New York and London, 1974); John Foster, *Class Struggle and the Industrial Revolution: Early Industrial Capitalism in Three English Towns* (London, 1974). But most English urban history, like the urban history of other countries, focuses on individual cities. An enormous amount has been written about London. Francis Sheppard, *London, 1808–1870: The Infernal Wen* (Berkeley and Los Angeles, 1971), is part of a multivolume series, in which the preceding volume is George Rudé, *Hanoverian London, 1714–1808* (Berkeley and Los Angeles, 1971). Two important contributions to the social history of London in the second half of the nineteenth century are Gareth Stedman Jones, *Outcast London: A Study in the Relationship between Classes in Victorian Society* (New York, 1971), and his "Working-Class Culture and Working-Class Politics in London, 1870–1900: Notes on the Remaking of a Working Class," *Journal of Social History* 7 (1974):

460–508. Two of the classic works of contemporary urban social description deal with London: Henry Mayhew, *London Labour and the London Poor* (4 vols., London, 1861–62), a gold mine of shrewd and colorful reporting, and Charles Booth, *Life and Labour of the People in London* (17 vols., 3rd ed., London, 1902–1903). Booth's work, a major statistical source for urban historians, can be sampled in a volume of excerpts entitled *Charles Booth on the City: Physical Pattern and Social Structure,* ed. Harold W. Pfautz (Chicago and London, 1967). These analyses can be supplemented by a fascinating volume of illustrations done by Gustav Doré (with commentary by Blanchard Jerrold) entitled *London: A Pilgrimage* (London, 1872; reprinted 1968). Two of London's residential suburbs have been treated in H. J. Dyos, *Victorian Suburb: A Study of the Growth of Camberwell* (Leicester, 1961), and F. M. L. Thompson, *Hampstead: Building a Borough, 1650–1964* (London and Boston, 1974). There are also general social histories of several other English cities. The impact of urban growth upon market and cathedral towns is explored in Alan Armstrong, *Stability and Change in an English County Town: A Social Study of York, 1801–51* (Cambridge, Eng., and New York, 1974), and Robert Newton, *Victorian Exeter, 1837–1914* (Leicester, 1968). The development of industrial cities is treated in Asa Briggs and Conrad Gill, *History of Birmingham* (2 vols., London and New York, 1952); Malcolm I. Thomis, *Politics and Society in Nottingham, 1785–1835* (Oxford, 1965); Roy A. Church, *Economic and Social Change in a Midland Town: Victorian Nottingham, 1815–1900* (London, 1966); and T. C. Barker and J. R. Harris, *A Merseyside Town in the Industrial Revolution: St. Helens, 1750–1900* (Liverpool, 1954).

The offerings in the area of modern German urban history are far less rich, especially for readers who are limited to works in English. A valuable reference work is Erich Keyser, ed., *Deutsches Städtebuch: Handbuch städtischer Geschichte* (5 vols., Stuttgart, 1939–71), which contains articles on hundreds of individual cities, including a great deal of both statistical and bibliographical information. The general work by Hans Mauersberg cited above under "Early Modern Cities" is also useful for the first half of the nineteenth century. Two regional studies by Wilhelm Brepohl treat the area of most rapid urbanization in Germany, the industrial Ruhr Valley: *Der Aufbau des Ruhrvolkes im Zuge der Ost-West-Wanderung: Beiträge zur deutschen Sozialgeschichte des 19. und 20. Jahrhunderts* (Recklinghausen, 1948), and

Industrievolk im Wandel von der agraren zur industriellen Daseinsform dargestellt am Ruhrgebiet (Tübingen, 1957). Wolfgang Köllmann's book on Barmen is still in a class by itself as a case study of a German city in the nineteenth century. There are, however, a number of useful works on the history of Berlin. Hans Herzfeld has edited a large collection of essays on many aspects of life in the city and the surrounding area, *Berlin und die Provinz Brandenburg im 19. und 20. Jahrhundert* (Berlin, 1968). The changing social structure of Berlin in the first half of the nineteenth century is explored in another lengthy collection of essays, edited by Otto Büsch: *Untersuchungen zur Geschichte der frühen Industrialisierung vornehmlich im Wirtschaftsraum Berlin/Brandenburg* (Berlin, 1971). A more popular survey of life in the city during the later part of the century is Annemarie Lange, *Berlin zur Zeit Bebels und Bismarcks* (Berlin-East, 1971). Gerhard Masur's *Imperial Berlin* (New York, 1970) is both a study and a memoir, which gives considerable attention to cultural history. The history of Nuremberg can be approached through the relevant chapters of Gerhard Pfeiffer, ed., *Nürnberg: Geschichte einer europäischen Stadt* (Munich, 1971). There are also chapters on the nineteenth century in Hans Mauersberg, *Die Wirtschaft und Gesellschaft Fuldas in neuerer Zeit: Eine städtegeschichtliche Studie* (Göttingen, 1969). Middle-class life in Germany's second largest city is described in Percy Ernst Schramm, *Hamburg, Deutschland und die Welt: Leistung und Grenzen hanseatischen Bürgertums in der Zeit zwischen Napoleon I. und Bismarck* (2nd ed., Hamburg, 1952). Statistical methods are employed in David Crew, "Definitions of Modernity: Social Mobility in a German Town, 1880–1901," *Journal of Social History* 7 (1973): 51–74, a study of the industrial city of Bochum. There are interesting comparisons between German and Austrian urbanization in William H. Hubbard, "Politics and Society in the Central European City: Graz, Austria, 1861–1918," *Canadian Journal of History* 5 (1970): 25–45.

There is a real dearth of works in the area of French urban history. For the first half of the nineteenth century, there is the survey by Jean Vidalenc of the French urban population, *La société française de 1815 à 1848: Le peuple des villes et des bourgs* (Paris, 1973). Surprisingly, there is no general work on the history of Paris which covers the whole century, although Jean Tulard, *Nouvelle histoire de Paris: Le Consulat et l'Empire, 1800–1815* (Paris, 1970) paints a broad picture of the city during the Napoleonic period. Philippe Wolffe is editing a series of general histories of French cities, each of which goes from their beginning to the present. The following volumes have appeared so far: Jean Meyer, ed., *Histoire de Rennes* (Toulouse, 1972); Edouard Baratier, ed., *Histoire de Marseille* (Toulouse, 1973); and Philippe Wolffe, ed., *Histoire de Toulouse* (Toulouse, 1974). Much of the most interesting work on French cities focuses specifically on the working classes and/or the associated problem of urban violence. Three studies concentrating on urban workers are Maurice Agulhon, *Une ville ouvrière au temps du socialisme utopique: Toulon de 1815 à 1851* (Paris, 1970); Pierre Pierrard, *La vie ouvriere â Lille sous le Second Empire* (Paris, 1965); and Joan Wallach Scott, *The Glassworkers of Carmaux: French Craftsmen and Political Action in a Nineteenth-Century City* (Cambridge, Mass., 1974). Working-class violence is analyzed in Robert Bezucha, *The Lyon Uprising of 1834: Social and Political Conflict in the Early July Monarchy* (Cambridge, Mass., 1974), and Charles Tilly and Lynn Lees, "Le Peuple de Juin 1848," *Annales: Économies, Sociétés, Civilizations* 29 (1974): 1061–91, to be reprinted in English as "The People of June 1848," in Roger Price, ed., *1848 and the Second French Republic* (London, 1976).

Urban Government

The development of political institutions designed to cope with the problems posed by cities is a large subject that we have intentionally omitted from this book. Those who wish to pursue the subject on their own can begin with the chapter on "Local Government" in Eugene N. and Pauline R. Anderson, *Political Institutions and Social Change in Continental Europe in the Nineteenth Century* (Berkeley and Los Angeles, 1967). A detailed contemporary account of city government in the early twentieth century is William Bennett Munro, *The Government of European Cities* (New York, 1909). See also the late-nineteenth-century accounts of Albert Shaw, *Municipal Government in Continental Europe* and *Municipal Government in Great Britain* (both New York, 1895). More recent studies of English urban politics are A. Temple Patterson, *Radical Leicester: A History of Leicester, 1780–1850* (Leicester, 1954); François Vigier, *Change and Apathy: Liverpool and Manchester during the Industrial Revolution*

(Cambridge, Mass. and London, 1970); and E. P. Hennock, *Fit and Proper Persons: Ideal and Reality in Nineteenth-Century Urban Government* (London, 1973). For Germany, the place to start is with William Harbutt Dawson, *Municipal Life and Government in Germany* (London, 1914), which was intended to elicit imitation in England of German administrative achievements. James J. Sheehan, "Liberalism and the City in Nineteenth-Century Germany," *Past and Present,* no. 51 (May 1971), pp. 116–137, examines the struggle for political power between liberals and socialists. The following German works may also be consulted: Helmuth Croon, Wolfgang Hofmann, and George-Christoph von Unruh, *Selbstverwaltung im Zeitalter der Industrialisierung* (Stuttgart, 1971); Helmuth Croon, "Bürgertum und Verwaltung in den Städten des Ruhrgebiets im 19. Jahrhundert," *Tradition* 9 (1964): 23–41; Helmut Böhme, *Frankfurt und Hamburg: Des deutschen Reiches Silber- und Goldloch und die allerenglischste Stadt des Kantinents* (Frankfurt am Main, 1968); and Wolfgang Hofmann, *Die Bielefelder Stadtverordneten: Ein Beitrag zu bürgerlicher Selbstverwaltung und sozialem Wandel, 1850 bis 1914* (Lübeck, 1964). The absence of works on urban government in nineteenth-century France is traceable in large part to the nature of the French administrative system, in which cities possessed far less autonomy than was the case in Britain or Germany.

Perceptions of Cities and the History of City Planning

A stimulating essay on the attitudes of intellectuals toward urban experience is Carl Schorske, "The Idea of the City in European Thought: Voltaire to Spengler," in Oscar Handlin and John Burchard, eds., *The Historian and the City* (Cambridge, Mass., 1963). For Britain, see B. I. Coleman, ed., *The Idea of the City in Nineteenth-Century Britain* (London and Boston, 1973), a wide-ranging anthology of contemporary accounts with a useful introduction. Raymond Williams, *The Country and the City* (New York, 1973), discusses attitudes toward cities in English literature during the past several centuries. An introduction to the problem of the city in Germany is Andrew Lees, "Debates about the Big City in Germany, 1890–1914," *Societas: A Review of Social History* 5 (1975): 31–47. A useful summary of the views of nineteenth-century German sociologists appears in the opening chapters of Elisabeth Pfeil, *Grossstadtforschung* (Bremen-Horn, 1950). Anti-urbanism, which became especially virulent in Germany in the late nineteenth and early twentieth centuries, is the subject of Klaus Bergmann, *Agrarromantik und Grossstadtfeindschaft* (Meisenheim am Glan, 1970).

Perceptions of cities frequently led to proposals for redesigning them so as to make them more habitable. City planning is another important aspect of nineteenth-century urban history for which we provide bibliographical references in lieu of any treatment in the text itself. Two useful introductions are Leonard Benevolo, *The Origins of Modern Town Planning,* trans. Judith Landry (Cambridge, Mass., 1967), and Françoise Choay, *The Modern City: Planning in the Nineteenth Century,* trans. Marguerite Hugo and George R. Collins (New York, 1969). Françoise Choay has also edited a useful anthology of nineteenth- and twentieth-century writings, *L'urbanisme: Utopies et réalités* (Paris, 1965). The following works illuminate the architectural side of city planning: Siegfried Giedion, *Space, Time and Architecture: The Growth of a New Tradition* (5th ed., Cambridge, Mass., 1971); Pierre Lavedan, *Histoire de l'urbanisme* (3 vols., Paris, 1926–52); and E. A. Gutkind, *International History of City Development* (8 vols., New York, 1964–72), which also deals with urban geography. For Britain, there are several works: note particularly William Ashworth, *The Genesis of Modern British Town Planning: A Study in Economic and Social History of the Nineteenth and Twentieth Centuries* (London, 1954); and Colin and Rose Bell, *City Fathers: Town Planning in Britain from Roman Times to 1900* (New York and Washington, 1969). The development of London is treated in Steen Eiler Rasmussen, *London: The Unique City* (London and New York, 1937), and Donald J. Olsen, *Town Planning in London: The Eighteenth and Nineteenth Centuries* (New Haven, 1964). For France, there are several works on city planning in Paris: David H. Pinkney, *Napoleon III and the Rebuilding of Paris* (Princeton, 1958); Howard Saalman, *Haussmann: Paris Transformed* (New York, 1971); and Anthony Sutcliffe, *The Autumn of Central Paris: The Defeat of Town Planning, 1850–1970* (London, 1970). See also Charlene Marie Leonard, *Lyon Transformed: Public Works of the Second Empire, 1853–1864* (Berkeley and Los Angeles, 1961). For Germany, where the influence of the Austrian critic of uniformity in city planning, Camillo Sitte, was enormous, see George R. and Christiane Craseman Collins, *Camillo Sitte and the Birth of Modern City Planning* (New York, 1965). A classic German work is the harsh portrait of Berlin by Werner Hegemann, *Das steinerne Berlin: Geschichte der grössten Mietskasernenstadt der Welt* (Berlin, 1930).